Ste

Windows® 8 Apps
with HTML5 and JavaScript

UNLEASHED

SAMS | 800 East 96th Street, Indianapolis, Indiana 46240 USA

Windows® 8 Apps with HTML5 and JavaScript Unleashed

Copyright © 2013 by Pearson Education, Inc.

All rights reserved. No part of this book shall be reproduced, stored in a retrieval system, or transmitted by any means, electronic, mechanical, photocopying, recording, or otherwise, without written permission from the publisher. No patent liability is assumed with respect to the use of the information contained herein. Although every precaution has been taken in the preparation of this book, the publisher and author assume no responsibility for errors or omissions. Nor is any liability assumed for damages resulting from the use of the information contained herein.

ISBN-13: 978-0-672-33605-8

ISBN-10: 0-672-33605-7

Library of Congress Cataloging-in-Publication Data is on file.

Printed in the United States of America

First Printing November 2012

Trademarks

All terms mentioned in this book that are known to be trademarks or service marks have been appropriately capitalized. Sams Publishing cannot attest to the accuracy of this information. Use of a term in this book should not be regarded as affecting the validity of any trademark or service mark.

Warning and Disclaimer

Every effort has been made to make this book as complete and as accurate as possible, but no warranty or fitness is implied. The information provided is on an "as is" basis. The author and the publisher shall have neither liability nor responsibility to any person or entity with respect to any loss or damages arising from the information contained in this book or from the use of the programs accompanying it.

Bulk Sales

Sams Publishing offers excellent discounts on this book when ordered in quantity for bulk purchases or special sales. For more information, please contact

    U.S. Corporate and Government Sales
    1-800-382-3419
    corpsales@pearsontechgroup.com

For sales outside of the U.S., please contact

    International Sales
    international@pearsoned.com

Editor-in-Chief
Greg Wiegand

Executive Editor
Neil Rowe

Development Editor
Mark Renfrow

Managing Editor
Kristy Hart

Project Editor
Betsy Harris

Indexer
Tim Wright

Proofreader
Williams Woods Publishing

Technical Editor
Jeff Burtoft

Publishing Coordinator
Cindy Teeters

Cover Designer
Mark Shirar

Senior Compositor
Gloria Schurick

Contents at a Glance

	Introduction	1
1	Building Windows Store Apps	5
2	WinJS Fundamentals	45
3	Observables, Bindings, and Templates	77
4	Using WinJS Controls	109
5	Creating Forms	141
6	Menus and Flyouts	161
7	Using the `ListView` Control	185
8	Creating Data Sources	223
9	App Events and States	253
10	Page Fragments and Navigation	273
11	Using the Live Connect API	293
12	Graphics and Games	319
	Index	333

Table of Contents

Introduction **1**

1 Building Windows Store Apps 5

What Is a Windows Store App? 5
    Microsoft Design Style Principles 6
    Common Features of Windows Store Apps 8
Creating Your First Windows Store App 13
    Creating the Visual Studio Project 13
    Declaring App Capabilities 15
    Creating the HTML Page 16
    Creating the Style Sheet 17
    Creating the JavaScript File 18
    Running the App 20
Elements of a Windows Store App 21
    JavaScript 21
    HTML5 21
    Cascading Style Sheets 3 22
    Windows Runtime 22
    Windows Library for JavaScript 23
    What about jQuery? 23
Building Windows Store Apps with Visual Studio 26
    Windows Store App Project Templates 26
    Running a Windows Store App 34
Debugging a Windows Store App 35
    Using the Visual Studio JavaScript Console Window 35
    Setting Breakpoints 37
    Using the DOM Explorer 37
Publishing to the Windows Store 38
    Register as a Windows Developer 38
    Submitting Your App 39
    Passing App Certification 41
Summary 42

2 WinJS Fundamentals 45

Namespaces, Modules, and Classes 45
    Using Namespaces 46
    Using the Module Pattern 48
    Using Classes 51

Contents   v

Asynchronous Programming with Promises..56
    Using Promises...57
    Using `then()` versus `done()`...58
    Creating Promises..60
    Creating a Timeout Promise..61
    Canceling Promises...62
    Composing Promises..63
Retrieving DOM Elements with Query Selectors..63
    Performing Queries with the `WinJS.Utilities.query()` Method....64
    Retrieving a Single Element with the
        `WinJS.Utilities.id()` Method..66
    Using the `WinJS.Utilities.children()` Method..........................67
    Working with the `QueryCollection` Class......................................68
Performing Ajax Calls with the `xhr` Function..69
    Specifying Different Response Types..72
    Customizing the Properties of the `XmlHttpRequest` Object......73
Summary...75

3 Observables, Bindings, and Templates   77

Understanding Observables..77
    Creating an Observable...78
    Creating Observable Listeners...79
    Coalescing Notifications..81
    Bypassing Notifications...82
    Working with the `WinJS.Binding.List` Object..............................83
    Creating an Observable Collection of Observables......................86
Understanding Declarative Data Binding..86
    Declarative Data Binding and Observables....................................89
    Capturing the Contents of an HTML Form.....................................91
    Declarative Data Binding and WinJS Controls...............................94
    Declarative Data Binding and Binding Converters......................96
Understanding Templates...100
    Creating an Imperative Template..100
    Creating a Declarative Template...103
    Applying a Template with a Query Selector................................104
    Creating External Templates..106
    Summary..108

4 Using WinJS Controls   109

Introduction to WinJS Controls...109
    Creating a WinJS Control Declaratively...111
    Creating Controls Imperatively..113

vi Windows® 8 Apps with HTML5 and JavaScript Unleashed

  Setting Control Options 114
  Retrieving Controls from an HTML Document 115
 Using the `Tooltip` Control 116
  Using the `contentElement` Property 117
  Styling a Tooltip 117
 Using the `ToggleSwitch` Control 118
  Determining the State of a `ToggleSwitch` 118
 Using the `Rating` Control 120
  Customizing the Ratings 121
  Submitting a Rating 121
 Using the `DatePicker` Control 123
  Formatting the Year, Month, and Date 124
  Displaying Only Years, Months, or Days 126
  Capturing the Selected Date 127
 Using the `TimePicker` Control 128
  Getting and Setting the Current Time 130
  Formatting the Hour, Minute, and Period 131
 Using the `FlipView` Control 132
  Displaying Page Numbers 135
  Creating Custom `FlipView` Buttons 137
 Summary 139

5 Creating Forms   **141**

 Using HTML5 Form Validation 141
  Using the `required` Attribute 142
  Using the `pattern` Attribute 142
  Performing Custom Validation 143
  Customizing the Validation Error Style 144
  Resetting a Form 146
 Using HTML5 Input Elements 147
  Labeling Form Fields 148
  Entering a Number 149
  Entering a Value from a Range of Values 151
  Entering Email Addresses, URLs, Telephone Numbers,
   and Search Terms 151
  Entering a Value from a List of Values 153
  Selecting Files 154
 Creating a Rich Text Editor 155
 Displaying Progress 156
 Summary 158

6 Menus and Flyouts — 161

Using the `Flyout` Control — 161
Using the `Menu` Control — 163
Using the `AppBar` Control — 167
    Creating a Simple App Bar — 168
    Using App Bar Commands — 170
    Showing Contextual Commands — 173
Configuring App Settings — 175
    Creating About Page Settings — 176
    Creating Personal Settings — 178
Displaying Windows Dialogs — 182
Summary — 184

7 Using the `ListView` Control — 185

Introduction to the `ListView` Control — 185
    Using List Layout versus Grid Layout — 190
    Preventing Overlapping `ListView` Items — 193
Selecting Items in a `ListView` Control — 197
    Creating a Master/Detail View — 198
    Selecting Multiple Items — 202
Sorting Items in a `ListView` Control — 204
Filtering Items in a `ListView` Control — 206
Grouping Items in a `ListView` Control — 208
Switching Views with Semantic Zoom — 211
Switching a `ListView` Template Dynamically — 216
Loading `ListView` Items Incrementally — 219
Summary — 221

8 Creating Data Sources — 223

Creating Custom Data Sources — 223
    Creating the Data Source Class — 224
    Creating a Data Adapter — 224
    Implementing the `getCount()` Method — 225
    Implementing the `itemsFromIndex()` Method — 225
    Implementing the `insertAtEnd()` Method — 227
    Implementing the `remove()` Method — 227
    Implementing the `change()` Method — 228
    Handling Errors — 228
    Implementing the `setNotificationHandler()` Method — 229
Creating a File Data Source — 230
    Using the File Data Source — 231

		Creating a Web Service Data Source	236
		Creating the Data Source	236
		Creating the Web Service	237
		Using the Web Service Data Source	240
		Creating an `IndexedDB` Data Source	241
		Overview of `IndexedDB`	241
		Using the `IndexedDB` Data Source	245
		Summary	252
9	**App Events and States**		**253**
		App Events	253
		Handling the Activated Event	254
		Handling the Error Event	255
		Deferring Events with Promises	256
		Creating Custom Events	257
		Suspending, Terminating, and Resuming an App	257
		Detecting When an App Is Suspended and Terminated	258
		Detecting the Previous Execution State	258
		Testing Application State with Visual Studio	259
		Storing State with Session State	260
		Application View States	261
		Snapped, Filled, Portrait, and Landscape	261
		Using Media Queries	264
		Using the JavaScript `mediaMatch` Method	266
		Defining a Viewport	267
		Summary	270
10	**Page Fragments and Navigation**		**273**
		Using the `HtmlControl` Control	273
		Creating a Page Control	276
		Creating Multipage Apps	280
		Creating a Navigation App	280
		Understanding the Navigation App default.html Page	281
		Adding New Page Controls to a Navigation App	283
		Navigating to Another Page	285
		Understanding the Navigation API	286
		Understanding the `PageControlNavigator` Control	287
		Understanding Navigation State	287
		Summary	291

Contents ix

11 Using the Live Connect API   **293**

  Installing the Live SDK 294
    Adding a Reference to the Live SDK 294
    Registering Your App 294
    Initializing the Live Connect SDK 296
    Specifying Different Scopes 296
  Authenticating a User 299
    Using `WL.login()` 299
    Using the `signIn` Control 300
    Authentication Events 302
  Passing an Authentication Token to a Web Service 303
    Sending the Authentication Token from a Windows Store App 303
    Verifying the Authentication Token in a Web Service 306
    Retrieving the User ID 308
  Retrieving Basic User Information 309
  Uploading and Downloading Files from SkyDrive 311
    Listing SkyDrive Folders and Files 312
    Downloading Files from SkyDrive 314
    Uploading Files to SkyDrive 316
    Summary 318

12 Graphics and Games   **319**

  Overview of the Game 320
  Creating the Game Tiles 321
  Playing the Game Sounds 322
  Creating the Game Canvas 323
  Capturing User Interaction 325
  Creating the Update Loop 327
  Creating the Render Loop 329
  Summary 331

Index   **333**

About the Author

Formerly a Senior Program Manager at Microsoft, **Stephen Walther** now runs his own consulting and training company, www.SuperexpertTraining.com. He flies to companies and provides hands-on training on building Windows Store apps.

Stephen was completing his Ph.D. at MIT and teaching classes on metaphysics at MIT and Harvard when he abruptly realized that there is no money in metaphysics. He dropped out to help found two successful Internet startups. He created the Collegescape website, a website used by more than 200 colleges including Stanford, Harvard, and MIT for online college applications (sold to ETS). He also was a founder of CityAuction, which was one of the first and largest auction websites (sold to CitySearch).

Dedication

This book is dedicated to Ada Reason Walther, who just learned to read (Congratulations!). And who wants a goldfish (I'm working on it). And who just kicked her older sister, Athena (Stop that!).

Acknowledgments

Yikes, it takes too much work to write a technical book—don't ever do it! I would like to blame my editor, Neil Rowe, for talking me into writing another book. I also want to blame my wife, Ruth Walther, for failing to talk me out of it. Finally, I want to blame my technical editor, Jeff Burtoft, for doing such a careful job of coming up with ways to improve the book and forcing me to spend even more time working on the book. Really, don't ever agree to write a book....

We Want to Hear from You!

As the reader of this book, *you* are our most important critic and commentator. We value your opinion and want to know what we're doing right, what we could do better, what areas you'd like to see us publish in, and any other words of wisdom you're willing to pass our way.

We welcome your comments. You can email or write to let us know what you did or didn't like about this book—as well as what we can do to make our books better.

Please note that we cannot help you with technical problems related to the topic of this book.

When you write, please be sure to include this book's title and author as well as your name and email address. We will carefully review your comments and share them with the author and editors who worked on the book.

Email: consumer@samspublishing.com

Mail: Sams Publishing
ATTN: Reader Feedback
800 East 96th Street
Indianapolis, IN 46240 USA

Reader Services

Visit our website and register this book at informit.com/register for convenient access to any updates, downloads, or errata that might be available for this book.

Introduction

If you want to build a software application and reach the largest possible market of customers and make the most money, then it makes sense to build a Windows 8 app.

Microsoft Windows is the most popular operating system in the world. Windows accounts for more than 90% of the operating system market. As of June 2012, over 600 million licenses for Windows 7 have been sold. The size of the Windows market dwarfs the size of every other marketplace for software applications (including the iPhone and Android markets).

Now, it is true that not everyone who is using earlier versions of Windows will upgrade to Windows 8. But, it is fairly safe to predict that a very large number of people will make the jump. Microsoft CEO Steve Ballmer—admittedly, not the most unbiased of people—predicts that more than 500 million people will be using Windows 8 by the end of 2013.

I want to own a toilet made of solid gold, Nathan Myhrvold's jet, and a Tesla Roadster (orange). These are modest goals and I know that many of you reading this book share the same goals. The most likely way for you or me (hopefully me) to reach these goals is to build Windows 8 apps.

When you build a Windows 8 app, you can sell your app right within Windows 8 itself. Windows 8 includes the Windows Store where you can list your app for anywhere between free and $999.99. You can sell a variety of different types of apps including productivity apps (think time trackers and contact managers) and games (think *Angry Birds* and *Cut the Rope*).

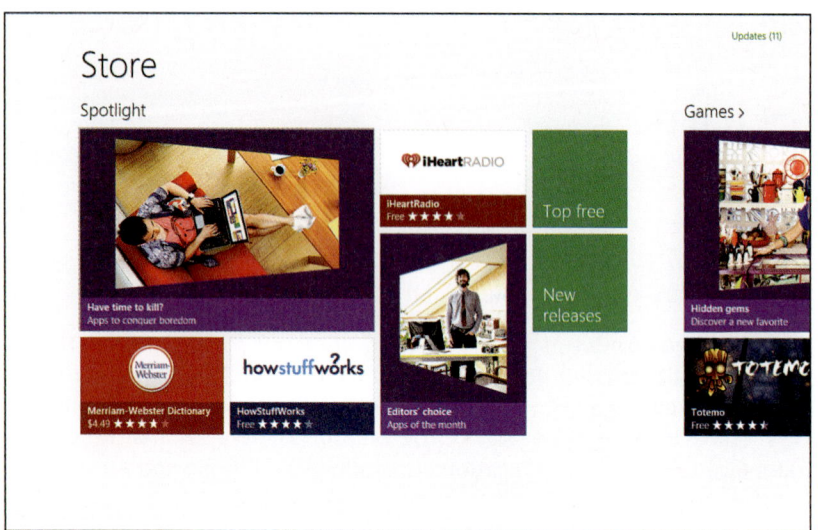

FIGURE I.1

This book is all about building Windows Store apps that you can sell in the Windows Store. In particular, you learn how to build Windows Store apps using JavaScript and HTML5.

Why JavaScript and HTML5? You can build Windows Store apps using other technologies such as C# and XAML or C++, but this book focuses exclusively on building Windows Store apps with JavaScript and HTML5.

The advantage of building Windows Store apps with JavaScript and HTML5 is that you can leverage your existing skills building websites to build Windows applications. If you are already comfortable programming with JavaScript, HTML, and Cascading Style Sheets, then you should find it easy to build Windows Store apps.

This book covers everything you need to know to build Windows Store apps. You learn how to use the Windows Library for JavaScript (WinJS) to create JavaScript applications. In particular, you learn how to use WinJS controls such as the `Rating`, `Menu`, and `ListView` controls.

You also learn how to work with the Windows Runtime. By taking advantage of the Windows Runtime, you can access Windows 8 functionality to do things that you could not normally do in a pure web app, such as capture video and sound.

By the end of this book, you will understand how to create Windows Store apps such as productivity and game apps. For example, in Chapter 7 and 8, you learn how to use the `ListView` control to create a simple task list app. And, in Chapter 12, you learn how to create a simple arcade game—the Brain Eaters game.

Read this book, build a Windows Store app, sell lots of copies, and buy a jet.

Prerequisites for This Book

If you can build a website using JavaScript, HTML, and Cascading Style Sheets, then you have the skills that you need to read and understand this book.

There are two software requirements for building Windows Store apps and using the code from this book.

First, you must build a Windows Store app on the Windows 8 operating system. Let me repeat this: You must have Windows 8 installed on your computer to use the code from this book.

Second, in order to use the code from this book, you need Microsoft Visual Studio 2012. There is a free version of Visual Studio 2012—Microsoft Visual Studio 2012 Express for Windows 8—which you can download from the Microsoft.com website.

> **NOTE**
> Occasionally in the printed book, when a line of code is too long to fit across the page, a code-continuation character (➥) has been inserted to mark the continuation.

Source Code

All of the source code associated with this book can be downloaded from GitHub by visiting: https://github.com/StephenWalther/Windows8AppsUnleashed

Click the Downloads link to download the latest version of the code in a ZIP file.

CHAPTER 1
Building Windows Store Apps

IN THIS CHAPTER

- ▶ What Is a Windows Store App?
- ▶ Creating Your First Windows Store App
- ▶ Elements of a Windows Store App
- ▶ Building Windows Store Apps with Visual Studio
- ▶ Debugging a Windows Store App
- ▶ Publishing to the Windows Store

In this chapter, I introduce you to the basics of building Windows Store apps. I start off by explaining how a Windows Store app differs from a traditional Windows desktop application. You learn what makes a Windows Store app a Windows Store app.

Feeling fearless and bold, and hoping that *you too* feel fearless and bold, I next guide you through building your first Windows Store app. You learn how to take advantage of the features of Microsoft Visual Studio 2012 to build, run, and debug a Windows Store app.

Next, we dive into a discussion of the fundamental elements of a Windows Store app. You learn how a Windows Store app is forged out of HTML5, JavaScript, the Windows Library for JavaScript, and the Windows Runtime.

Finally, we get to the money part. I explain how you can publish your Windows Store app to the Windows Store and start collecting those dollars.

What Is a Windows Store App?

I can still remember the first time that I used an iPhone. When you scroll the screen on an iPhone, the screen actually bounces! And when you add an email to the trash, the email gets sucked into the trashcan! It's as if there is a little universe inside an iPhone and it follows our physical laws.

For some reason—that I have not explored and that I do not completely understand—this illusion that there is a second universe inside my iPhone makes me happy. It makes interacting with an iPhone fun.

Now we come to Windows. Except for the dancing card thing in Windows Solitaire, I can't think of anything in Windows that has ever created this same sense of fun. I can't remember the last time that Windows made me laugh or brought me joy.

With Windows Store apps, Microsoft has finally acknowledged that user experience matters—in a big way. The heart of Windows Store apps is a set of user experience principles named the *Microsoft design style principles*. By embracing the Microsoft design style principles, you can create Windows Store apps that seem more alive and that are a pleasure to use.

Microsoft Design Style Principles

The Microsoft design style principles is a set of user experience design principles developed by Microsoft in the context of building the Windows Phone, Xbox Live, and the (now defunct) Zune. You also can see the Microsoft design principles applied to Microsoft websites such as Microsoft SkyDrive and the Windows Azure Portal. Get ready. Here they are:

1. Show pride in craftsmanship.

    ▶ Devote time and energy to small things that are seen often by many.

    ▶ Engineer the experience to be complete and polished at every stage.

2. Do more with less.

    ▶ Solve for distractions, not discoverability. Let people be immersed in what they love and they will explore the rest.

    ▶ Create a clean and purposeful experience by leaving only the most relevant elements on screen so people can be immersed in the content.

3. Be fast and fluid.

    ▶ Let people interact directly with content, and respond to actions quickly with matching energy.

    ▶ Bring life to the experience, create a sense of continuity and tell a story through meaningful use of motion.

4. Be authentically digital.

    ▶ Take full advantage of the digital medium. Remove physical boundaries to create experiences that are more efficient and effortless than reality.

    ▶ Embrace the fact that we are pixels on a screen. Design with bold, vibrant and crisp colors and images that go beyond the limits of real world material.

5. **Win as one.**

    ▶ Leverage the ecosystem and work together with other apps, devices and the system to complete scenarios for people.

    ▶ Fit into the UI model to reduce redundancy. Take advantage of what people already know to provide a sense of familiarity, control, and confidence.

> **NOTE**
>
> The Microsoft design style principles were originally known as *Metro design principles*. This list of Microsoft design style principles was taken from http://msdn.microsoft.com/en-us/library/windows/apps/hh464920 and http://msdn.microsoft.com/en-us/library/windows/apps/hh465424.aspx.

When I first read these principles, my initial reaction was that they seemed overly abstract and squishy. Exactly the type of principles which would be created by beret wearing user experience guys.

But then, when I saw how the principles were applied in practice—when building actual Windows Store apps—I started to develop a better appreciation for these principles.

Take the "Do more with less" design principle. One of the distinctive features of a Windows Store app is the lack of chrome. Ironically, a Windows Store app is a Windows app without the Window. Windows Store apps are full screen apps.

This lack of chrome makes it easier to concentrate on the content of the application. For example, Windows 8 includes two versions of Internet Explorer: a desktop version and a full-throated Windows 8 version which follows the Microsoft design style principles.

I really prefer using the Windows 8 version of Internet Explorer over the desktop version. When using the Windows 8 version, all you see is the web page which is the point of the application in the first place.

Or consider the "Be fast and fluid" principle. The reason that I like interacting with my iPhone so much is the illusion of motion and this illusion is created by the judicious use of animations: On an iPhone, objects bounce and wobble.

When building a Windows Store app, you are encouraged to take advantage of animations. For example, if you use the standard ListView control—which we discuss in detail later in this book—then you get animations when you add or remove items. When you add an item to a ListView, it not only appears, it glides into place. When you remove an item, it doesn't just disappear, items above and below it collapse into place.

> **NOTE**
>
> There is a technical word for when a computer app imitates physical reality. The word is *skeuomorphism*.

Common Features of Windows Store Apps

Windows Store apps are applications which follow the Microsoft design style principles. Furthermore, Windows Store apps are designed to run on the Windows 8 or Windows RT operating system.

All Windows Store apps have a common set of features. Let me explain these features by pointing them out in the context of the Windows 8 version of Internet Explorer.

Support for Keyboard, Mouse, Touch, and Stylus

One of the most distinctive characteristics of a Windows Store app is its over-sized tiles and buttons and generous use of whitespace. All of this UI roominess makes Windows Store apps friendly to fat fingers.

Windows Store apps are designed to work equally well when used on a touch-only tablet and when used on a desktop computer with a keyboard and mouse. Windows Store apps are designed to be gropeable.

The nice thing about how Windows 8 works is that you don't need to put a lot of thought into supporting touch as a developer. As long as you stick with the standard WinJS controls, you get both keyboard and touch support for free.

Using the App Bar and Nav Bar

Figure 1.1 contains a screenshot of the Windows 8 version of Internet Explorer with the home page of the New York Times open. Notice that the only thing that you see is the content of the New York Times. No toolbars, no buttons, no status bars.

FIGURE 1.1   Windows 8 Internet Explorer

What Is a Windows Store App? 9

In a Windows Store app, you hide all of your commands in the app bar. The app bar appears only when you swipe from the bottom or top of the screen or you right-click the screen.

The app bar for Internet Explorer includes the address bar and buttons such as the back button and refresh button (see Figure 1.2).

FIGURE 1.2   Using the app bar and nav bar

Notice in Figure 1.2 that there is another bar at the top of the screen. This bar is called the nav bar and you use it to navigate. In the case of Internet Explorer, the nav bar contains thumbnails of all of your open browser tabs.

Using Charms

If you swipe from the right edge of the screen or mouse to either of the right corners or press the keyboard combination Win+c, then the charms are revealed (see Figure 1.3).

10   CHAPTER 1   Building Windows Store Apps

FIGURE 1.3   Viewing charms

Here's a list of the standard charms:

- **Search**—Enables you to search content in the current app and other apps.
- **Share**—Enables you to share content in the current app with other apps.
- **Start**—Navigates you to the Start screen.
- **Devices**—Enables you to connect to a device.
- **Settings**—Enables you to configure both app settings and system settings.

These charms provide you with standard locations to place common application functionality. For example, all Windows Store app settings should appear in the Settings charm (see Figure 1.4). This makes it much easier for users to find your settings.

What Is a Windows Store App?   11

FIGURE 1.4 The Settings charm

When you are building a Windows Store app, you don't build your own settings menu. Instead, you extend the Settings charm with your custom app settings. I discuss the details of doing this in Chapter 6, "Menus and Flyouts."

Full Screen, Snapped, and Filled
A Windows Store app can be in three different *view states*: Full screen, snapped, and filled. The default state is full screen—the app takes over all of the available screen real estate.

You can switch an app between the different view states by pressing the keyboard combination Win+. (period) or by swiping from the top-edge to the left edge of the screen or by mousing to the top-left corner and dragging down.

> **WARNING**
>
> You can switch an app to snapped state only on a Windows device with a horizontal resolution of 1,366 pixels or higher. Otherwise, there is not enough screen real estate to see more than one app at a time.

Figure 1.5 shows two Windows 8 apps on the screen at one time. The Weather app is in a snapped state and the Internet Explorer app is in a filled state. A snapped app always has a horizontal resolution of 320 pixels. The filled app takes up the remainder of the screen real estate.

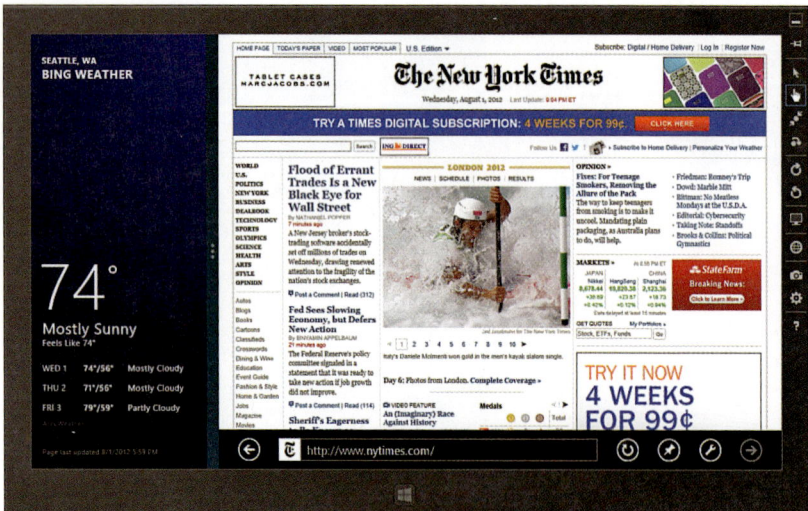

FIGURE 1.5   Snapped and filled apps

When building Windows Store apps, you need to design the app so it works in full screen, snapped, or filled state. At any moment, the horizontal resolution of your app could be dramatically changed. I discuss how to handle switching between different view states in Chapter 9, "App Events and States."

Closing a Windows Store App

Now close a Windows Store app by moving your cursor over the x at the top-right of the screen. Ha! Tricked You! There is no close button in a Windows Store app because there is no chrome.

> **NOTE**
>
> Even though it is not obvious how to close a Windows Store app, it is possible. You can close a Windows Store app by swiping down from the top of the screen to the very bottom of the screen or pressing the keyboard combination ALT+F4.

When interacting with Windows Store apps, there is no obvious way to close an app. This is intentional. Instead of closing a Windows Store app, you are encouraged to simply switch to another running app (by swiping from the left edge of the screen) or launch a new app (by selecting a new app from the Start screen).

When you design a Windows Store app, you must design the app with the knowledge that a user might switch back and forth to your running app at any time. In Chapter 9, I discuss how you can gracefully resume an app after it has been suspended.

Creating Your First Windows Store App

Let's be fearless. In this section, I guide you through building your first Windows Store app. Doing a *Hello World* app would be predictable and boring. Therefore, I suggest that we do something a little more advanced.

I'll show you how you can create an app which enables you to take pictures. When you click the Take Picture command in the app bar, you can take a picture, and then the picture is displayed in the app (see Figure 1.6, which shows a picture of my dog Rover).

> **NOTE**
>
> The code for the completed app can be found in the Chapter1 folder with the name App1.

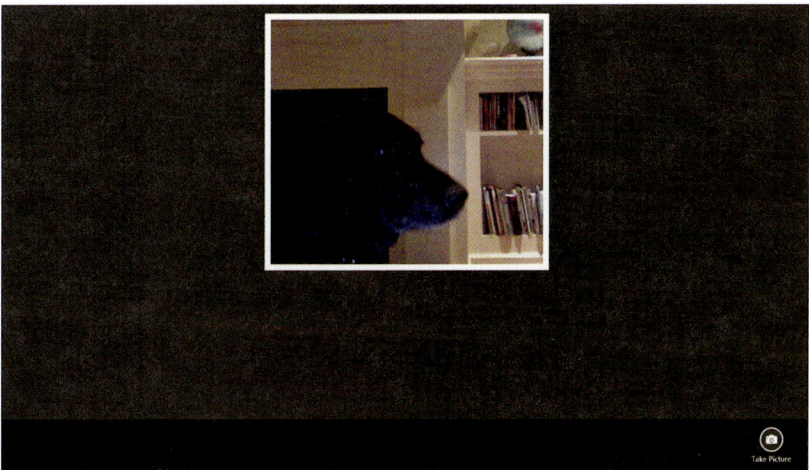

FIGURE 1.6   Your first Windows Store app

Creating the Visual Studio Project

The first step is to create the Microsoft Visual Studio Project. I used Visual Studio 2012 to create almost all of the code samples for this book. In most cases, I used the free version of Visual Studio—Visual Studio 2012 Express for Windows 8—which you can download from Microsoft.com.

> **NOTE**
>
> In chapters in which I created a web service project, I used Visual Studio Professional 2012 because I needed to create both a Windows Store app and an ASP.NET project in the same solution.

NOTE

You can create Windows Store apps with either Microsoft Visual Studio 2012 or Microsoft Blend. If you need to release to the Windows Store, then I recommend using Microsoft Visual Studio 2012.

In order to build Windows Store apps, you must use Visual Studio on Windows 8. If you don't have a dedicated Windows 8 computer, you can use a virtual machine running Windows 8 such as VMware Player.

Go ahead and launch Visual Studio. Next, select the menu option File, New Project. On the left-side of the New Project dialog, select JavaScript and select the *Blank App* project template. Enter the name App1 for your project and click the OK button (see Figure 1.7).

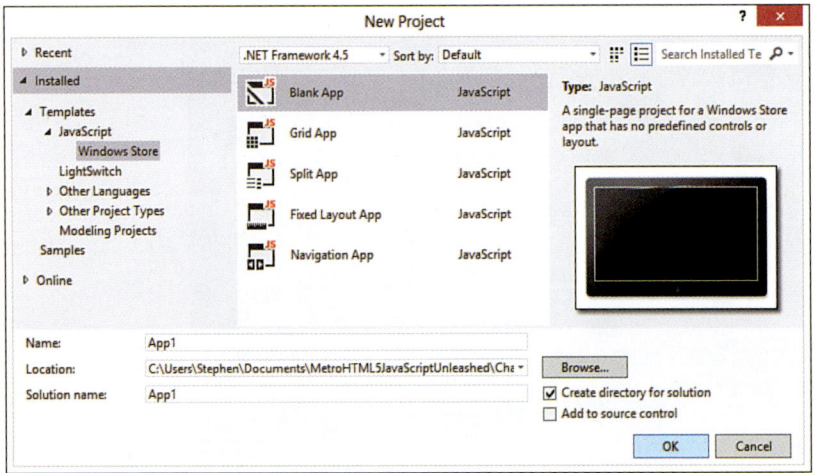

FIGURE 1.7 Using the Visual Studio New Project dialog

After you create your project, you can see all of the files for your project in the Solution Explorer window (Figure 1.8). When you create a new Windows Store app, you get a default.html file (in the root of your project), a default.js file (in the js folder), and a default.css file (in the css folder). These three files are the starting point for your app.

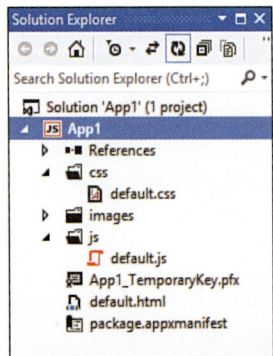

FIGURE 1.8 Windows Store app default files

Declaring App Capabilities

Before we can jump into writing code, there is one other thing which we must do first. We are building an app which takes pictures. That is scary. Potentially, an app could take pictures of you without your knowledge and send the pictures back to an evil hacker lurking on the Internet (or Steve Ballmer sitting behind his desk at Microsoft).

When your app does something scary, you must declare that your app will do this scary thing up front so the user can consent. You declare the capabilities of your app in your application manifest file. You can open the editor for your application manifest by double-clicking the package.appxmanifest file in the Solution Explorer window.

Click the Capabilities tab to view all of the declared capabilities of your application. For example, if you want your app to be able to record from the computer microphone, then you need to select the Microphone capability, or if you want your app to be able to save new photos in the user's Pictures library, then you need to select the Pictures Library capability. For our app, we need to enable the Webcam capability so we can take pictures (see Figure 1.9).

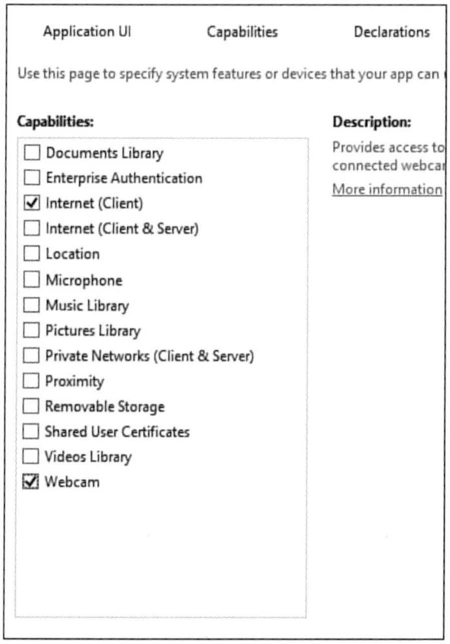

FIGURE 1.9 Enabling the capability to take pictures

When a user first runs our app, the user will need to consent to allowing the app to access the Webcam (see Figure 1.10). The user only needs to consent once.

16 CHAPTER 1 Building Windows Store Apps

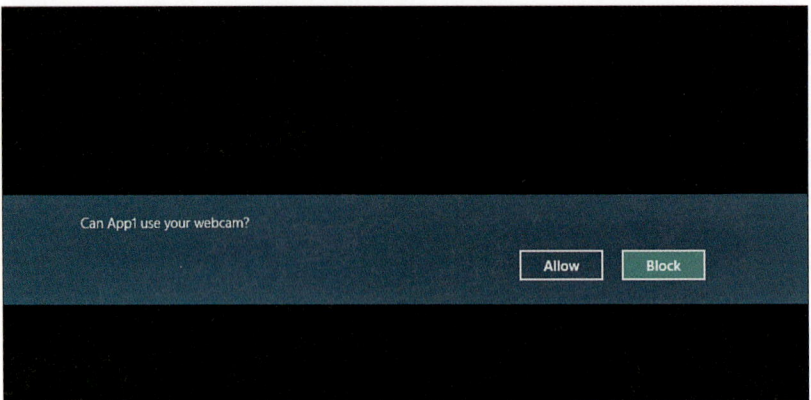

FIGURE 1.10 Asking for consent to access your webcam

> **NOTE**
>
> After a user consents, the user can deny an app permissions to use a particular capability by using the Permissions setting under the Settings charm.

Creating the HTML Page

When you create a Windows Store app, you get a default.html file in the root of your application. This is the first page which is opened when you run your app. Let's go ahead and customize this page for our picture app (see Listing 1.1).

LISTING 1.1 Modified default.html Page

```html
<!DOCTYPE html>
<html>
<head>
    <meta charset="utf-8" />
    <title>App1</title>

    <!-- WinJS references -->
    <link href="//Microsoft.WinJS.1.0/css/ui-dark.css" rel="stylesheet" />
    <script src="//Microsoft.WinJS.1.0/js/base.js"></script>
    <script src="//Microsoft.WinJS.1.0/js/ui.js"></script>

    <!-- App1 references -->
    <link href="/css/default.css" rel="stylesheet" />
    <script src="/js/default.js"></script>
</head>
<body>
```

```html
        <img id="imgPhoto" src="/images/placeholder.png" />

        <!-- AppBar Control -->
        <div id="appBar1"
            data-win-control="WinJS.UI.AppBar">
            <button data-win-control="WinJS.UI.AppBarCommand"
                data-win-options="{
                    id:'cmdTakePicture',
                    label:'Take Picture',
                    icon:'camera',
                    tooltip:'Take Picture'
                }">
            </button>
        </div>
    </body>
</html>
```

The HTML page in Listing 1.1 has been modified so it contains new content in the body of the page. First, notice that the page contains an IMG tag with the ID `imgPhoto`. We'll display the photo which we take from the camera here.

Notice, furthermore, that the page contains a DIV tag with a `data-win-control="WinJS.UI.AppBar"` attribute. This is an example of a WinJS control. This control renders an app bar which contains a command for taking a picture (see Figure 1.11).

FIGURE 1.11   The Take Picture command in the app bar

Creating the Style Sheet

When you create a new Windows Store app, you also get a default style sheet named default.css which is located in the css folder. This file contains default style rules for handling Windows Store apps in different view states.

> **NOTE**
>
> I discuss the different Windows Store app view states in detail in Chapter 9.

For our app, I've modified the default.css to format the appearance of the photo which appears in the IMG tag like this:

```css
#imgPhoto {
    display:block;
    margin: 15px auto;
    border: 10px solid white;
    max-width: 90%;
    max-height: 90%;
}
```

Creating the JavaScript File

The third file that we need to modify is the JavaScript file named default.js which is located in the js folder. This file contains all of the code associated with the default.html page.

We are going to delete all of the default content of this file and start over. The complete contents of the modified version of default.js are contained in Listing 1.2.

LISTING 1.2 The default.js JavaScript File

```javascript
(function () {
    "use strict";

    // Aliases
    var capture = Windows.Media.Capture;

    // Executed immediately after page content is loaded
    function init() {
        // Process all of the controls
        WinJS.UI.processAll().done(function () {
            // References to DOM elements
            var cmdTakePicture = document.getElementById("cmdTakePicture");
            var imgPhoto = document.getElementById("imgPhoto");

            // Handle Take Picture command click
            cmdTakePicture.addEventListener("click", function () {
                var captureUI = new capture.CameraCaptureUI();
                captureUI.photoSettings.format =
➥capture.CameraCaptureUIPhotoFormat.png;

                captureUI.captureFileAsync(capture.CameraCaptureUIMode.photo).
➥done(function (photo) {
                    if (photo) {
                        // Use HTML5 File API to create object URL to refer to the
➥photo file
```

```
                    var photoUrl = URL.createObjectURL(photo);

                    // Show photo in IMG element
                    imgPhoto.src = photoUrl;
                }
            });
        });
    });
    }

    document.addEventListener("DOMContentLoaded", init);
})();
```

> **NOTE**
>
> The JavaScript code contained in the `Default.js` file which we deleted is used to handle app lifecycle events such as app activation and suspension. I discuss these app events in detail in Chapter 9.

There is a lot of interesting stuff happening in the JavaScript code in Listing 1.2. Let's walk through the code.

First, I've created an `init()` function which is executed when the `DOMContentLoaded` event is raised. The `DOMContentLoaded` event is a standard DOM event which is raised when a browser finishes parsing an HTML document.

I put all of my code into the `init()` function so the code won't be executed until the DOM is ready. Otherwise, if I attempted to access any of the HTML elements in the page, I would get an exception because the elements would not yet exist.

The first thing that I do within the `init()` method is call the `WinJS.UI.processAll()` method. This method processes all of the controls in a page. In particular, it converts the DIV tag with the `data-win-control="WinJS.UI.AppBar"` attribute into an actual app bar.

Next, I set up an event handler for the Take Picture command. When you click the Take Picture command in the app bar, an instance of the `Windows.Media.Capture.CameraCaptureUI` class is created. The `CameraCaptureUI` class is an example of a Windows Runtime class.

The `CameraCaptureUI.captureFileAsync()` method displays the screen for taking a picture (see Figure 1.12). When you click the OK button, the `done()` method is called and the picture is displayed in the page.

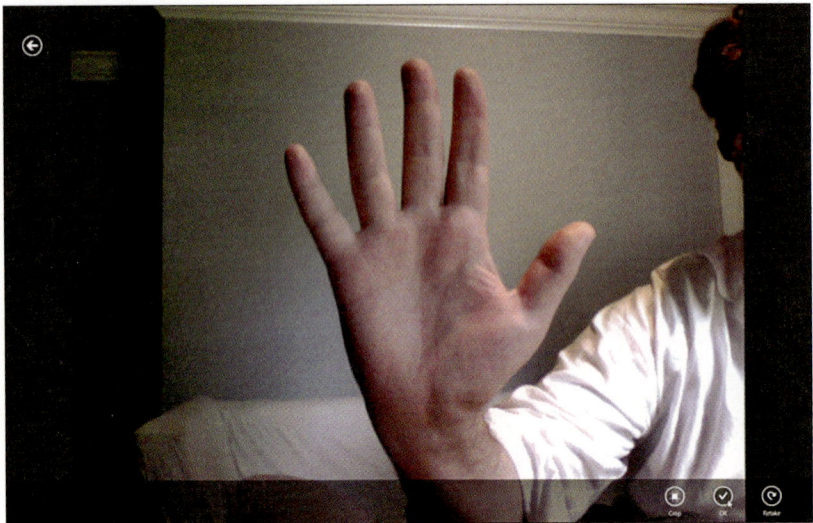

FIGURE 1.12 The camera capture UI screen

An object URL is created for the photo blob (the actual image data) returned by the `captureFileAsync()` method by calling the `URL.createObjectURL()` method. This `createObjectURL()` method is part of the HTML5 File API.

The photo is displayed in the HMTL page with the following lines of code:

```
// Show photo in IMG element
imgPhoto.src = photoUrl;
```

And that is all there is to it! We built an app which enables us to take pictures from our computer and display the pictures in an HTML page.

Notice that our JavaScript file contains a combination of standard JavaScript methods, HTML5 methods, Windows Library for JavaScript methods, and Windows Runtime methods. This is normal for all of the JavaScript files which you create when creating a Windows Store app.

Running the App

After you create the app, you can run it by hitting the green Run button in the Visual Studio toolbar (see Figure 1.13) or just hit the F5 key.

FIGURE 1.13 Running a Windows Store style app

Assuming that your laptop or tablet has a camera, you can start taking pictures.

> **WARNING**
> Remember that the Take Picture command is contained in the app bar and the app bar does not appear by default. You need to either right-click the app or swipe from the top or bottom edge of your computer to display the app bar.

Elements of a Windows Store App

As we saw in the previous section, a Windows Store app is built using several technologies. A Windows Store app is built out of a combination of open and familiar web technologies such as HTML5, JavaScript, and CSS 3 and Microsoft technologies such as the Windows Library for JavaScript and the Windows Runtime. Let me say a little more about each of these elements of a Windows Store app.

JavaScript

This book is all about writing Windows Store apps using JavaScript. As an alternative to JavaScript, you also could write Windows Store apps using C#, Visual Basic, or even C++.

When writing Windows Store apps, you can take advantage of the features of ECMAScript 5 which is the latest version of JavaScript. This means that you can use the new JavaScript Array methods like `indexOf()` and `forEach()`. You also can use property setters and getters and "use strict".

HTML5

When writing Windows Store apps, you can take advantage of many of the new features of HTML5 and related standards. Here is a list of some of the most important of these new features:

- **Form Validation Attributes**—You can take advantage of the new validation attributes in the HTML5 standard to perform form validation. I discuss these new validation attributes and how you can use them in a Windows Store app in Chapter 5, "Creating Forms."

- **data-*** —The *data dash star* standard enables you to add custom attributes to existing HTML5 elements. The WinJS library uses data-* for declarative data-binding and declarative control instantiation.

- **Indexed Database API (IndexedDB)**—The Indexed Database API exposes a database in the browser. If you need to store a list of products in a database within a Windows Store app, then you can take advantage of IndexedDB. I explain how to use IndexedDB in Chapter 8, "Creating Data Sources."

- **File API**—The HTML5 File API enables you work with files in the browser. We used the HTML5 API in the previous section when building our first Windows Store app.

- **Canvas**—Enables you to draw graphics using JavaScript. I provide you with an introduction to Canvas in chapter 12, "Graphics and Games."

▶ **Web Workers**—Enables you to execute background tasks without blocking the user interface thread.

Cascading Style Sheets 3

When you build Windows Store apps, you can take advantage of several new features of the Cascading Style Sheets 3 standard (and related standards) including:

▶ **Media Queries**—Enables you to apply different styles depending on the characteristics of a device such as the height, width, or view state of the device. I discuss Media Queries in Chapter 9.

▶ **CSS3 Grid Layout**—Enables you to lay out HTML content in columns and rows without using HTML tables.

▶ **CSS3 Flexible Box Layout (FlexBox)**—Enables you to preserve relative element position and size when displaying HTML content in different devices.

Windows Runtime

The Windows Runtime (WinRT) contains a class library which you can use in your Windows Store apps. These classes are projected directly into JavaScript so they appear to be built-in JavaScript objects.

For example, when we wrote our first Windows Store app, we took advantage of the WinRT `Windows.Media.Capture.CameraCaptureUI` class. When we called the `CameraCaptureUI.captureFileAsync()` method, we were able to take a picture.

All of the WinRT classes are exposed in JavaScript from the root Windows namespace. For example, you create an instance of the `CameraCaptureUI` class with the following code:

```
var captureUI = new Windows.Media.Capture.CameraCaptureUI();
```

> **NOTE**
>
> Notice that WinRT class names can get silly long. For this reason, it is a good idea to alias the namespaces like this:
>
> ```
> var capture = Windows.Media.Capture;
> ```

The WinRT classes extend JavaScript with all of the functionality that you need when building a Windows application. All of the stuff that you are not allowed to do—or that it does not even make sense to do—when building a website. These classes enable you to do fun and amazing things such as:

▶ **Geolocation**—Use the WinRT `Windows.Devices.Geolocation.Geolocator` class to get your current latitude and longitude.

▶ **File Access**—Read and write to the file system by taking advantage of the WinRT classes in the `Windows.Storage` namespace.

▶ **Compass**—Always know the direction of True North with the `Windows.Devices.Sensors.Compass` class.

▶ **Print**—Print from your Windows Store app by using the `Windows.Printing.PrintManager` class.

▶ **Compress Files**—Compress and decompress files using the classes in the WinRT `Windows.Storage.Compression` namespace.

Windows Library for JavaScript

The Windows Library for JavaScript (WinJS) is a pure JavaScript library created by Microsoft specifically for building Windows Store apps. Understanding how to use this library is the primary focus of this book

The WinJS library contains all of the WinJS controls. These are the controls that you use to build the user interface for your Windows Store app. For example, the WinJS library includes a `DatePicker` control, which displays a user interface widget for selecting a date.

What about jQuery?

jQuery is the most popular JavaScript library in the universe. An obvious question, therefore, is whether or not you can use jQuery when building Windows store apps?

> **NOTE**
>
> According to BuiltWith, over 57% of the top 10,000 websites use jQuery. This is (by a wide margin) the most common JavaScript framework used on websites. See http://trends.BuiltWith.com/javascript.

The answer is yes. Let me show you.

The easiest way to add jQuery to a Windows Store app project is to use the Library Package Manager in Visual Studio. Select the menu option Tools, Library Package Manager, Package Manager Console. Enter the command install-package jQuery into the Package Manager Console window (see Figure 1.14).

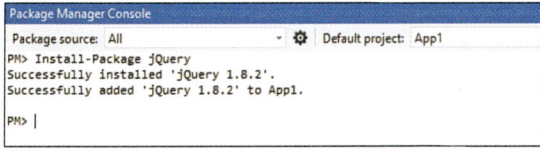

FIGURE 1.14 Adding jQuery with the Library Package Manager Console

Executing the **install-package** jQuery command adds a Scripts folder with three files: the full version of jQuery, the minified version of jQuery, and an intellisense file. The intellisense file enables Visual Studio to provide jQuery intellisense when you use jQuery methods.

Listing 1.3 contains a combined HTML and JavaScript file which uses jQuery.

LISTING 1.3   Using jQuery in a Windows Store App

```html
<!DOCTYPE html>
<html>
<head>
    <meta charset="utf-8" />
    <title>jQueryWindows8</title>

    <!-- WinJS references -->
    <link href="//Microsoft.WinJS.1.0/css/ui-dark.css" rel="stylesheet" />
    <script src="//Microsoft.WinJS.1.0/js/base.js"></script>
    <script src="//Microsoft.WinJS.1.0/js/ui.js"></script>

    <!-- jQueryWindows8 references -->
    <script type="text/javascript" src="Scripts/jquery-1.7.2.js"></script>

    <style type="text/css">
        #divMessage {
            display:none;
            padding:10px;
            border: solid 1px white;
            background-color: #ff6a00;
        }
    </style>
</head>
<body>
    <button id="btnShow">Click Here</button>
    <div id="divMessage">
        Secret Message
    </div>
```

```
    <script type="text/javascript">
        $("#btnShow").click(function () {
            $("#divMessage").fadeToggle("slow");
        });
    </script>

</body>
</html>
```

The page in Listing 1.3 contains a Button and a DIV element. The contents of the DIV element are hidden by default (with `display:none`). When you click the button, the contents of the DIV fade slowly into view (see Figure 1.15).

FIGURE 1.15 Using jQuery to animate a DIV element

> **NOTE**
>
> The code in Listing 1.3 is contained in the Chapter1 project in a folder named jQueryWindows8.

> **WARNING**
>
> In a Windows Store app, JavaScript code executed in the local context has extra security restrictions to prevent script injection attacks. In particular, you cannot assign HTML which contains potentially dangerous content such as scripts or malformed HTML to an element's innerHTML property.
>
> If you are using a JavaScript library which was not written with these security restrictions in mind, such as jQuery, then you might need to modify the library to work with a Windows Store app. If you trust the content being assigned to the innerHTML property, then instead of using the innerHTML property, you can use the `WinJS.Utilities.setInnerHTMLUnsafe()` method.

Building Windows Store Apps with Visual Studio

This book focuses on building Windows Store apps with Visual Studio. In this section, I want to devote a few pages to describing the features of Visual Studio which matter when building Windows Store apps. You learn how to select a project template for a Windows Store app, how to run a Windows Store app, and how to debug a Windows Store app.

Windows Store App Project Templates

When you select the File, New Project menu option in Visual Studio, you can select from five different project templates as your starting point for your Windows Store app:

1. **Blank App**—The simplest of the templates. Contains a single default.html, default.css, and default.js file.

2. **Navigation App**—Use this template for apps which require multiple pages.

3. **Grid App**—Contains two pages. One page displays a list of items in different groups. The second page displays details for the item which you click.

4. **Split App**—Contains two pages. One page displays a list of groups. The second page displays a list of items and details for one item.

5. **Fixed Layout App**—Always scales an element to the same size with the same aspect ratio regardless of the screen resolution.

We already used the Blank App project template when creating our first Windows app above. Let me discuss the other project templates in more detail.

Navigation App Project Template

The Blank App template is a good template to use when building a simple, single-page app. If you need to support multiple pages, on the other hand, then you should use the Navigation App template.

The Navigation App project template includes a single page named home. You can add additional pages by adding new Page Controls to the pages subfolder (see Figure 1.16). I describe how you can create multi-page applications in detail in Chapter 10, "Page Fragments and Navigation."

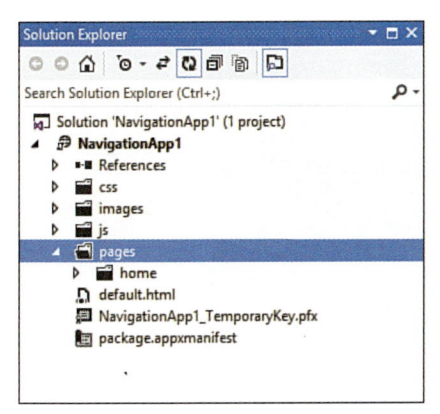

FIGURE 1.16 Creating a multi-page app with the Navigation App project template

The next two project templates—the Grid App project template and the Split App project template—are built on top of the Navigation App template. In other words, the Grid and Split App templates are multi-page apps with additional pages.

Grid App Project Template

The Grid App project template displays sets of items in different groups. You can click an item to view details on an item.

Imagine, for example, that you are creating a product catalog. In that case, you might create different product categories such as Beverages and Fruit. Each category is a group and each category contains a set of product items.

The Grid App project template displays different pages depending on the view state of your app. If your app is not snapped, then there are two pages. The `groupedItems` page displays the groups and their items (see Figure 1.17). When you click an item, the `itemDetail` page shows details for a particular item (see Figure 1.18).

FIGURE 1.17 The Grid App groupedItems page

FIGURE 1.18 The Grid App itemDetails page

If your Windows Store app is snapped, then there is an extra page. You select a group (see Figure 1.19), then you select an item (see Figure 1.20), and then you see the item details (see Figure 1.21).

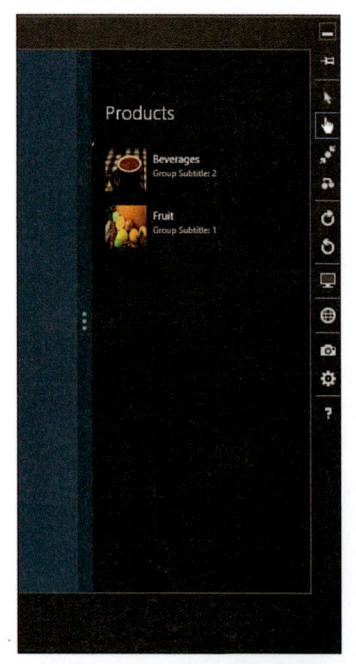

FIGURE 1.19 The Grid App groupedItems page in a snapped app

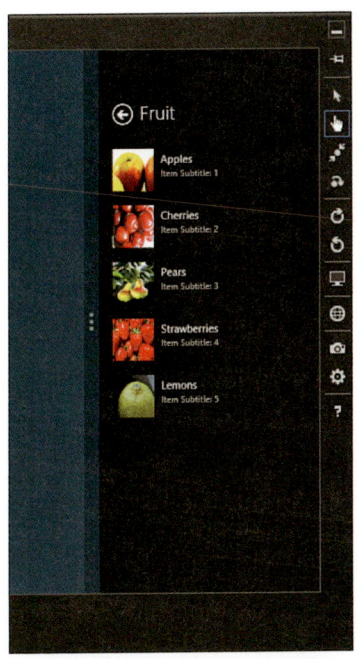

Building Windows Store Apps with Visual Studio   29

FIGURE 1.20   The Grid App groupDetail page in a snapped app

FIGURE 1.21   The Grid App itemDetail page in a snapped app

Split App Project Template

The Split App project template also can be used to display groups of items such as products grouped into product categories. The Split App project template has two pages: items and split.

The items page displays the list of groups. For example, in Figure 1.22, the items page displays the product categories.

FIGURE 1.22 The Split App items page

If you click a group, then you navigate to the split page. This page displays a list of items in the group—the products in the category—and enables you to select an item to see item details (see Figure 1.23).

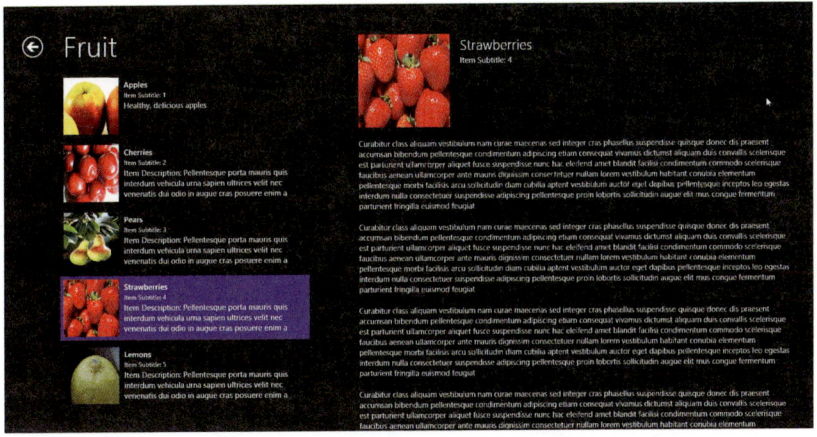

Building Windows Store Apps with Visual Studio   31

FIGURE 1.23   The Split App split page

Like the Grid App template, the Split App project template provides a different user experience when the app is snapped. When a Split App is snapped, you navigate from the group, to the items in the group, to the item detail.

Fixed Layout App Project Template
The Fixed Layout template is for a very specific scenario. The HTML page in this template includes a `ViewBox` control, which resizes its content to fit the available screen real estate while retaining the correct aspect ratio.

Imagine, for example, that you happen to have a picture of a Tesla and the picture measures 800px by 484px. You want the page to fill the entire available space but not get distorted.

Figure 1.24 illustrates the appearance of the picture on a device with a resolution of 1,024px by 768px. Notice that the picture has been scaled automatically to fit the available space.

FIGURE 1.24 Picture shown with 1,024px by 768px resolution

If you view the very same picture on a device with a different resolution, then the picture will be scaled automatically to fit the new resolution. For example, Figure 1.25 illustrates what happens when you display the picture on a device with a resolution of 1,920px by 1,080px. Notice that you get pillars on either edge of the photo so that the photo will not be distorted.

FIGURE 1.25 Picture shown with 1,920px by 1,080px resolution

The `ViewBox` even resizes its child element automatically when you snap an app (see Figure 1.26).

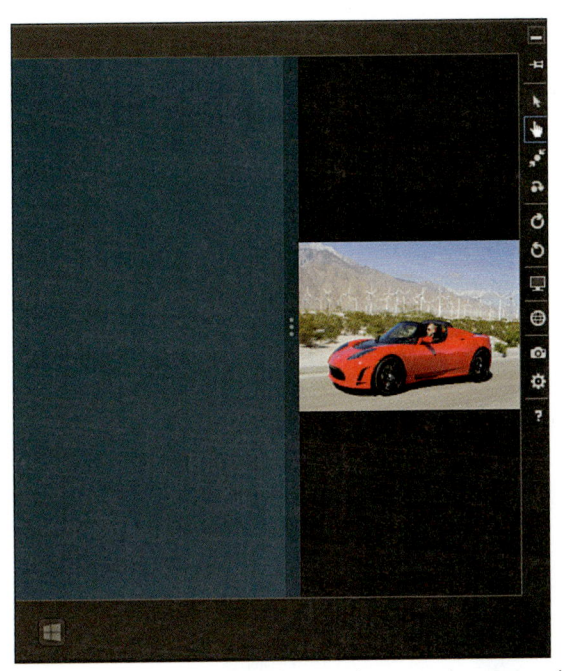

FIGURE 1.26   Resized picture when app is snapped

The `ViewBox` control has some significant limitations. You can add only one child element to a `ViewBox`. It won't work, for example, with a set of pictures.

Furthermore, the `ViewBox` does not work with text. You can use the `ViewBox` to resize a picture or a canvas.

The main scenario in which it makes sense to use the `ViewBox` (and the Fixed Layout project template) is when you want to create a game and you want the game to look good on computers and tablets with different resolutions. You don't want your angry bird to look fat on one computer and skinny on another.

> **NOTE**
>
> Behind the scenes, the `ViewBox` control uses the Cascading Style Sheet 3 translate and scale functions.

Running a Windows Store App

Visual Studio provides you with three different options for running a Windows Store app:

- Local Machine
- Simulator
- Remote Machine

The Local Machine option runs a Windows Store app as if the app was installed on the local machine. The Windows Store app will run using the screen resolution and capabilities of your development machine (the machine running Visual Studio).

The Simulator option runs your app in a separate window (see Figure 1.27). The advantage of using the simulator is that you can simulate different types of devices. For example, you can switch from *mouse mode* to *basic touch mode* to simulate a touch device such as a tablet PC. You also can switch to different screen resolutions to test your app at different resolutions.

FIGURE 1.27   Using the Visual Studio simulator

The final option is to deploy and run your Windows Store app on a remote machine. Before you can run your app on a remote machine, you must first specify the remote machine name in the Project Property Pages window (see Figure 1.28).

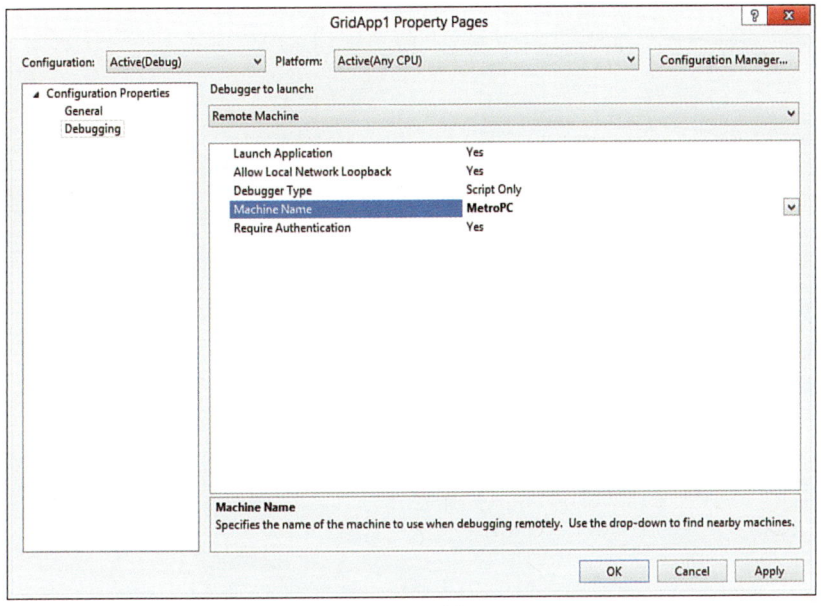

FIGURE 1.28 Specifying the remote machine name

After you specify the name of the remote machine, you can deploy and run your app on the remote machine by picking this option from the Visual Studio toolbar.

> **WARNING**
>
> To deploy and run an app on a remote machine, you need to install the Remote Tools for Visual Studio 2012 on the remote machine. You can download the Remote Tools from the Microsoft.com website.

Debugging a Windows Store App

I'm always optimistic and believe that any code that I write will run without error the first time that I run it. To date, that has never happened. I spend a significant amount of my time debugging code which does not do what I want.

In this section, I discuss the tools in Visual Studio which you can use to debug your code. I discuss how you can use the JavaScript Console window, use breakpoints, and use the DOM Explorer.

Using the Visual Studio JavaScript Console Window

When I write JavaScript code for pages used in websites, I use the JavaScript console window to view JavaScript errors. I also write custom messages to the console window using `console.log()` so I can debug my code (see Figure 1.29).

36   CHAPTER 1   Building Windows Store Apps

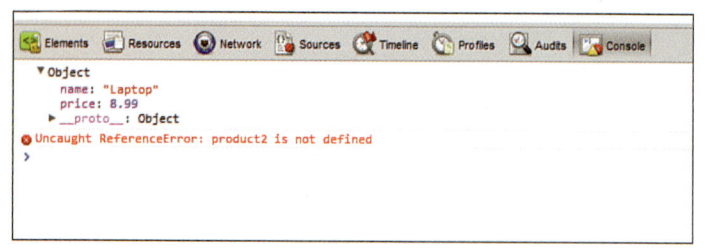

FIGURE 1.29   Debugging with the Google Chrome JavaScript console

When running a Windows Store app, you don't have access to the browser JavaScript Console. Instead of using the browser JavaScript Console, you need to use the *Visual Studio* JavaScript Console (see Figure 1.30).

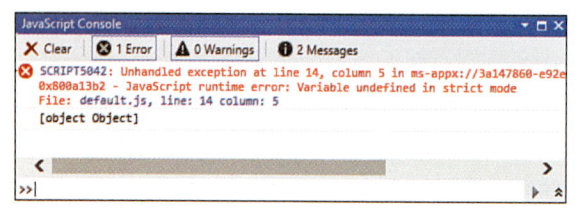

FIGURE 1.30   The Visual Studio JavaScript Console window

You can view JavaScript errors and write debug messages to the Visual Studio JavaScript Console window by using `console.log()` in exactly the same way as you would write to a browser console window.

If you hit an error and you want to display the value of a JavaScript variable, then you can enter the variable name in the bottom of the JavaScript Console (see Figure 1.31).

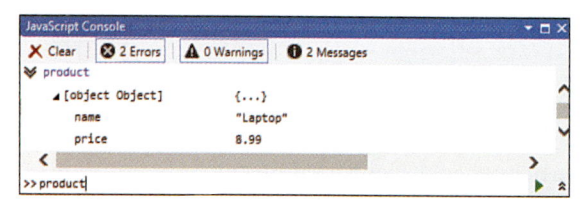

FIGURE 1.31   Dumping a JavaScript variable to the JavaScript Console window

> **NOTE**
>
> The Visual Studio Console window only appears when an app is running. If you can't find the window, use the menu option Debug, Windows, JavaScript Console.

Setting Breakpoints

If you are building a Windows Store app, and the Windows Store app is behaving in ways that you don't understand, then it is useful to set breakpoints and step through your code.

You set a breakpoint by clicking in the left gutter of the Visual Studio code editor next to the line that you want to break on (see Figure 1.32). When you run your app in debug mode, and the breakpoint is hit, then you can examine the values of your variables by hovering over them with a mouse.

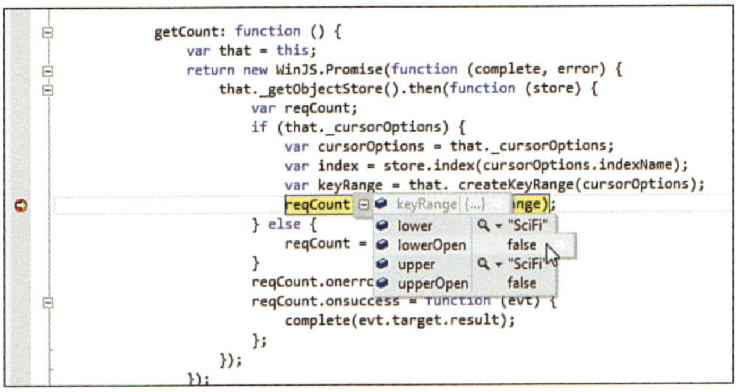

```
getCount: function () {
    var that = this;
    return new WinJS.Promise(function (complete, error) {
        that._getObjectStore().then(function (store) {
            var reqCount;
            if (that._cursorOptions) {
                var cursorOptions = that._cursorOptions;
                var index = store.index(cursorOptions.indexName);
                var keyRange = that.createKeyRange(cursorOptions);
                reqCount        keyRange  [...]    inge);
            } else {        lower      "SciFi"
                reqCount =  lowerOpen   false
            }               upper      "SciFi"
            reqCount.onerrc upperOpen   false
            reqCount.onsuccess = function (evt) {
                complete(evt.target.result);
            };
        });
    });
};
```

FIGURE 1.32 Setting a breakpoint

You can step through your code, line by line, by using the Step Into toolbar button or by pressing F11.

> **NOTE**
> As an alternative to setting a breakpoint with Visual Studio, you can create a breakpoint in code by using the JavaScript *debugger* statement.

Using the DOM Explorer

Another of my favorite browser developer tools is the HTML inspector (this is a feature, for example, of Firebug). You can use this tool to view the live HTML and CSS in a document.

Visual Studio supports a similar tool named the DOM Explorer. You can use the DOM Explorer to inspect the property of any HTML element in a running Windows Store app.

After running a Windows Store app in Visual Studio, you can view the DOM Explorer window by selecting the menu option Debug, Windows, DOM Explorer. Within the DOM Explorer window, you can click any element and view all of the properties of the element including information about all of the styles associated with the element (see Figure 1.33).

38   CHAPTER 1   Building Windows Store Apps

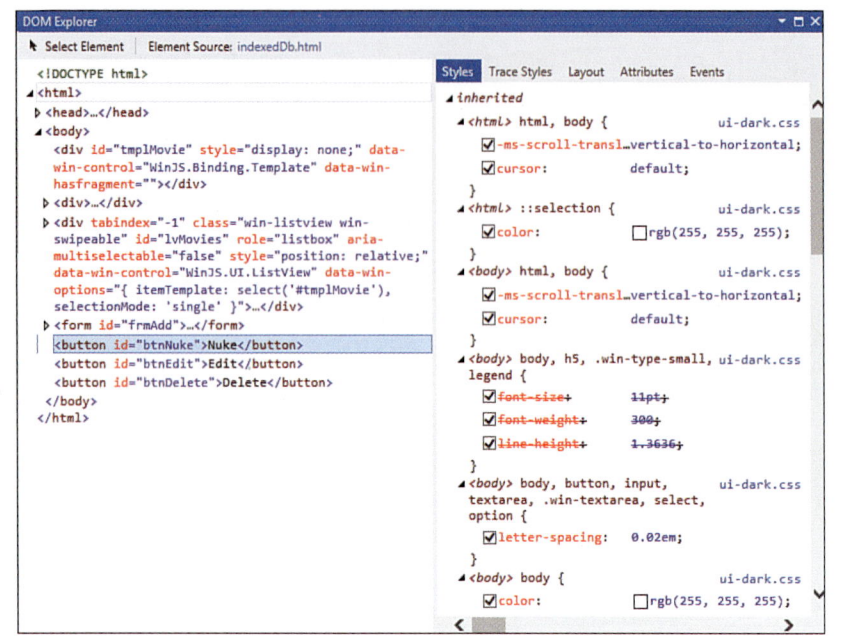

FIGURE 1.33   Using the DOM Explorer Window

If you click an element associated with a WinJS control, then you can see all of the HTML attributes and elements rendered by the control. Adding a `ListView` control to a page, for example, adds a lot of new DIV elements to the page.

Publishing to the Windows Store

One of the main motivations for building a Windows Store app is to sell your app in the Windows Store for either fame or profit. In this section, I discuss the steps you need to follow to publish your Windows Store app to the Windows Store.

> **NOTE**
>
> You can distribute your app without publishing to the Windows Store by taking advantage of a feature called *sideloading*. In order to take advantage of sideloading, you must sign your app and configure the right group policy settings on the target computers. You can learn about sideloading by visiting http://technet.microsoft.com/en-us/library/hh852635.aspx.

Register as a Windows Developer

Before you can publish an app to the Windows Store, you must first register as a Windows Store developer. You can sign up at the Windows Store Dashboard on the Windows Dev Center.

The sign-up procedure is painless. Currently, it costs $99 a year to become a registered Windows Store developer (see Figure 1.34) or it is free with an MSDN subscription.

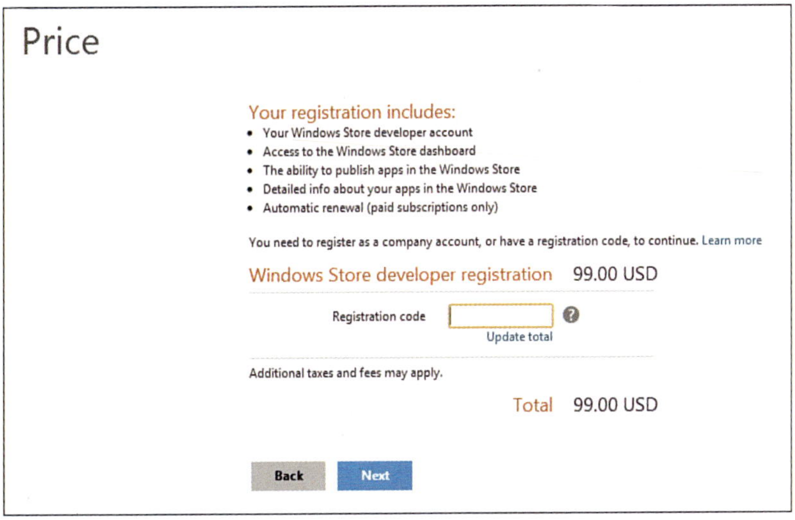

FIGURE 1.34 Register as a Windows Store developer

Submitting Your App

After you register, you can access the Windows Store dashboard and submit a new app. The process of submitting an app is broken down into eight steps (see Figure 1.35).

One of the most important steps is selecting the name for your app. You can reserve an app name in the Windows Store even before you have finished creating the app. Picking an app name is similar to picking a domain name—so I recommend that you acquire the name that you want as soon as possible.

You also need to decide on how much you want to charge for your app. Currently, you can charge anywhere from $1.49 to $999.99 in increments of 50 cents. You also have the option of providing your app for free.

> **NOTE**
>
> There are iPhone apps which sell for $999.99. For example, the iVIP Black iPhone app sells for $999.99. But to purchase it, you need to prove that you are a "High Net Worth" individual with "assets and/or income in excess of £1 million."

MyTasks: Release 1

- App name — Complete — You reserved an app name. You can also reserve another name for your app to use in another language or to change your app's name. Learn more
- Selling details (5 minutes) — Pick your app's price, listing categories, and where you want to sell it. Learn more
- Advanced features (5 minutes) — Configure push notifications and Live Services and define in-app offers. Learn more
- Age rating and rating certificates (5 minutes) — Describe the audience for your app and upload your rating certificates. Learn more
- Cryptography (5 minutes) — Declare whether your app uses cryptography and enable package upload. Learn more
- Packages (10 minutes) — Upload your app to the Windows Store. To enable this step, complete the Cryptography page. Learn more
- Description (10 minutes) — Briefly describe for your customers what your app does. Learn more
- Notes to testers (2 minutes) — Add notes about this release for the people who will review your app. Learn more

FIGURE 1.35 Submitting an app to the Windows Store

When you reach the sixth step, the Packages step, you can upload your finished Windows Store app to the Windows Store. Within Visual Studio, use the menu option Project, Store, Create App Package to package up your Windows Store app (see Figure 1.36). Next, you can click the Packages step to upload the package.

Create App Package

Create Your Package

Do you want to build a package to upload to the Windows Store?
- ● Yes
- ○ No

Visual Studio will download the required information for the package to be uploaded to the Store or used locally. You must sign into the Store with a Microsoft account. You can create an account if you don't have one.

Sign In   Cancel

FIGURE 1.36 Creating your App Package

Passing App Certification

Microsoft must review your app before it gets published to the Windows Store. In other words, your app must go through a certification process. Part of this certification process is automated and part of the certification process must be done by a human.

There are many requirements for certification. Some of these requirements are obvious. For example, your app can't contain programming errors that causes it to immediately crash. Also, your app cannot simply be a big ad for your business.

Some of the certification requirements are not so obvious. For example, to be certified, your app must fully support both snapped and filled view states. Your app also cannot unexpectedly transport large amounts of data over a metered network connection.

> **NOTE**
>
> The Windows Store certification requirements are detailed at http://msdn.microsoft.com/en-us/library/windows/apps/hh694083.aspx.

You can use the Windows App Certification Kit to run the automated certification tests on your app before you upload your package to the Windows Store. The easiest way to run the Windows Certification Kit is to package your app within Visual Studio by selecting the menu option Package, Store, Create App Package. The last step in the Create App Package wizard enables you to launch the Windows App Certification Kit (see Figure 1.37).

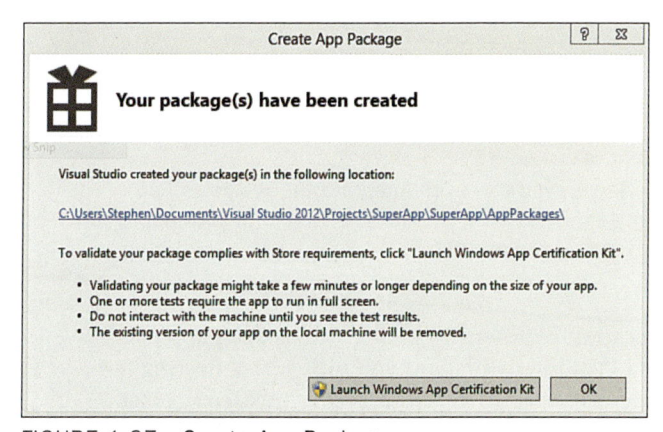

FIGURE 1.37 Create App Package

> **NOTE**
>
> The Windows App Certification Kit is installed at the same time as you install Visual Studio. You can run it independently of Visual Studio by launching the Windows App Cert Kit from the Start screen.

When you run the Windows App Certification Kit, the App Certification Kit will launch and run your app and then, after your computer does crazy stuff for a while, a report is generated which details whether your app passes or fails (see Figure 1.38).

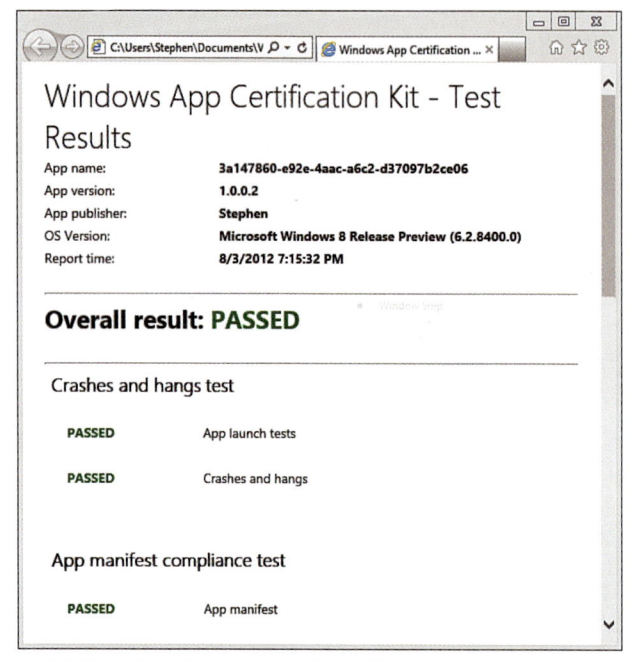

FIGURE 1.38 A (successful) certification report generated by the Windows App Certification Kit

> **NOTE**
>
> If you are using Team Foundation Server, you can even integrate the Windows App Certification Kit into your build process. Every time you do a new build of your app, you can run the technical certification tests automatically.

After your app passes all the certification requirements—after it has been approved by Microsoft—your app appears in the Windows Store and you can start collecting money. When anyone buys your app, money is added to a payout account which you set up on the Windows Store dashboard.

Summary

The goal of this chapter was to introduce you to Windows Store apps. I started this chapter by providing you with an overview of the Microsoft design style principles. You also learned about the standard features of Windows Store apps such as the app bar, charms, and snapped view state.

I then led you, step-by-step, through the process of building your first Windows Store app. We created a really cool camera app which you could never create as a standard web application.

You learned about the standard elements of a Windows Store app. You learned how a Windows Store app is composed out of standard HTML5, JavaScript, and CSS3. You also learned how Windows Store apps take advantage of Microsoft technologies such as the Windows Runtime and the Windows Library for JavaScript.

I also explained how you can take advantage of the features of Visual Studio for Windows 8 when building a Windows Store app. You learned how to run a Windows Store app using the simulator. You also learned how to debug a Windows Store app by using breakpoints and the Visual Studio JavaScript Console window.

Finally, you learned how you can make money from your Windows Store app by publishing your app to the Windows Store. You learned how to register your app, submit your app, and pass certification.

CHAPTER 2

WinJS Fundamentals

IN THIS CHAPTER

▶ Namespaces, Modules, and Classes

▶ Asynchronous Programming with Promises

▶ Retrieving DOM Elements with Query Selectors

▶ Performing Ajax Calls with the `xhr` Function

The goal of this chapter is to explain the features included in the base WinJS library. These are the features that you will use in just about any application that you build.

The first part of this chapter is devoted to the topic of namespaces, modules, and classes. You learn the recommended patterns for organizing your JavaScript code.

Next, you learn how to take advantage of another feature of the base WinJS library called *promises*. Promises provide you with an elegant way to perform asynchronous programming in your JavaScript code.

In this chapter, you also learn how to use *Query Selectors* when working with the WinJS library. Query Selectors enable you to efficiently retrieve DOM elements from an HTML document (think jQuery selectors).

Finally, you learn how to work with a function included in the base WinJS library named the `xhr()` function. The `xhr()` function enables you to perform Ajax calls—including cross-domain calls.

Namespaces, Modules, and Classes

When you build Windows Store apps with the WinJS library, Microsoft recommends that you follow particular patterns when organizing your JavaScript code. In particular, they recommend that you organize your code into namespaces, modules, and classes.

By following these patterns, you can build JavaScript code which is less buggy and easier to maintain over time.

Using Namespaces

Let me start by explaining the methods in the WinJS library for defining namespaces.

Before we do anything else, we should start by answering the questions: Why do we need namespaces? What function do they serve? Do they just add needless complexity to our Windows Store apps?

After all, plenty of JavaScript libraries do just fine without introducing support for namespaces. For example, jQuery has no support for namespaces and jQuery is the most popular JavaScript library in the universe. If jQuery can do without namespaces, why do we need to worry about namespaces at all?

Namespaces perform two functions in a programming language. First, namespaces prevent naming collisions. In other words, namespaces enable you to create more than one object with the same name without conflict.

For example, imagine that two companies—company A and company B—both want to make a JavaScript shopping cart control and both companies want to name the control `ShoppingCart`. By creating a `CompanyA` namespace and `CompanyB` namespace, both companies can create a ShoppingCart control: a `CompanyA.ShoppingCart` and a `CompanyB.ShoppingCart` control.

The second function of a namespace is organization. Namespaces are used to group related functionality even when the functionality is defined in different physical files. For example, I know that all of the methods in the WinJS library related to working with classes can be found in the WinJS.Class namespace. Namespaces make it easier to understand the functionality available in a library.

If you are building a simple JavaScript application, then you won't have much reason to care about namespaces. If you need to use multiple libraries written by different people, then namespaces become very important.

Using `WinJS.Namespace.define()`

In the WinJS library, the most basic method of creating a namespace is to use the `WinJS.Namespace.define()` method. This method enables you to declare a namespace (of arbitrary depth).

The `WinJS.Namespace.define()` method has the following parameters:

- `name`—A string representing the name of the new namespace. You can add nested namespace by using dot notation
- `members`—An optional collection of objects to add to the new namespace

For example, the code sample in Listing 2.1 declares two new namespaces named `CompanyA` and `CompanyB.Controls`. Both namespaces contain a `ShoppingCart` object which has a `checkout()` method.

LISTING 2.1 Creating Namespaces (namespaces\namespaces.html)

```
// Create CompanyA namespace with ShoppingCart
WinJS.Namespace.define("CompanyA");
CompanyA.ShoppingCart = {
    checkout: function () { return "Checking out from A"; }
};

// Create CompanyB.Controls namespace with ShoppingCart
WinJS.Namespace.define(
    "CompanyB.Controls",
    {
        ShoppingCart: {
            checkout: function () { return "Checking out from B"; }
        }
    }
);

// Call CompanyA ShoppingCart checkout method
console.log(CompanyA.ShoppingCart.checkout());  // Writes "Checking out from A"

// Call CompanyB.Controls checkout method
console.log(CompanyB.Controls.ShoppingCart.checkout());  // Writes "Checking out
➥from B"
```

In the previous code, the `CompanyA` namespace is created by calling `WinJS.Namespace.define("CompanyA")`. Next, the `ShoppingCart` is added to this namespace. The namespace is defined and an object is added to the namespace in separate lines of code.

A different approach is taken in the case of the `CompanyB.Controls` namespace. The namespace is created and the `ShoppingCart` object is added to the namespace with the following code:

```
WinJS.Namespace.define(
    "CompanyB.Controls",
    {
        ShoppingCart: {
            checkout: function () { return "Checking out from B"; }
        }
    }
);
```

Notice that `CompanyB.Controls` is a nested namespace. The top level namespace `CompanyB` contains the namespace Controls. You can declare a nested namespace using dot notation and the WinJS library handles the details of creating one namespace within the other.

After the namespaces have been defined, you can use either of the two shopping cart controls in the same JavaScript file without conflict. You call `CompanyA.ShoppingCart.checkout()` or you can call `CompanyB.Controls.ShoppingCart.checkout()`.

Using `WinJS.Namespace.defineWithParent()`

The `WinJS.Namespace.defineWithParent()` method is similar to the `WinJS.Namespace.define()` method. Both methods enable you to define a new namespace. The difference is that the `defineWithParent()` method enables you to add a new namespace to an existing namespace.

The `WinJS.Namespace.defineWithParent()` method has the following parameters:

- `parentNamespace`—An object which represents a parent namespace
- `name`—A string representing the new namespace to add to the parent namespace
- `members`—An optional collection of objects to add to the new namespace

The following code sample demonstrates how you can create a root namespace named `CompanyA` and add a Controls child namespace to the `CompanyA` parent namespace:

```
WinJS.Namespace.define("CompanyA");
WinJS.Namespace.defineWithParent(CompanyA, "Controls",
    {
        ShoppingCart: {
            checkout: function () { return "Checking out"; }
        }
    }
);

console.log(CompanyA.Controls.ShoppingCart.checkout()); // Writes "Checking out"
```

One significant advantage of using the `defineWithParent()` method over the `define()` method is the `defineWithParent()` method is strongly-typed. In other words, you use an object to represent the base namespace instead of a string. If you misspell the name of the object (`CompnyA`), then you get a runtime error.

Using the Module Pattern

When you are building a JavaScript library, you want to be able to create both public and private methods. Some methods, the public methods, are intended to be used by consumers of your JavaScript library. The public methods act as your library's public API.

Other methods, the private methods, are *not* intended for public consumption. Instead, these methods are internal methods required to get the library to function. You don't want people calling these internal methods because you might need to change them in the future.

Namespaces, Modules, and Classes 49

JavaScript does not support access modifiers. You can't mark an object or method as public or private. Anyone gets to call any method and anyone gets to interact with any object.

The only mechanism for encapsulating (hiding) methods and objects in JavaScript is to take advantage of functions. In JavaScript, a function determines variable scope. A JavaScript variable either has global scope—it is available everywhere—or it has function scope—it is available only within a function. If you want to hide an object or method, then you need to place it within a function.

For example, the following code contains a function named `doSomething()` which contains a nested function named `doSomethingElse()`:

```
function doSomething() {
    console.log("doSomething");

    function doSomethingElse() {
        console.log("doSomethingElse");
    }
}

doSomething(); // Writes "doSomething"
doSomethingElse(); // Throws ReferenceError
```

You can call `doSomethingElse()` only within the `doSomething()` function. The `doSomethingElse()` function is encapsulated in the `doSomething()` function.

The WinJS library takes advantage of function encapsulation to hide all of its internal methods. All of the WinJS methods are defined within self-executing anonymous functions. Everything is hidden by default. Public methods are exposed by explicitly adding the public methods to namespaces defined in the global scope.

Imagine, for example, that I want a small library of utility methods. I want to create a method for calculating sales tax and a method for calculating the expected ship date of a product. The library in Listing 2.2 encapsulates the implementation of my library in a self-executing anonymous function:

LISTING 2.2 Encapsulating Functions with a Module (modules\modules.html)

```
(function (global) {

    // Public method which calculates tax
    function calculateTax(price) {
        return calculateFederalTax(price) + calculateStateTax(price);
    }

    // Private method for calculating state tax
    function calculateStateTax(price) {
```

```
        return price * 0.08;
    }

    // Private method for calculating federal tax
    function calculateFederalTax(price) {
        return price * 0.02;
    }

    // Public method which returns the expected ship date
    function calculateShipDate(currentDate) {
        currentDate.setDate(currentDate.getDate() + 4);
        return currentDate;
    }

    // Export public methods
    WinJS.Namespace.define("CompanyA.Utilities",
        {
            calculateTax: calculateTax,
            calculateShipDate: calculateShipDate
        }
    );

})(this);

// Show expected ship date
var shipDate = CompanyA.Utilities.calculateShipDate(new Date());
console.log(shipDate);

// Show price + tax
var price = 12.33;
var tax = CompanyA.Utilities.calculateTax(price);
console.log(price + tax);
```

In the previous code, the self-executing anonymous function contains four functions: `calculateTax()`, `calculateStateTax()`, `calculateFederalTax()`, and `calculateShipDate()`. The following statement is used to expose only the `calcuateTax()` and the `calculateShipDate()` functions:

```
// Export public methods
WinJS.Namespace.define("CompanyA.Utilities",
    {
        calculateTax: calculateTax,
        calculateShipDate: calculateShipDate
    }
);
```

Because the `calculateTax()` and `calculateShipDate()` functions are added to the `CompanyA.Utilities` namespace, you can call these two methods outside of the self-executing function. These are the public methods of your library which form the public API.

The `calculateStateTax()` and `calculateFederalTax()` methods, on the other hand, are forever hidden within the black hole of the self-executing function. These methods are encapsulated and can never be called outside of the scope of the self-executing function. These are the internal methods of your library.

Using Classes

Unlike other popular computer languages—such as C# or Java—JavaScript does not have any built-in support for classes. In JavaScript, you do not distinguish between a type (a class) and an instance of that type (an object). Everything in JavaScript is an object.

The WinJS library includes extensions to JavaScript for creating classes. These methods are used extensively within the WinJS library itself. For example, all of the WinJS JavaScript controls are created using these methods. In this section, we discuss how you can define new classes by taking advantage of the methods in the WinJS library.

Using `WinJS.Class.define()`

In the WinJS library, new JavaScript classes are created by calling the `WinJS.Class.define()` method. This method accepts three arguments:

- `constructor`—The constructor function used to initialize the new object. If you pass null then an empty constructor is created
- `instanceMembers`—A collection of instance properties and methods
- `staticMembers`—A collection of static properties and methods

The code in Listing 2.3 demonstrates how to create a Robot class and then create a Roomba robot object from the Robot class:

LISTING 2.3 Creating a Class (classes\classes.html)

```
var Robot = WinJS.Class.define(
    function (name, price) {
        this.name = name;
        this.price = price;
    },
    {
        _name: undefined,
        _price: 0,

        price: {
            set: function (value) {
                if (value < 0) {
                    throw new Error("Invalid price!");
```

52 CHAPTER 2 WinJS Fundamentals

```
            }
            this._price = value;
        },
        get: function () { return this._price; }
    },
    makeNoise: function () {
        return "Burp, Wow!, oops!";
    }
  }
);

// Create a robot
var roomba = new Robot("Roomba", 200.33);

console.log(roomba.price); // Writes "200.33"
console.log(roomba.makeNoise()); // Writes "Burp, Wow!, oops!"

// Set invalid price
roomba.price = -88; // Throws "Invalid price!"
```

The Robot class is defined using the `WinJS.Class.define()` method. The first argument passed to this method is the constructor function for the Robot class. This constructor function initializes the Robot name and price properties.

The next argument passed to the `WinJS.Class.define()` method is a collection of instance members. This collection is used to define the _name and _price fields and the price property. This collection also contains the definition of the `makeNoise()` method.

> **NOTE**
>
> There is a convention of naming all private members of a class—fields, properties, and methods—with a leading underscore. For example, the private field backing the price property in Listing 2.3 is named _price instead of price.

Notice that the price property includes a getter and a setter. If you attempt to assign an invalid price to the Robot then the setter throws an Error as illustrated in Figure 2.1.

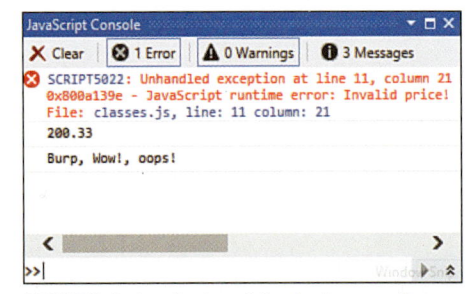

FIGURE 2.1   An Invalid price! exception

Namespaces, Modules, and Classes

Using `WinJS.Class.derive()`

The `WinJS.Class.derive()` method enables you to use prototype inheritance to derive one class from another class. The `WinJS.Class.derive()` method accepts the following four arguments:

- `baseClass`—The class to inherit from.
- `constructor`—A constructor function that can be used to initialize the new class
- `instanceMembers`—New instance properties and methods
- `staticMembers`—New static properties and methods

Here is a basic example. In the code in Listing 2.4, three classes are defined: `Robot`, `Roomba`, and `AIBO`. The `Robot` class is the base class and the `Roomba` and `AIBO` classes derive from the `Robot` class.

LISTING 2.4 Deriving a Class (derive\derive.html)

```
var Robot = WinJS.Class.define(
    function () {
        this.type = "Robot"
    },
    {
        sayHello: function () {
            return "My name is " + this.name
                + " and I am a " + this.type;
        }
    }
);

var Roomba = WinJS.Class.derive(
    Robot,
    function (name) {
        this.name = name;
        this.type = "Roomba";
    }
);

var AIBO = WinJS.Class.derive(
    Robot,
    function (name) {
        this.name = name;
        this.type = "AIBO";
    }
);

// Create a Roomba
```

```
var myRoomba = new Roomba("rover");
console.log(myRoomba.sayHello());

// Create an AIBO
var myAIBO = new AIBO("spot");
console.log(myAIBO.sayHello());
```

When you run the previous code, the following messages are written to the Visual Studio JavaScript Console (see Figure 2.2).

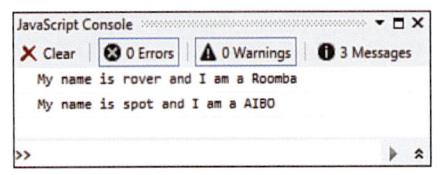

```
JavaScript Console                          ▼ □ ×
✗ Clear   ⊗ 0 Errors  ⚠ 0 Warnings  ⓘ 3 Messages
My name is rover and I am a Roomba
My name is spot and I am a AIBO

>>                                        ▶ ⌃
```

FIGURE 2.2   Derived robots

In the previous code, the constructor function for the Robot class is never called. The Roomba and the AIBO constructor functions are called instead. However, both the Roomba and AIBO classes inherit the `sayHello()` method from the base Robot class.

Using `WinJS.Class.mix()`
As an alternative to using the `WinJS.Class.derive()` method, you can use the `WinJS.Class.mix()` method. This method enables you to create mixins. A mixin enables you to combine methods from multiple JavaScript objects into a single object.

Behind the scenes, the `WinJS.Class.derive()` method which we discussed in the previous section uses prototype inheritance and prototype inheritance has performance drawbacks. Following a prototype chain requires processor time. Therefore, the suggestion is that you avoid prototype inheritance by using mixins instead.

When you use a mixin instead of prototype inheritance, the methods and properties are combined into a single object. You don't get a long prototype chain.

The `WinJS.Class.mix()` method has the following parameters:

▶ **constructor**—a constructor function used to initialize the new class

▶ **mixin**—a parameter array which contains the mixin methods

The code in Listing 2.5 demonstrates how you can use the `WinJS.Class.mix()` method to simulate single inheritance.

LISTING 2.5   Creating a Mixin (mixins\mixins.html)

```
var Robot = {
    makeNoise: function () {
        return "beep";
    }
```

Namespaces, Modules, and Classes

```
};

var Roomba = WinJS.Class.mix(
    function (name) {
        this.name = name;
    },
    Robot
);

var myRoomba = new Roomba("rover");
console.log(myRoomba.makeNoise()); // Writes "beep"
```

In the previous code, the `Roomba` class contains all of the methods of the `Robot` class.

One of the advantages of mixins is that you can use mixins to support something like multiple inheritance. You can use a mixin to combine as many sets of methods and properties as you need. For example, the code sample in Listing 2.6 demonstrates how you can build a Roomba from Robot methods, Product methods, and Vacuum methods.

LISTING 2.6   Combining Multiple Objects (mixinMultiple\mixinMultiple.html)

```
"use strict";

var Robot = {
    makeNoise: function () {
        return "beep";
    }
};

var Product = {
    price: {
        set: function (value) {
            if (value < 0) {
                throw new Error("Invalid price!");
            }
            this._price = value;
        },
        get: function () { return this._price; }
    },
    sayName: function () {
        return this.name;
    }
}

var Vacuum = {
    vacuum: function () { return "bzzzzzz"; }
```

56 CHAPTER 2 WinJS Fundamentals

```
}

var Roomba = WinJS.Class.mix(
    function (name) {
        this.name = name;
    },
    Robot, Product, Vacuum
);

var myRoomba = new Roomba("rover");
console.log(myRoomba.makeNoise()); // Writes "beep"
console.log(myRoomba.sayName()); // Writes "rover"
console.log(myRoomba.vacuum()); // Writes "bzzzzz"
myRoomba.price = -88 // Throws Error
```

Notice that a mixin can contain both methods and properties. Furthermore, a mixin property can contain a setter and getter. For example, the price property included in the Product mixin includes a setter which performs validation.

When you execute the code above, the following results are displayed in your Visual Studio JavaScript Console window as illustrated by Figure 2.3.

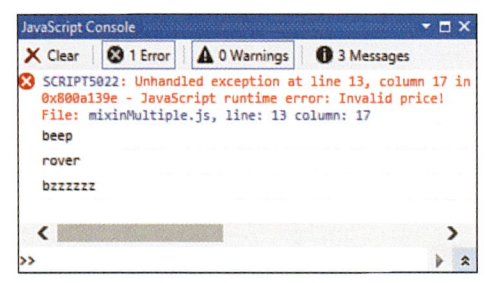

FIGURE 2.3 Robot noises

> **NOTE**
>
> The WinJS library includes several mixins which you can use in your code including the WinJS.Utilities.eventMixin, WinJS.UI.DOMEventMixin, and the WinJS.Binding.dynamicObserversableMixin.

Asynchronous Programming with Promises

Some code executes immediately, some code requires time to complete or might never complete at all. For example, retrieving the value of a local variable is an immediate operation. Retrieving data from a remote website with an Ajax request takes longer or might not complete at all.

When an operation might take a long time to complete, you should write your code so that it executes asynchronously. Instead of waiting for an operation to complete, you should start the operation and then do something else until you receive a signal that the operation is complete.

An analogy: Some telephone customer service lines require you to wait on hold—listening to really bad music—until a customer service representative is available. This is synchronous programming and very wasteful of your time.

Some newer customer service lines enable you to enter your telephone number so a customer service representative can call you back when a customer representative becomes available. This approach is much less wasteful of your time because you can do useful things while waiting for the callback.

There are several patterns that you can use to write code which executes asynchronously. The most popular pattern in JavaScript is the callback pattern. When you call a function which might take a long time to return a result, you pass a callback function to the function.

Using callbacks is a natural way to perform asynchronous programming with JavaScript. Instead of waiting for an operation to complete, sitting there and listening to really bad music, you can get a callback when the operation is complete.

Using Promises

The CommonJS website defines a promise like this (http://wiki.commonjs.org/wiki/Promises):

"Promises provide a well-defined interface for interacting with an object that represents the result of an action that is performed asynchronously, and may or may not be finished at any given point in time. By utilizing a standard interface, different components can return promises for asynchronous actions and consumers can utilize the promises in a predictable manner."

A promise provides a standard pattern for specifying callbacks. In the WinJS library, when you create a promise, you can specify three callbacks: a complete callback, a failure callback, and a progress callback (both the failure and progress callbacks are optional).

Promises are used extensively in the WinJS library. The methods in the animation library, the control library, and the binding library all use promises.

For example, the `xhr()` method included in the WinJS base library returns a promise. The `xhr()` method wraps calls to the standard `XmlHttpRequest` object in a promise. The code in Listing 2.7 illustrates how you can use the `xhr()` method to perform an Ajax request which retrieves the feed from my blog at StephenWalther.com:

LISTING 2.7   Making a Promise (promises\promises.html)

```
var options = {
    url: "http://stephenwalther.com/blog/feed",
    responseType: "document"
```

CHAPTER 2 WinJS Fundamentals

```
};

WinJS.xhr(options).done(
    function (xmlHttpRequest) {
        console.log("success");

        // Display title of first blog entry
        var firstTitle = xmlHttpRequest.response.querySelector("item>title");
        console.log(firstTitle.textContent);
    },
    function (xmlHttpRequest) {
        console.log("fail");
    },
    function (xmlHttpRequest) {
        console.log("progress");
    }
)
```

The `WinJS.xhr()` method returns a promise. The Promise class includes a `done()` method which accepts three callback functions: a complete callback, an error callback, and a progress callback:

`Promise.done(completeCallback, errorCallback, progressCallback)`

In the code in Listing 2.7, three anonymous functions are passed to the `done()` method. Unless there is a network error, the error function is never called. The progress function is called repeatedly during the Ajax request. Finally, the complete callback is done when the Ajax call completes. The complete callback displays the title of the first blog entry retrieved (see Figure 2.4).

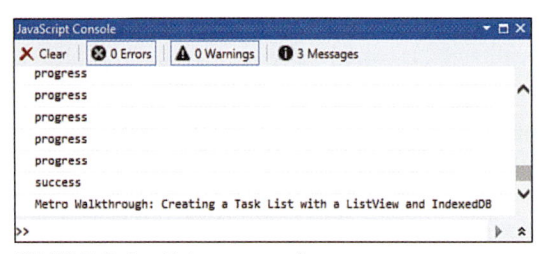

FIGURE 2.4 Using a promise

Using `then()` versus `done()`

In the previous section, we used the Promise object `done()` method to set up our complete, error, and progress callbacks. The Promise object exposes another method which is closely related to `done()`: the `then()` method.

Asynchronous Programming with Promises   59

The `then()` method—just like the `done()` method—enables you to set up a complete, error, and progress callback function. So why does the `then()` method exist? There are two important differences between `then()` and `done()`.

The `then()` method, unlike the `done()` method, supports chaining. If you need to chain multiple promises together, then you are forced to use the `then()` method. For example, the code in Listing 2.8 illustrates how you can make one Ajax call which downloads the URL of the most recent blog entry from my blog and *then* make a second Ajax call which downloads the contents of that blog entry. The second Ajax call is not made until the first Ajax call completes.

LISTING 2.8   Chaining Promises (promiseChain\promiseChain.html)

```
var options = {
    url: "http://stephenwalther.com/blog/feed",
    responseType: "document"
};


WinJS.xhr(options).then(
    function (xmlHttpRequest) {
        // Get link for first blog entry
        var firstLink = xmlHttpRequest.response.querySelector("item>link");

        // Make second Ajax request (returns a promise)
        return WinJS.xhr({
            url: firstLink.textContent,
            responseType: "document"
        });
    }
).done(
    function (xmlHttpRequest) {
        // Get body of blog post
        var postBody = xmlHttpRequest.response.querySelector("div.entry");

        // Write first 200 characters of blog post
        console.log(postBody.textContent.trim().substr(0, 200));
    }
);
```

In Listing 2.8, notice that the complete function passed to the `then()` method returns a second promise. Calling `WinJS.xhr()` returns a new promise.

If the second promise completes successfully, then the complete function passed to the `done()` method executes. This method displays the first 200 characters of the blog entry.

CHAPTER 2 WinJS Fundamentals

You can chain together as many promises as you need by calling `then().then().then()...` The last call in the chain should be a call to `done()`.

The second difference between `then()` and `done()` concerns error handling. You can pass an error function to both the `then()` and `done()` methods as the second parameter to handle errors and, as a best-practice, you should do this. But, if you don't supply an error function, then the `done()` method throws an exception but the `then()` method does not. Instead, the `then()` method returns a promise in the error state.

For example, the code in Listing 2.9 performs an Ajax request with a bad URL. The request made with the `then()` method does not raise an error. An error message is written to the JavaScript Console, but execution of the app is not halted.

LISTING 2.9   done() versus then() (promiseErrors\promiseErrors.html)

```
var options = {
    url: "http://BadURL"
};

WinJS.xhr(options).then();   // DOES NOT throw an exception

WinJS.xhr(options).done();   // DOES throw an exception
```

If you don't want your code to fail silently, like the `then()` method in Listing 2.9, then you should use `done()` instead of `then()`. If you are chaining promises, always use `done()` as the last link in the chain.

Creating Promises

You can create your own promises by creating a new instance of the Promise class. The constructor for the Promise class requires a function which accepts three parameters: a complete, error, and progress function parameter.

For example, the code in Listing 2.10 illustrates how you can create a method named `wait10Seconds()` which returns a promise. The progress function is called every second and the complete function is not called until 10 seconds have passed:

LISTING 2.10   Creating a Promise (promiseCreate\promiseCreate.html)

```
function wait10Seconds() {
    return new WinJS.Promise(function (complete, error, progress) {
        var seconds = 0;
        var intervalId = window.setInterval(function () {
            seconds++;
            progress(seconds);
            if (seconds > 9) {
                window.clearInterval(intervalId);
                complete();
```

```
        }
    }, 1000);
});
}

wait10Seconds().done(
    function () { console.log("complete") },
    function () { console.log("error") },
    function (seconds) { console.log("progress:" + seconds) }
);
```

All of the work happens in the constructor function for the promise. The `window.setInterval()` method is used to execute code every second. Every second, the `progress()` callback method is called. If more than 10 seconds have passed, then the `complete()` callback method is called and the `clearInterval()` method is called.

When you execute the previous code, you can see the output in the Visual Studio JavaScript Console in Figure 2.5.

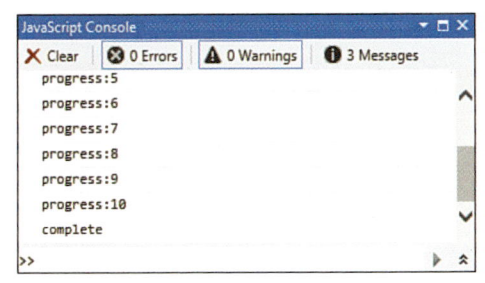

FIGURE 2.5   Output of a custom promise

Creating a Timeout Promise

In the previous section, we created a custom Promise which uses the `window.setInterval()` method to complete the promise after 10 seconds. We really did not need to create a custom promise because the Promise class already includes a static method for returning promises which complete after a certain interval.

The code in Listing 2.11 illustrates how you can use the `timeout()` method. The `timeout()` method returns a promise which completes after a certain number of milliseconds.

LISTING 2.11   A Timeout Promise (promiseTimeout\promiseTimeout.html)

```
WinJS.Promise.timeout(3000).then(
    function () { console.log("complete") },
    function () { console.log("error") },
    function () { console.log("progress") }
);
```

In the previous code, the Promise completes after 3 seconds (3000 milliseconds). The Promise returned by the `timeout()` method does not support progress events. Therefore, the only message written to the console is the message "complete" after 10 seconds.

Canceling Promises

Some promises, but not all, support cancellation. When you cancel a promise, the promise's error callback is executed.

For example, the code in Listing 2.12 uses the `WinJS.xhr()` method to perform an Ajax request. However, immediately after the Ajax request is made, the request is cancelled.

LISTING 2.12 Canceling a Promise (promiseCancel\promiseCancel.html)

```
// Specify Ajax request options
var options = {
    url: "http://StephenWalther.com"
};

// Make the Ajax request
var request = WinJS.xhr(options).then(
    function (xmlHttpRequest) {
        console.log("success");
    },
    function (xmlHttpRequest) {
        console.log("fail: " + xmlHttpRequest.message);
    },
    function (xmlHttpRequest) {
        console.log("progress");
    }
);

// Cancel the Ajax request
request.cancel();
```

When you run the previous code, the message "fail: Canceled" is written to the Visual Studio JavaScript Console (see Figure 2.6). Canceling is only supported when using `then()` and not `done()`.

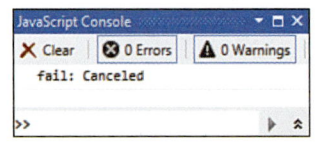

FIGURE 2.6 Canceling a promise (promiseCancel\promiseCancel.html)

Composing Promises

You can build promises out of other promises. In other words, you can compose promises.

There are two static methods of the Promise class which you can use to compose promises: the `join()` method and the `any()` method. When you join promises, a promise is complete when all of the joined promises are complete. When you use the `any()` method, a promise is complete when any of the promises complete.

The following code illustrates how to use the `join()` method. A new promise is created out of two timeout promises. The new promise does not complete until both of the timeout promises complete:

```
WinJS.Promise.join([WinJS.Promise.timeout(1000), WinJS.Promise.timeout(5000)])
    .done(function () { console.log("join complete"); });
```

The message "complete" will not be written to the JavaScript Console until both promises passed to the `join()` method complete. The message won't be written for 5 seconds (5,000 milliseconds).

The `any()` method completes when any promise passed to the `any()` method completes:

```
WinJS.Promise.any([WinJS.Promise.timeout(1000), WinJS.Promise.timeout(5000)])
    .done(function () { console.log("any complete"); });
```

The code above writes the message "any complete" to the JavaScript Console after 1 second (1,000 milliseconds). The message is written to the JavaScript console immediately after the first promise completes and before the second promise completes.

Retrieving DOM Elements with Query Selectors

When you are building a Windows Store app with JavaScript, you need some way of easily retrieving elements from an HTML document. For example, you might want to retrieve all of the input elements which have a certain CSS class. Or, you might want to retrieve the one and only element with an id of `favoriteColor`.

The standard way of retrieving elements from an HTML document is by using a selector. Anyone who has ever created a Cascading Style Sheet has already used selectors. You use selectors in Cascading Style Sheets to apply formatting rules to elements in a document.

For example, the following Cascading Style Sheet rule changes the background color of every INPUT element with a class of .required in a document to the color red:

```
input.required { background-color: red }
```

The "`input.required`" part is the selector which matches all INPUT elements with a class of required.

The W3C standard for selectors (technically, their recommendation) is entitled "Selectors Level 3" and the standard is located here:

http://www.w3.org/TR/css3-selectors/

Selectors are not only useful for adding formatting to the elements of a document. Selectors are also useful when you need to apply behavior. For example, you might want to select a particular BUTTON element with a selector and add a click handler to the element so that something happens whenever you click the button.

jQuery is famous for its support for selectors. Using jQuery, you can use a selector to retrieve matching elements from a document and modify the elements. The WinJS library enables you to perform the same types of queries as jQuery using the W3C selector syntax.

> **NOTE**
>
> The W3C selector standard is supported for all modern browsers, including recent versions of Google Chrome, Apple Safari, and Mozilla Firefox.

Performing Queries with the `WinJS.Utilities.query()` Method

When using the WinJS library, you perform a query using a selector by using the `WinJS.Utilities.query()` method.

The following HTML document contains a BUTTON and a DIV element:

LISTING 2.13 A Document with a Secret Message (selectorsQuery\selectorsQuery.html)

```
<!DOCTYPE html>
<html>
<head>
    <meta charset="utf-8">
    <title>Selectors Query</title>

    <!-- WinJS references -->
    <link href="//Microsoft.WinJS.1.0/css/ui-dark.css" rel="stylesheet" />
    <script src="//Microsoft.WinJS.1.0/js/base.js"></script>
    <script src="//Microsoft.WinJS.1.0/js/ui.js"></script>

    <!-- Chapter02 references -->
    <link href="/css/default.css" rel="stylesheet">
    <script type="text/javascript" src="selectorsQuery.js"></script>
</head>
<body>

    <button>Click Me!</button>

    <div style="display:none">
```

Retrieving DOM Elements with Query Selectors

```
        <h1>Secret Message</h1>

    </div>

</body>
</html>
```

The document contains a reference to the JavaScript file in Listing 2.14 named selectorsQuery.js.

LISTING 2.14 Using a Selector (selectorsQuery\selectorsQuery.js)

```
(function () {
    "use strict";

    function initialize() {
        WinJS.Utilities.query("button").listen("click", function () {
            WinJS.Utilities.query("div").clearStyle("display");
        });
    };

    document.addEventListener("DOMContentLoaded", initialize);
})();
```

The `selectorsQuery.js` script uses the `WinJS.Utilities.query()` method to retrieve all of the BUTTON elements in the page. The `listen()` method is used to wire an event handler to the BUTTON click event. When you click the BUTTON, the secret message contained in the hidden DIV element is displayed. The `clearStyle()` method is used to remove the `display:none` style attribute from the DIV element (see Figure 2.7).

FIGURE 2.7 Displaying the secret message

> **WARNING**
>
> Make sure that you don't try to use the `WinJS.Utilities.query()` method until after the document is loaded. In Listing 2.14, the call to `WinJS.Utilities.query()` is contained within the `initialize()` function which is triggered by the `DOMContentLoaded` event.

Under the covers, the `WinJS.Utilities.query()` method uses the standard `querySelectorAll()` method. This means that you can use any selector which is compatible with the `querySelectorAll()` method. The `querySelectorAll()` method is defined in the W3C Selectors API Level 1 standard located here:

http://www.w3.org/TR/selectors-api/

Unlike the `querySelectorAll()` method, the `WinJS.Utilities.query()` method returns a `QueryCollection`. I talk about the methods of the `QueryCollection` class below.

Retrieving a Single Element with the `WinJS.Utilities.id()` Method

If you want to retrieve a single element from a document, instead of matching a set of elements, then you can use the `WinJS.Utilities.id()` method. For example, the following line of code changes the background color of an element to the color red:

```
WinJS.Utilities.id("message").setStyle("background-color", "red");
```

Retrieving DOM Elements with Query Selectors   67

The statement above matches the one and only element with an id of message. For example, the statement matches the following DIV element:

```
<div id="message">Hello!</div>
```

Notice that you do not use a hash when matching a single element with the `WinJS.Utilities.id()` method. You would need to use a hash when using the `WinJS.Utilities.query()` method to do the same thing like this:

```
WinJS.Utilities.query("#message").setStyle("background-color", "red");
```

Under the covers, the `WinJS.Utilities.id()` method calls the standard `document.getElementById()` method. The `WinJS.Utilities.id()` method returns the result as a QueryCollection.

If no element matches the identifier passed to `WinJS.Utilities.id()` then you do not get an error. Instead, you get a `QueryCollection` with no elements (length=0).

Using the `WinJS.Utilities.children()` Method

The `WinJS.Utilities.children()` method enables you to retrieve a `QueryCollection` which contains all of the children of a DOM element. For example, imagine that you have a DIV element which contains children DIV elements like this:

```
<div id="discussContainer">
    <div>Message 1</div>
    <div>Message 2</div>
    <div>Message 3</div>
</div>
```

You can use the following code to add borders around all of the child DIV elements and not the container DIV element (see Figure 2.8):

```
var discussContainer = WinJS.Utilities.id("discussContainer").get(0);
WinJS.Utilities.children(discussContainer).setStyle("border", "2px dashed red");
```

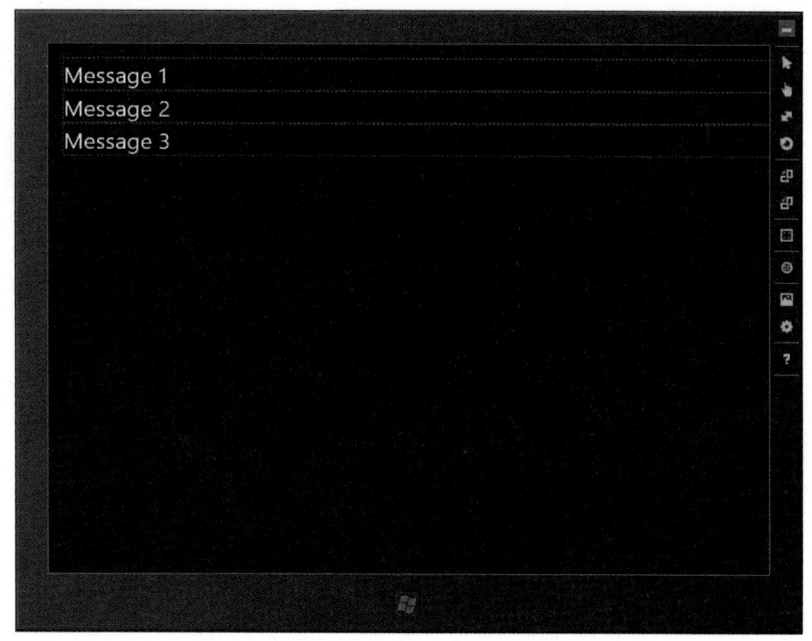

FIGURE 2.8 Retrieving children

It is important to understand that the `WinJS.Utilities.children()` method only works with a DOM element and not a `QueryCollection`. Notice that the `get()` method is used to retrieve the DOM element which represents the `discussContainer`.

Working with the `QueryCollection` Class

Both the `WinJS.Utilities.query()` method and the `WinJS.Utilities.id()` method return an instance of the `QueryCollection` class. The `QueryCollection` class derives from the base JavaScript Array class and adds several useful methods for working with HTML elements:

- `addClass(name)`—Adds a class to every element in the `QueryCollection`
- `clearStyle(name)`—Removes a style from every element in the `QueryCollection`
- `control(ctor, options)`—Enables you to transform the items in the `QueryCollection` into WinJS controls
- `forEach(callbackFn, thisArg)`—Enables you to perform an operation on each item in the `QueryCollection`
- `get(index)`—Retrieves the element from the `QueryCollection` at the specified index
- `getAttribute(name)`—Retrieves the value of an attribute for the first element in the `QueryCollection`
- `hasClass(name)`—Returns true if the first element in the `QueryCollection` has a certain class

- `include(items)`—Includes a collection of items in the `QueryCollection`
- `listen(eventType, listener, capture)`—Adds an event listener to every element in the `QueryCollection`
- `query(query)`—Performs an additional query on the `QueryCollection` and returns a new `QueryCollection`
- `removeClass(name)`—Removes a class from the every element in the `QueryCollection`
- `removeEventListener(eventType, listener, capture)`—Removes an event listener from every element in the `QueryCollection`
- `setAttribute(name, value)`—Adds an attribute to every element in the `QueryCollection`
- `setStyle(name, value)`—Adds a style attribute to every element in the `QueryCollection`
- `template(templateElement, data, renderDonePromiseContract)`—Renders a template using the supplied data for each item in the Query collection
- `toggleClass(name)`—Toggles the specified class for every element in the `QueryCollection`

Because the `QueryCollection` class derives from the base Array class, it also contains all of the standard Array methods like `indexOf()` and `slice()`.

Performing Ajax Calls with the `xhr` Function

The WinJS `xhr()` function is a thin wrapper around the browser `XMLHttpRequest` object. Unlike working with the `XMLHttpRequest` object, the `xhr()` function returns a promise. You use the `xhr()` function whenever you want to make an Ajax request.

Listings 2.15 and 2.16 contain the code for making a simple Ajax request. The home page of the Microsoft site is retrieved and the list of all of the links extracted from this page is displayed (see Figure 2.9).

LISTING 2.15 Making a Simple Ajax Request (xhr\xhr.html)

```
<!DOCTYPE html>
<html>
<head>
    <meta charset="utf-8">
    <title>Simple XHR</title>

    <!-- WinJS references -->
    <link href="//Microsoft.WinJS.1.0/css/ui-dark.css" rel="stylesheet" />
    <script src="//Microsoft.WinJS.1.0/js/base.js"></script>
```

CHAPTER 2 WinJS Fundamentals

```html
    <script src="//Microsoft.WinJS.1.0/js/ui.js"></script>

    <!-- Chapter02 references -->
    <link href="/css/default.css" rel="stylesheet">
    <script type="text/javascript" src="xhr.js"></script>
</head>
<body>

    <h1>Here are the Microsoft Site Links:</h1>


    <ul id="ulResults"></ul>

</body>
</html>
```

LISTING 2.16   Making a Simple Ajax Request (xhr\xhr.js)

```javascript
(function () {
    "use strict";

    function initialize() {
        // Create the xhr options
        var options = {
            url: "http://Microsoft.com",
            responseType: "document"
        };

        // Make the Ajax request
        WinJS.xhr(options).done(
            function (xhr) {
                var li;
                var ulResults = document.getElementById("ulResults");
                var links = xhr.response.querySelectorAll("a");
                for (var i = 0; i < links.length; i++) {
                    li = document.createElement("LI");
                    li.innerText = links[i].href;
                    ulResults.appendChild(li);
                }
            },
            function () {
                var messageDialog = new Windows.UI.Popups.MessageDialog("Could not
➥download page!");
                messageDialog.showAsync();
            }
```

            );
        };

        document.addEventListener("DOMContentLoaded", initialize);
    })();
```

![Figure 2.9: Screenshot showing "Here are the Microsoft Site Links:" followed by a list of Microsoft URLs including http://www.microsoft.com/en-us/, ms-appx:///dde5138e-ef8e-48c5-86d9-957bfc5406c0/en-us/default.aspx?bldi=1-0, http://windows.microsoft.com/en-US/windows/home, http://office.microsoft.com/en-us/, http://www.xbox.com/en-US/, and many others.]

FIGURE 2.9  Requesting and displaying links from the Microsoft homepage

The `WinJS.xhr()` function returns a promise. Two anonymous functions are passed to the `WinJS.xhr()` method in Listing 2.16: a promise complete function and a promise error function. The complete function displays the list of links in an HTML UL element and the error page shows a warning message to the user.

Notice that the code in Listing 2.15 makes a request against a remote website. This should be surprising. Normally, the `XMLHttpRequest` object is subject to the same origin policy which prevents you from requesting content from another domain. However, in the context of a Windows Store app, you don't have this restriction.

> **NOTE**
>
> Internet Explorer 10, but not earlier versions, supports the W3C Cross-Origin Resource Sharing (CORS) standard. If the remote server returns the right HTTP header then you can make Ajax requests against the remote server. In the context of a Windows Store app, you can ignore CORS and make cross-origin requests without doing anything special.

Notice that you pass the URL used by the Ajax request in the second parameter passed to the `WinJS.xhr()` function in an option object. You can pass any of the following options:

- ▶ `type`—Enables you to specify the HTTP method used in the Ajax request. For example, "POST", "GET", "PUT", "DELETE", "HEAD".

- ▶ `url`—Enables you to specify the URL used when making the Ajax request.
```

- **user**—Enables you to specify credentials when making the Ajax request.
- **Password**—Enables you to specify credentials when making the Ajax request.
- **headers**—Enables you to customize the HTTP headers used in the Ajax request.
- **data**—Enables you to specify the data passed to the remote server in the Ajax request. You can pass a string, array of unsigned bytes, or even a document. Use `JSON.stringify()` to convert other types of JavaScript objects into a string.
- **responseType**—Enables you to specify the type of data returned from the server. Possible values are "arraybuffer", "blob", "document", "ms-stream", or "text".
- **customRequestInitializer**—Enables you to customize the properties of the underlying `XmlHttpRequest` object.

I'll talk more about both the `responseType` and `customRequestInitializer` in the following sections.

Specifying Different Response Types

The `XmlHttpRequest` object—and therefore, the `WinJS.xhr()` function—can be used to return several different types of data including blobs, documents, and text. You can use the `responseType` option to specify how you want the data returned.

The default value of `responseType` is "text". For example, the following request will return the contents of the XML feed as a string:

```
var options = {
    url: "http://stephenwalther.com/blog/feed"
};

WinJS.xhr(options).done(
    function (xhr) {
        var result = xhr.response;   // xhr.response is a string
    }
);
```

Most likely, you don't want to return an XML document as a string because then you can't use methods like `querySelector()` and `querySelectorAll()` to extract elements from the document. Instead, you want to return an XML document as a document like this:

```
var options = {
    url: "http://stephenwalther.com/blog/feed",
    responseType: "document"
};

WinJS.xhr(options).done(
    function (xhr) {
```

```
        var result = xhr.response;   // xhr.response is a document
    }
);
```

Notice that the options object includes a `responseType` property with the value "document". When you call the `WinJS.xhr()` method, the data is returned as a document instead of a string. That means that you can query the results using methods like `querySelector()` and `querySelectorAll()`.

> **NOTE**
> For backwards compatibility, the `XmlHttpRequest` object also has `responseText` and `responseXML` properties. You should favor the new `XmlHttpRequest` response property over these legacy properties.

Customizing the Properties of the `XmlHttpRequest` Object

The `WinJS.xhr()` function is nothing more than a wrapper around the native browser `XmlHttpRequest` object. There are some cases in which you might need to use features of the underlying `XmlHttpRequest` object that are not exposed through the options of the `WinJS.xhr()` function. In these cases, you can take advantage of the `WinJS.xhr()` function's `customRequestInitializer` option to customize the `XmlHttpRequest` object.

Imagine, for example, that you want to request and display the contents of a text file. Furthermore, you want to display download progress during the Ajax request.

The page in Listing 2.17 contains an HTML5 PROGRESS element (for displaying the download progress) and a DIV element (for displaying the contents of the text file).

LISTING 2.17 Customizing the `XmlHttpRequest` Object (xhrCustom\xhrCustom.html)

```html
<!DOCTYPE html>
<html>
<head>
    <meta charset="utf-8">
    <title>XHR Custom</title>

    <!-- WinJS references -->
    <link href="//Microsoft.WinJS.1.0/css/ui-dark.css" rel="stylesheet" />
    <script src="//Microsoft.WinJS.1.0/js/base.js"></script>
    <script src="//Microsoft.WinJS.1.0/js/ui.js"></script>

    <!-- Chapter02 references -->
    <link href="/css/default.css" rel="stylesheet">
    <script type="text/javascript" src="xhrCustom.js"></script>
</head>
<body>
```

74   CHAPTER 2   WinJS Fundamentals

```html
    <progress id="prgResults" max="100"></progress>

    <div id="divResults"></div>

</body>
</html>
```

The code in Listing 2.18 illustrates how you can take advantage of the `customRequestInitializer` option to hook up a progress event handler to the `XmlHttpRequest` object used by the `WinJS.xhr()` function. The progress event handler updates the PROGRESS element so you can watch while a long running Ajax request completes (see Figure 2.10).

LISTING 2.18   Customizing the `XmlHttpRequest` Object (xhrCustom\xhrCustom.js)

```javascript
(function () {
    "use strict";

    function initialize() {
        // Cache references to DOM elements
        var prgResults = document.getElementById("prgResults");
        var divResults = document.getElementById("divResults");

        // Create xhr options
        var options = {
            url: "products.txt",
            customRequestInitializer: function (xhr) {
                xhr.onprogress = function (evt) {
                    if (evt.lengthComputable) {
                        var percentComplete = (evt.loaded / evt.total) * 100;
                        prgResults.value = percentComplete;
                    }
                };
            }
        };

        // Perform Ajax request
        WinJS.xhr(options).done(
            function (xhr) {
                divResults.innerHTML = xhr.response;
            }
        );
    }

    document.addEventListener("DOMContentLoaded", initialize);
})();
```

Notice that the options object has a `customRequestInitializer` property which represents a function for initializing the `XmlHttpRequest` object. The function adds a `onprogress` handler which displays the amount of progress completed using the HTML5 PROGRESS element.

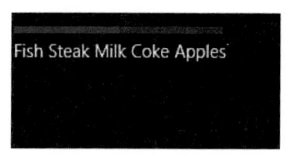

FIGURE 2.10 Showing Ajax request progress

Summary

The goal of this chapter was to introduce you to the features of the base WinJS library. In the first section, you learned how to organize your JavaScript code into modules, namespaces, and classes. By taking advantage of modules and namespaces, you can avoid polluting the global namespace and make your app easier to maintain over time.

Next, I discussed how you can take advantage of promises whenever you need to write asynchronous code. I discussed, for example, how you can use promises when performing Ajax requests. You learned how to create promises, cancel promises, chain promises, and compose new promises from existing promises.

I also discussed how you can use WinJS query selectors to retrieve DOM elements. You learned how to use `WinJS.Utilities.query()` to perform a query using a selector and return a query set. You also learned how to retrieve individual elements with `WinJS.Utilities.id()`.

Finally, I explained how you can use the `WinJS.xhr()` function to perform Ajax queries in a Windows Store app. You learned how to control the type of data returned by the `WinJS.xhr()` function by setting the responseType option. For example, you learned how to return the results of an Ajax query as a string or a document.

CHAPTER 3

Observables, Bindings, and Templates

IN THIS CHAPTER

▶ Understanding Observables

▶ Understanding Declarative Data Binding

▶ Understanding Templates

In this chapter, I explain how you can display JavaScript objects, such as a single product or array of products, in the pages of your Windows Store apps.

I start by explaining observables. An observable enables you to detect when a JavaScript property has been changed automatically. I also explain how you can take advantage of the `WinJS.Binding.List` object to detect when elements of an array are changed.

Next, I focus on the topic of declarative data binding. You learn how to use both ordinary JavaScript objects and observable JavaScript objects with declarative data binding.

Finally, I discuss how you can display an array of objects using a WinJS template. A template enables you to format and display multiple JavaScript objects at a time.

Understanding Observables

An *observable* is an object which can notify one or more listeners when the value of a property is changed.

Observables enable you to keep your user interface and your application data in sync. For example, by taking advantage of observables, you can update your user interface automatically whenever the properties of a product change. Observables are the foundation of declarative binding in the WinJS library.

> **NOTE**
>
> The WinJS library is not the first JavaScript library to include support for observables. For example, Backbone, Knockout, Ember, and the Microsoft Ajax Library (now part of the Ajax Control Toolkit) all support observables.

Creating an Observable

Imagine that I have created a product object like this:

```
var product = {
    name: "Milk",
    description: "Something to drink",
    price: 12.33
};
```

Nothing very exciting about this product. It has three properties named name, description, and price.

Now, imagine that I want to be notified automatically whenever any of these properties are changed. In that case, I can create an observable product from my product object like this:

```
var observableProduct = WinJS.Binding.as(product);
```

This line of code creates a new JavaScript object named `observableProduct` from the existing JavaScript object named product. This new object also has a name, description, and price property. However, unlike the properties of the original product object, the properties of the observable product object trigger notifications when the properties are changed.

Each of the properties of the new observable product object has been changed into accessor properties which have both a getter and a setter. For example, the observable product price property looks something like this:

```
price: {
        get: function () { return this.getProperty("price"); }
        set: function (value) { this.setProperty("price", value); }
}
```

When you read the price property, then the `getProperty()` method is called and when you set the price property, then the `setProperty()` method is called. The `getProperty()` and `setProperty()` methods are methods of the observable product object.

The observable product object supports the following methods and properties:

- **addProperty(name, value)**—Adds a new property to an observable and notifies any listeners.
- **backingData**—An object which represents the value of each property.
- **bind(name, action)**—Enables you to execute a function when a property changes.
- **getProperty(name)**—Returns the value of a property using the string name of the property.
- **notify(name, newValue, oldValue)**—A private method which executes each function in the _listeners array.

- ▶ `removeProperty(name)`—Removes a property and notifies any listeners.
- ▶ `setProperty(name, value)`—Updates a property and notifies any listeners.
- ▶ `unbind(name, action)`—Enables you to stop executing a function in response to a property change.
- ▶ `updateProperty(name, value)`—Updates a property and notifies any listeners.

So when you create an observable, you get a new object with the same properties as an existing object. However, when you modify the properties of an observable object, then you can notify any listeners of the observable that the value of a particular property has changed automatically.

Imagine that you change the value of the price property like this:

```
observableProduct.price = 2.99;
```

In that case, the following sequence of events is triggered:

The price setter calls the `setProperty("price", 2.99)` method

The `setProperty()` method updates the value of the `backingData.price` property and calls the `notify()` method

The `notify()` method executes each function in the collection of listeners associated with the price property

When an observable property is updated, you can execute one or more functions (listeners) automatically.

> **WARNING**
>
> If you call the `WinJS.Binding.as()` method on a WinRT object, then you will get an exception. The problem is that WinRT objects are immutable and the `WinJS.Binding.as()` method attempts to add a new method named `_getObservable()` to the immutable object. You can make JavaScript objects observable, but not WinRT objects.

Creating Observable Listeners

If you want to be notified when a property of an observable object is changed, then you need to register a listener. You register a listener by using the `bind()` method like in Listing 3.1.

LISTING 3.1 Binding an Object Property to a Listener (observables\observables.html)

```javascript
// Simple product object
var product = {
    name: "Milk",
    description: "Something to drink",
```

80   CHAPTER 3   Observables, Bindings, and Templates

```
    price: 12.33
};

// Create observable product
var observableProduct = WinJS.Binding.as(product);

// Execute a function when price is changed
observableProduct.bind("price", function (newValue, oldValue) {
    console.log(newValue + " was " + oldValue);
});

// Change the price
observableProduct.price = 2.99;
```

In the code above, the `bind()` method is used to associate the price property with a function. When the price property is changed, the function logs the new value and old value of the price property to the Visual Studio JavaScript console (see Figure 3.1).

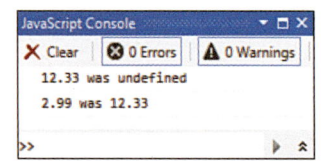

FIGURE 3.1   Binding to a property

The price property is associated with the function using the following lines of code:

```
// Execute a function when price is changed
observableProduct.bind("price", function (newValue, oldValue) {
    console.log(newValue + " was " + oldValue);
});
```

Notice that the function bound to the price property is called twice. It is called for the initial value of the property and it is called when the property is changed.

> **NOTE**
>
> You can bind a listener to a complex property by supplying an object to the second parameter of the `WinJS.Binding.bind()` method like this:
>
> ```
>     // Create object with complex property
> var customer = {
>     shippingAddress: {
>         street: "312 Main Street"
>     }
> };
> ```

```
// Create observable
var observableCustomer = WinJS.Binding.as(customer);


// Bind to complex property
WinJS.Binding.bind(observableCustomer, {
    shippingAddress: {
        street: function (newValue) {
            console.log("Modified shipping address to "
                + newValue);
        }
    }
});


// Change value of complex property
observableCustomer.shippingAddress.street = "100 Grant Street";
```

Coalescing Notifications

If you make multiple changes to a property—one change immediately following another—then separate notifications won't be sent. Instead, any listeners are notified only once. The notifications are coalesced into a single notification.

For example, in the code in Listing 3.2, the product price property is updated three times. However, only two messages are written to the JavaScript console. Only the initial value and the last value assigned to the price property are written to the JavaScript Console window:

LISTING 3.2 Coalescing Notifications (observablesCoalesce\observablesCoalesce.html)

```
// Simple product object
var product = {
    name: "Milk",
    description: "Something to drink",
    price: 12.33
};


// Create observable product
var observableProduct = WinJS.Binding.as(product);


// Execute a function when price is changed
observableProduct.bind("price", function (newValue, oldValue) {
    console.log(newValue + " was " + oldValue);
});
```

CHAPTER 3 Observables, Bindings, and Templates

```
// Change the price
observableProduct.price = 3.99;
observableProduct.price = 2.99;
observableProduct.price = 1.99;
```

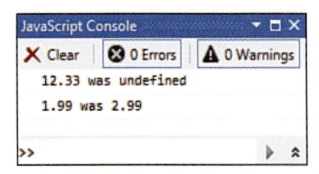

```
JavaScript Console
X Clear    0 Errors    0 Warnings
12.33 was undefined
1.99 was 2.99
```

FIGURE 3.2 Coalescing notifications

If there is a time delay between changes to a property, then the changes result in different notifications.

If you need to prevent multiple notifications from being coalesced into one—and you don't want to create an artificial time delay—then you can take advantage of promises. Because the `updateProperty()` method returns a promise, you can create different notifications for each change in a property by using the following code:

```
// Change the price
observableProduct.updateProperty("price", 3.99)
    .then(function () {
        observableProduct.updateProperty("price", 2.99)
            .then(function () {
                observableProduct.updateProperty("price", 1.99);
            });
    });
```

In this case, even though the price is immediately changed from 3.99 to 2.99 to 1.99, separate notifications for each new value of the price property are sent (see Figure 3.3).

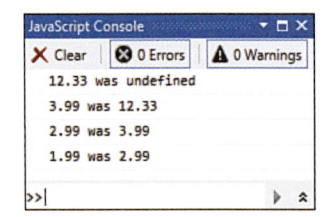

```
JavaScript Console
X Clear    0 Errors    0 Warnings
12.33 was undefined
3.99 was 12.33
2.99 was 3.99
1.99 was 2.99
```

FIGURE 3.3 Using promises with observables

Bypassing Notifications

Normally, if a property of an observable object has listeners and you change the property, then the listeners are notified. However, there are certain situations in which you might want to bypass notification. In other words, you might need to change a property value silently without triggering any functions registered for notification.

If you want to change a property without triggering notifications, then you should change the property by using the `backingData` property. The code in Listing 3.3 illustrates how you can change the price property silently:

LISTING 3.3 Bypassing Notifications (observablesBypass\observablesBypass.html)

```
// Simple product object
var product = {
    name: "Milk",
    description: "Something to drink",
    price: 12.33
};

// Create observable product
var observableProduct = WinJS.Binding.as(product);

// Execute a function when price is changed
observableProduct.bind("price", function (newValue) {
    console.log(newValue);
});

// Change the price silently
observableProduct.backingData.price = 5.99;
console.log(observableProduct.price); // Writes 5.99
```

The price is changed to the value 5.99 by changing the value of `backingData.price`. Because the `observableProduct.price` property is not set directly, any listeners associated with the price property are not notified.

When you change the value of a property by using the `backingData` property, the change in the property happens synchronously. However, when you change the value of an observable property directly, the change is always made asynchronously.

Working with the `WinJS.Binding.List` Object

If you want to be notified whenever a change is made to an array of items—in other words, you want to work with an observable collection—then you should use the `WinJS.Binding.List` object.

The `WinJS.Binding.List` object wraps a standard JavaScript array in a new object and adds additional methods and events to support change notifications. The `WinJS.Binding.List` object supports the following events:

- ▶ `iteminserted`—Triggered when a new item is added to the list.
- ▶ `itemchanged`—Triggered when an item in the list is replaced with the `setAt()` method.

84   CHAPTER 3   Observables, Bindings, and Templates

- `itemmoved`—Triggered when an item in the list is moved with the `move()` method.
- `itemmutated`—Triggered by calling the `notifyMutated()` method.
- `itemremoved`—Triggered by removing an item from the list.
- `reload`—Triggered by reordering the items in a list by calling `sort()` or `reverse()`. Also triggered by calling the `notifyReload()` method.

The code in Listing 3.4 demonstrates how you can trigger each of these events and the information passed to each event handler.

LISTING 3.4   Using a `WinJS.Binding.List` (observablesList\observablesList.html)

```
var products = [
    { name: "Milk", price: 2.99 },
    { name: "Oranges", price: 2.50 },
    { name: "Apples", price: 1.99 }
];

// Create List
var productsList = new WinJS.Binding.List(products);

// Setup event handlers
productsList.oniteminserted = function (evt) {
    var message = "Item Inserted: " + evt.detail.value.name
        + " at index " + evt.detail.index
        + " with key " + evt.detail.key;
    console.log(message);
};

productsList.onitemchanged = function (evt) {
    var message = "Item Changed: " + evt.detail.oldValue.name
        + " to " + evt.detail.newValue.name
        + " at index " + evt.detail.index
        + " with key " + evt.detail.key;
    console.log(message);
};

productsList.onitemmutated = function (evt) {
    var message = "Item Mutated: " + evt.detail.value.name
        + " with key " + evt.detail.key;
    console.log(message);
};

productsList.onitemremoved = function (evt) {
    var message = "Item Removed: " + evt.detail.value.name
```

Understanding Observables

```
        + " at index " + evt.detail.index
        + " with key " + evt.detail.key;
    console.log(message);
};

productsList.onitemmoved = function (evt) {
    var message = "Item Moved: " + evt.detail.value.name
        + " from index " + evt.detail.oldIndex
        + " to index " + evt.detail.newIndex;
    console.log(message);
};

productsList.onreload = function (evt) {
    var message = "List Reloaded";
    console.log(message);
};

// Insert an item
productsList.push({ name: "Carrots", price: 2.33 }); // triggers iteminserted

// Replace an entire item
productsList.setAt(1, { name: "Navel Oranges", price: 2.50 }); // triggers
➥itemchanged

// Update an item property
productsList.getAt(1).price = 500.00;
productsList.notifyMutated(1); // triggers itemmutated

// Delete an item
productsList.splice(0, 1); // triggers itemremoved

// Move second item to top
productsList.move(1, 0); // triggers itemmoved

// Sort the list
productsList.sort(); // triggers reload
```

In Listing 3.4, a JavaScript array named products is created which represents a list of products with name and price properties. Next, a `WinJS.Binding.List` is created with the following line of code:

```
var productsList = new WinJS.Binding.List(products);
```

Event handlers for all of the `WinJS.Binding.List` events are created. Each event handler writes a message to the Visual Studio JavaScript Console (see Figure 3.4).

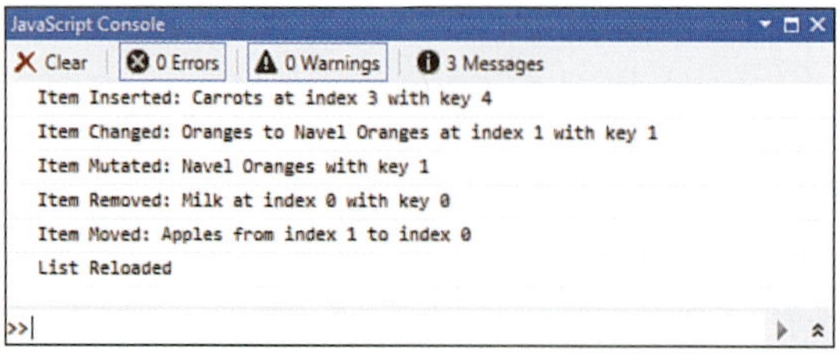

FIGURE 3.4 `WinJS.Binding.List` events

Creating an Observable Collection of Observables

By default, when you create a `WinJS.Binding.List` from a JavaScript array, the list is observable but not the items in the list. The `WinJS.Binding.List` simply contains the items from the array and the items are plain old JavaScript objects.

If you want to convert each of the items from the JavaScript array into an observable item, then you need to use the binding option when creating the `WinJS.Binding.List` like this:

```
var products = [
    { name: "Milk", price: 2.99 },
    { name: "Oranges", price: 2.50 },
    { name: "Apples", price: 1.99 }
];

// Create List
var productsList = new WinJS.Binding.List(products, { binding: true });

// Listen for changes in price
productsList.getAt(1).bind("price", function () {
    console.log("price changed");
});
```

The `productsList` in this code contains a list of observable objects. Because each object in the list is observable, you can hook up a listener function that gets triggered when a change is made to a property. In the code above, a message is written to the Visual Studio JavaScript console whenever the price property is modified.

Understanding Declarative Data Binding

Declarative data binding enables you to bind the attributes of an HTML element to the properties of a JavaScript object. You can take advantage of declarative data binding whenever you want to display data in an HTML page.

Let me start with a simple example. The page in Listing 3.5 displays product details (see Figure 3.5).

LISTING 3.5 Simple Declarative Data Binding (dataBinding\dataBinding.html)

```html
<!DOCTYPE html>
<html>
<head>
    <meta charset="utf-8" />
    <title>Chapter03</title>

    <!-- WinJS references -->
    <link href="//Microsoft.WinJS.1.0/css/ui-dark.css" rel="stylesheet" />
    <script src="//Microsoft.WinJS.1.0/js/base.js"></script>
    <script src="//Microsoft.WinJS.1.0/js/ui.js"></script>

    <!-- Chapter03 references -->
    <link href="/css/default.css" rel="stylesheet" />
    <script src="/dataBinding/dataBinding.js"></script>
</head>
<body>

    <h1>Product Details</h1>

    <div>
        Product Name:
    <span data-win-bind="innerText:name"></span>
</div>
<div>
    Product Price:
    <span data-win-bind="innerText:price"></span>
</div>
<div>
    Product Picture:
    <br />
    <img data-win-bind="src:photo;alt:name" />
</div>
</body>
</html>
```

The product name, price, and picture are displayed with HTML SPAN elements. Notice that each SPAN element includes a data-win-bind attribute. For example, the product name is displayed with the following SPAN element:

```html
<span data-win-bind="innerText:name"></span>
```

This `data-win-bind` attribute binds the value of the name property to the `innerText` property of the SPAN element.

You can use the data-win-bind attribute to bind (almost) any attribute of an HTML element to the value of a JavaScript property. For example, the picture of the Tesla is displayed by binding values to the IMG element's src and alt attributes:

```
<img data-win-bind="src:photo;alt:name" />
```

Notice that the data-win-bind attribute accepts a semicolon delimited list of HTML element attribute names and JavaScript object property names.

> **NOTE**
>
> The one attribute which you cannot use with declarative binding is the ID attribute. By default, the WinJS library generates a unique ID for each element automatically. You can disable this behavior by setting the `optimizeBindingReferences` property to false.

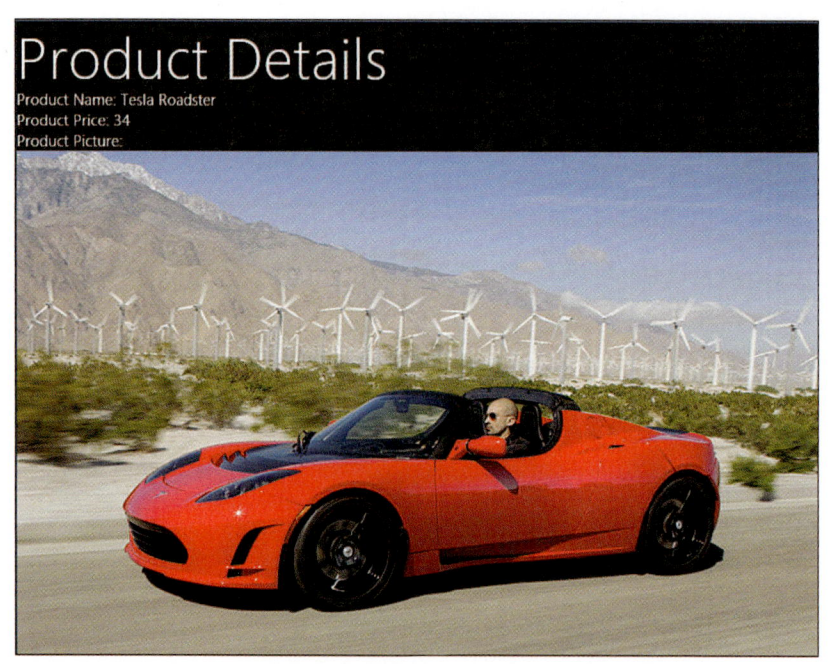

FIGURE 3.5   Showing product details with declarative data binding

The code in Listing 3.6 contains the product which is displayed by the HTML page in Listing 3.5.

LISTING 3.6   Simple Declarative Data Binding (databinding\databinding.js)

```
(function () {
    "use strict";

    function initialize() {
```

```
        var product = {
            name: "Tesla Roadster",
            price: 34,
            photo: "tesla.jpg"
        };

        WinJS.Binding.processAll(null, product);
    }

    document.addEventListener("DOMContentLoaded", initialize);

})();
```

There is nothing special about the product object in Listing 3.6—it is just a plain old JavaScript object.

Notice the call to `WinJS.Binding.processAll()` in Listing 3.6. The declarative data binding attributes in a page are not processed until you call this method. When you call the `WinJS.Binding.procesAll()` method, you must specify two parameters: the root element and the data context.

The root element determines which elements in a page get processed. If you pass the value null, then the entire document is parsed.

The data context contains the data which you want to bind to the HTML attributes. In Listing 3.6, the product object is passed to the `WinJS.Binding.processAll()` method as the data context.

> **WARNING**
> Don't call `WinJS.Binding.processAll()` until the document containing the HTML elements has been loaded. Otherwise, there is nothing to process. In Listing 3.6, the `WinJS.Binding.processAll()` method is called within a function triggered by the `DOMContentLoaded` event.

Declarative Data Binding and Observables

Declarative data binding and observables are a powerful combination. If you use observables with data binding, then you can update the contents of an HTML document automatically whenever you change the underlying JavaScript objects.

For example, the HTML page in Listing 3.7 contains a SPAN and a BUTTON element. The page displays the number of times the button has been clicked (see Figure 3.6).

FIGURE 3.6 Displaying a click count

LISTING 3.7 Using Data Binding with an Observable (dataBindingObservables\dataBindingObservables.html)

```html
<!DOCTYPE html>
<html>
<head>
    <meta charset="utf-8" />
    <title>Chapter03</title>

    <!-- WinJS references -->
    <link href="//Microsoft.WinJS.1.0/css/ui-dark.css" rel="stylesheet" />
    <script src="//Microsoft.WinJS.1.0/js/base.js"></script>
    <script src="//Microsoft.WinJS.1.0/js/ui.js"></script>

    <!-- Chapter03 references -->
    <link href="/css/default.css" rel="stylesheet" />
    <script src="dataBindingObservables.js"></script>
</head>
<body>

    <div>
        You have clicked the button
        <span data-win-bind="innerText:timesClicked"></span> times.
        <br />
        <button data-win-bind="onclick:click">Click Here!</button>
    </div>


</body>
</html>
```

Notice that the page in Listing 3.7 includes two data-win-bind attributes. The first data-win-bind attribute is used with a SPAN element to display the click count and the second data-win-bind attribute is used with a BUTTON element to handle the click event.

The JavaScript code in Listing 3.8 contains an observable object, named view model, which tracks the click count.

LISTING 3.8 Using Data Binding with an Observable (dataBindingObservables\
dataBindingObservables.html)

```
(function () {
    "use strict";

    function initialize() {

        // Create a view model
        var viewModel = {
            timesClicked: 0,
            click: function (evt) {
                evt.preventDefault();
                viewModel.timesClicked++;
            }
        };

        // Make the view model observable
        viewModel = WinJS.Binding.as(viewModel);

        // Bind the view model to the document
        WinJS.Binding.processAll(null, viewModel);
    }

    document.addEventListener("DOMContentLoaded", initialize);

})();
```

The `viewModel` object in Listing 3.8 has a property, named `timesClicked`, which is used to track the number of times the button has been clicked. The `viewModel` object also has a method named `click()` which is used to update the `timesClicked` property.

The `viewModel` is converted into an observable with the help of the `WinJS.Binding.as()` method. Finally, the `viewModel` is bound to the page and the `data-win-bind` attributes are processed by calling `WinJS.Binding.processAll()`.

Capturing the Contents of an HTML Form

The WinJS library does not support two-way data binding. Change notification is one-way. If you want to capture the contents of an HTML form, then you need to do the work of retrieving the values of the form elements yourself.

The page in Listing 3.9 contains an HTML form for creating a new product. It has two INPUT elements for the product name and price (see Figure 3.7). The form uses a single `data-win-bind` attribute. The FORM element has a `data-win-bind` attribute which wires up a form submit handler.

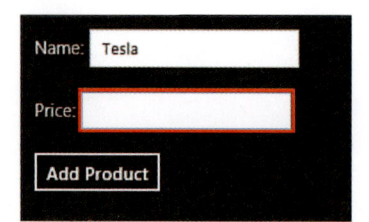

FIGURE 3.7 Creating a new product

LISTING 3.9 Two-Way Data Binding (dataBindingTwoWay\dataBindingTwoWay.html)

```html
<!DOCTYPE html>
<html>
<head>
    <meta charset="utf-8" />
    <title>Chapter03</title>

    <!-- WinJS references -->
    <link href="//Microsoft.WinJS.1.0/css/ui-dark.css" rel="stylesheet" />
    <script src="//Microsoft.WinJS.1.0/js/base.js"></script>
    <script src="//Microsoft.WinJS.1.0/js/ui.js"></script>

    <!-- Chapter03 references -->
    <link href="/css/default.css" rel="stylesheet" />
    <script src="dataBindingTwoWay.js"></script>
</head>
<body>
    <form data-win-bind="onsubmit:submit">
        <div class="field">
            <label>Name:</label>
            <input id="productName" required />
        </div>
        <div class="field">
            <label>Price:</label>
            <input id="productPrice" required />
        </div>
        <div class="field">
            <button>Add Product</button>
        </div>

    </form>

</body>
</html>
```

When you submit the HTML form, the `viewData.submit()` method in Listing 3.10 is invoked. This method grabs the HTML form fields and creates a new product object named `productToAdd`.

LISTING 3.10 Two-Way Data Binding (dataBindingTwoWay\dataBindingTwoWay.js)

```javascript
(function () {
    "use strict";

    function initialize() {

        var viewModel = {
            submit: function (evt) {
                // Prevent page from being posted
                evt.preventDefault();

                // Grab form field values
                var productToAdd = {
                    name: document.getElementById("productName").value,
                    price: document.getElementById("productPrice").value
                };

                // TODO: Add new product to database
            }
        };


        WinJS.Binding.processAll(null, viewModel);
    }

    document.addEventListener("DOMContentLoaded", initialize);

})();
```

The page in Listing 3.9 uses a data-win-bind attribute to wire up the form submit event handler. You might be wondering whether it would be easier to do without the data binding and directly wire up an event handler like this:

`<form onsubmit="submit">`

Why use declarative data binding at all? The advantage of using declarative data binding to wire up the event handler is that you do not need to expose the handler through a namespace. When using declarative data binding, a handler does not need to be a public method—the only requirement is that it be part of the data context used with the `WinJS.Binding.processAll()` method.

94   CHAPTER 3 Observables, Bindings, and Templates

> **NOTE**
>
> The HTML form in Listing 3.9 uses the HTML5 required attribute to ensure that values are entered in the name and price INPUT elements.

Declarative Data Binding and WinJS Controls

We discuss WinJS controls in detail in the next chapter; however, I want to make sure that you understand that you can use declarative data binding with WinJS controls properties in the same way as you can use declarative data binding with element attributes.

The trick is to use the `winControl` property which is exposed by every HTML element that is associated with a control. You can use the `winControl` property with the `data-win-bind` attribute.

For example, the page in Listing 3.11 contains a WinJS Rating control (see Figure 3.8).

FIGURE 3.8   Displaying an average rating with declarative data binding

LISTING 3.11   Using Declarative Data Binding with WinJS Controls (dataBindingControls\dataBindingControls.html)

```html
<!DOCTYPE html>
<html>
<head>
    <meta charset="utf-8" />
    <title>Chapter03</title>

    <!-- WinJS references -->
    <link href="//Microsoft.WinJS.1.0/css/ui-dark.css" rel="stylesheet" />
    <script src="//Microsoft.WinJS.1.0/js/base.js"></script>
    <script src="//Microsoft.WinJS.1.0/js/ui.js"></script>

    <!-- Chapter03 references -->
    <link href="/css/default.css" rel="stylesheet" />
    <script src="dataBindingControls.js"></script>
</head>
<body>

    <div
        data-win-control="WinJS.UI.Rating"
        data-win-bind="winControl.averageRating:averageRating">
    </div>
```

```html
    <div>
        The average rating for this product is:
        <span data-win-bind="innerText:averageRating"></span>
    </div>

</body>
</html>
```

Listing 3.11 contains a WinJS Rating control. The `averageRating` property of the WinJS Rating control is set with the following data-win-bind attribute:

```
data-win-bind="winControl.averageRating:averageRating"
```

The `winControl` property gets you from the HTML element to its associated control.

The JavaScript file in Listing 3.12 illustrates how you can bind the average rating to the Rating control.

LISTING 3.12 Using Declarative Data Binding with WinJS Controls (dataBindingControls\dataBindingControls.js)

```javascript
(function () {
    "use strict";

    function initialize() {

        // Create a view model
        var viewModel = {
            averageRating: 3
        };

        // Bind the view model to the document
        WinJS.UI.processAll()
            .done(function () {
                WinJS.Binding.processAll(null, viewModel);
            });
    }

    document.addEventListener("DOMContentLoaded", initialize);

})();
```

The code in Listing 3.12 contains two calls to the `processAll()` method. First, the `WinJS.UI.processAll()` method is called to process all of the WinJS controls in the page. Next, the `WinJS.Binding.processAll()` method is called to process all of the data binding attributes in the page. You must call the two `processAll()` methods in that order or there won't be controls with properties to bind to.

Declarative Data Binding and Binding Converters

Binding converters enable you to transform the value of a property when using the property in a data-win-bind attribute.

There are all sorts of situations in which a binding converter is useful; for example, formatting dates and times or hiding or displaying content depending on a property value. Whenever you need to alter a JavaScript property value before displaying it, use a binding converter.

Imagine, for example, that you want to display the text "On Sale!" only when a product is on sale. The page in Listing 3.13 displays two products (see Figure 3.9). It uses a binding converter to hide or display the contents of a DIV element which contains the text "On Sale!"

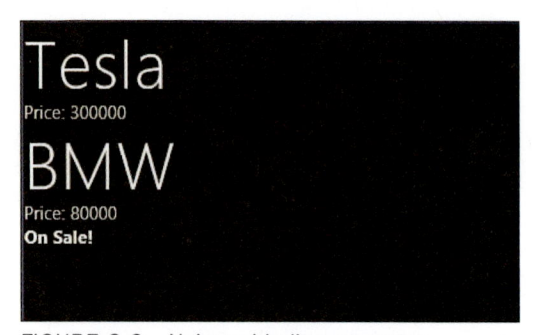

FIGURE 3.9 Using a binding converter

LISTING 3.13 Using a Binding Converter (dataBindingConverters/dataBindingConverters.html)

```html
<!DOCTYPE html>
<html>
<head>
    <meta charset="utf-8" />
    <title>Chapter03</title>

    <!-- WinJS references -->
    <link href="//Microsoft.WinJS.1.0/css/ui-dark.css" rel="stylesheet" />
    <script src="//Microsoft.WinJS.1.0/js/base.js"></script>
    <script src="//Microsoft.WinJS.1.0/js/ui.js"></script>

    <!-- Chapter03 references -->
    <link href="/css/default.css" rel="stylesheet" />
    <script src="dataBindingConverters.js"></script>
    <script type="text/javascript" src="myBindingConverters.js"></script>
</head>
<body>

    <div>
```

Understanding Declarative Data Binding

```
            <h1 data-win-bind="innerText:product1.name"></h1>
            <div>
                Price: <span data-win-bind="innerText:product1.price"></span>
            </div>
            <div data-win-bind="style.display:product1.onSale MyBindingConverters.
➥onSaleToDisplay">
                <b>On Sale!</b>
            </div>
        </div>
        <div>
            <h1 data-win-bind="innerText:product2.name"></h1>
            <div>
                Price: <span data-win-bind="innerText:product2.price"></span>
            </div>
            <div data-win-bind="style.display:product2.onSale MyBindingConverters.
➥onSaleToDisplay">
                <b>On Sale!</b>
            </div>
        </div>

</body>
</html>
```

The text "On Sale!" does not appear after the first product but it does appear after the second product. The text is displayed with the following DIV element:

```
<div data-win-bind="style.display:product2.onSale
➥MyBindingConverters.onSaleToDisplay">
    <b>On Sale!</b>
</div>
```

The binding converter is applied to the DIV element's style attribute. When the binding converter returns the value "none" then the contents of the DIV element are hidden with `display:none`. Otherwise, the binding converter returns the value "block" and the contents of the DIV element are displayed with `display:block`.

The binding converter appears in the value of the data-win-bind expression after the name of the JavaScript property being bound. In this case, the binding converter is a function named `MyBindingConverters.onSaleToDisplay`. This binding converter converts a Boolean value into either the value "none" or "block".

The binding converter is contained in a separate file—referenced by the HTML page—named `myBindingConverters.js` (see Listing 3.14).

CHAPTER 3 Observables, Bindings, and Templates

LISTING 3.14   A Binding Converter (dataBindingConverters\myBindingConverters.js)

```javascript
(function () {
    "use strict";

    var onSaleToDisplay = WinJS.Binding.converter(function (onSale) {
        return onSale ? "block" : "none";
    });

    WinJS.Namespace.define("MyBindingConverters",
        {
            onSaleToDisplay: onSaleToDisplay
        });

})();
```

You create a binding converter by passing a function to the `WinJS.Binding.converter()` method. The function converts the value passed to the function to some other value. In the code above, the function converts the product `onSale` property (a Boolean property) into either the value "block" or "none" (a value which can be used with the style display property).

The two products are created in Listing 3.15. Listing 3.15 contains an object named `viewModel` which has a product1 and product2 property.

LISTING 3.15   Using a Binding Converter (dataBindingConverters/dataBindingConverters.js)

```javascript
(function () {
    "use strict";

    function initialize() {

        var viewModel = {
            product1: {
                name: "Tesla",
                price: 300000.00,
                onSale: false
            },
            product2: {
                name: "BMW",
                price: 80000.00,
                onSale: true
            }
        };
```

```
            WinJS.Binding.processAll(null, viewModel);
    }

    document.addEventListener("DOMContentLoaded", initialize);

})();
```

Creating Date and Price Binding Converters

I can't let you stop reading this section until I mention how to create two other types of converters: date and price converters. I find that I need to use date and price converters in most Windows Store apps which I build in order to format dates and prices.

The JavaScript file in Listing 3.16 contains the two converters.

LISTING 3.16 The Date and Price Converters

```
(function () {
    "use strict";

    // Converts 77.8900 to $77.89
    var price = WinJS.Binding.converter(function (priceToConvert) {
        return "$" + priceToConvert.toFixed(2);
    });

    // Converts full date to 12/25/2013
    var shortDate = WinJS.Binding.converter(function (dateToConvert) {
        return dateToConvert.getMonth() + 1 +
            "/" + dateToConvert.getDate() +
            "/" + dateToConvert.getFullYear();
    });


    WinJS.Namespace.define("MyBindingConverters",
        {
            price: price,
            shortDate: shortDate
        });

})();
```

After you add a reference to the converters to an HTML page, you can use the date and price converters in your binding expressions, as demonstrated in Listing 3.17.

LISTING 3.17 Using the Date and Price Converters

```
<div>
    <h1 data-win-bind="innerText:product1.name"></h1>
    <div>
        Price:
        <span data-win-bind="innerText:product1.price MyBindingConverters.
➥price"></span>
    </div>
    <div>
        Date Available:
        <span data-win-bind="innerText:product1.dateAvailable MyBindingConverters.
➥shortDate"></span>
    </div>
</div>
```

The price converter causes the product price to be displayed as $100.00 instead of 99.999999. The `shortDate` converter causes the product `dateAvailable` property to be displayed as 12/25/2012 instead of Tue Dec 25 00:00:00 PST 2012.

> **NOTE**
>
> Sadly, you cannot pass additional parameters when using a binding converter. It would be nice if you could pass an additional parameter, for example, which represented the date format. However, you can't do this. Instead, you must create separate `dateShort` and `dateLong` binding converters.

Understanding Templates

If you need to display the same fragment of HTML more than one time in a page, then you should create a template. A template is a fragment of HTML which can include declarative data binding expressions. There are two ways to create a template: imperatively and declaratively.

Creating an Imperative Template

Imagine that you want to display an array of products in an HTML page. In that case, you can use a template to format each of the products in the array (see Figure 3.10).

Understanding Templates 101

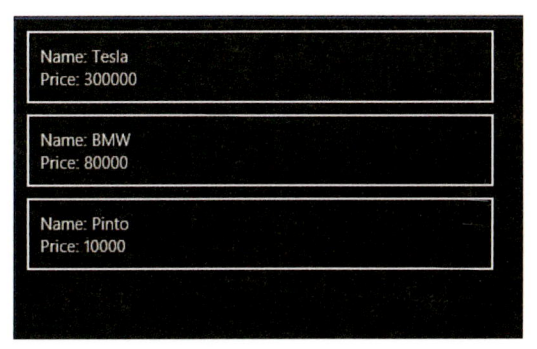

[Figure showing three product cards with Name/Price for Tesla 300000, BMW 80000, Pinto 10000]

FIGURE 3.10 Displaying a list of products with a template

The HTML page in Listing 3.18 contains a DIV element named `tmplProduct`. This DIV element is not displayed when the page is rendered. Instead, it contains the contents of the template.

The page also contains a second DIV element named `conProducts`. This DIV element acts as the target of the template. When each product is rendered, it is rendered into the `conProducts` DIV element.

LISTING 3.18 Creating an Imperative Template (templatesImperative\templatesImperative.html)

```html
<!DOCTYPE html>
<html>
<head>
    <meta charset="utf-8" />
    <title>Chapter03</title>

    <!-- WinJS references -->
    <link href="//Microsoft.WinJS.1.0/css/ui-dark.css" rel="stylesheet" />
    <script src="//Microsoft.WinJS.1.0/js/base.js"></script>
    <script src="//Microsoft.WinJS.1.0/js/ui.js"></script>

    <!-- Chapter03 references -->
    <link href="templatesImperative.css" rel="stylesheet" />
    <script src="templatesImperative.js"></script>
</head>
<body>

    <!-- Template -->
    <div id="tmplProduct">
        <div class="product">
            Name: <span data-win-bind="innerText:name"></span>
            <br />
            Price: <span data-win-bind="innerText:price"></span>
```

```
        </div>
    </div>

    <!-- Place Where Template is Rendered -->
    <div id="conProducts"></div>

</body>
</html>
```

The JavaScript code in Listing 3.19 illustrates how you can create a new template and render the template for each item in an array.

LISTING 3.19 Creating an Imperative Template (templatesImperative\templatesImperative.js)

```
(function () {
    "use strict";

    function initialize() {

        var products = [
            { name: "Tesla", price: 300000 },
            { name: "BMW", price: 80000 },
            { name: "Pinto", price: 10000 }
        ];

        // Get the template and template container
        var tmplProduct = document.getElementById("tmplProduct");
        var conProducts = document.getElementById("conProducts");

        // Create the template
        var template = new WinJS.Binding.Template(tmplProduct)

        // Render each array item using the template
        products.forEach(function (product) {
            template.render(product, conProducts);
        });
    }

    document.addEventListener("DOMContentLoaded", initialize);

})();
```

The template is created by creating a new instance of the WinJS Template control:

```
var template = new WinJS.Binding.Template(tmplProduct)
```

Next, the template is rendered for each item in the array within a `forEach()` method:

```
products.forEach(function (product) {
    template.render(product, conProducts);
});
```

When the template is rendered, only the inner contents of the template are rendered for each data item. The containing DIV element—named `tmplProduct` in the previous code—is not rendered.

Creating a Declarative Template

If you prefer, you can create the template declaratively instead of imperatively. The page in Listing 3.20 contains a WinJS Template control associated with a DIV element named `tmplProduct`.

LISTING 3.20 Creating a Template Declaratively (templatesDeclare\templatesDeclare.html)

```html
<!DOCTYPE html>
<html>
<head>
    <meta charset="utf-8" />
    <title>Chapter03</title>

    <!-- WinJS references -->
    <link href="//Microsoft.WinJS.1.0/css/ui-dark.css" rel="stylesheet" />
    <script src="//Microsoft.WinJS.1.0/js/base.js"></script>
    <script src="//Microsoft.WinJS.1.0/js/ui.js"></script>

    <!-- Chapter03 references -->
    <link href="templatesDeclare.css" rel="stylesheet" />
    <script src="templatesDeclare.js"></script>
</head>
<body>

    <!-- Template -->
    <div id="tmplProduct" data-win-control="WinJS.Binding.Template">
        <div class="product">
            Name: <span data-win-bind="innerText:name"></span>
            <br />
            Price: <span data-win-bind="innerText:price"></span>
        </div>
    </div>

    <!-- Place Where Template is Rendered -->
    <div id="conProducts"></div>
```

104   CHAPTER 3   Observables, Bindings, and Templates

```
</body>
</html>
```

In Listing 3.20, the Template control is declared with a `data-win-control= "WinJS.Binding.Template"` attribute.

Listing 3.21 contains the JavaScript code used to render the array of products using the template.

LISTING 3.21   Creating a Template Declaratively (templatesDeclare\templatesDeclare.js)

```
(function () {
    "use strict";

    function initialize() {

        var products = [
            { name: "Tesla", price: 300000 },
            { name: "BMW", price: 80000 },
            { name: "Pinto", price: 10000 }
        ];

        // Get the template and template container
        var tmplProduct = document.getElementById("tmplProduct");
        var conProducts = document.getElementById("conProducts");

        // Render each array item using the template
        WinJS.UI.processAll().done(function () {
            products.forEach(function (product) {
                tmplProduct.winControl.render(product, conProducts);
            });
        });
    }

    document.addEventListener("DOMContentLoaded", initialize);

})();
```

When using a declarative Template control, you must call the `WinJS.UI.processAll()` method. Otherwise, the DIV element won't be converted into a Template.

Applying a Template with a Query Selector

A query collection includes a `template()` method which you can use to quickly apply a template to either a single DOM element or set of DOM elements. For example, the page in Listing 3.22 displays a list of products.

LISTING 3.22 Using `WinJS.Utilities.id()` with a Template (templatesQuery\templatesQuery.html)

```html
<!DOCTYPE html>
<html>
<head>
    <meta charset="utf-8" />
    <title>Chapter03</title>

    <!-- WinJS references -->
    <link href="//Microsoft.WinJS.1.0/css/ui-dark.css" rel="stylesheet" />
    <script src="//Microsoft.WinJS.1.0/js/base.js"></script>
    <script src="//Microsoft.WinJS.1.0/js/ui.js"></script>

    <!-- Chapter03 references -->
    <link href="templatesQuery.css" rel="stylesheet" />
    <script src="templatesQuery.js"></script>
</head>
<body>

    <!-- Template -->
    <div id="tmplProduct" data-win-control="WinJS.Binding.Template">
        <div class="product">
            Name: <span data-win-bind="innerText:name"></span>
            <br />
            Price: <span data-win-bind="innerText:price"></span>
        </div>
    </div>

    <!-- Place Where Template is Rendered -->
    <div id="conProducts"></div>

</body>
</html>
```

The page in Listing 3.22 contains a declarative template named `tmplProduct`. The page also contains a DIV element named `conProducts` which is the place in the page where the template is rendered.

The JavaScript code in Listing 3.23 demonstrates how you can use the `WinJS.Utilities.id()` method to apply a template to the `conProducts` DIV element.

LISTING 3.23 Using `WinJS.Utilities.id()` with a Template (templatesQuery\templatesQuery.js)

```js
(function () {
    "use strict";
```

106 CHAPTER 3 Observables, Bindings, and Templates

```
    function initialize() {

        var products = [
            { name: "Tesla", price: 300000 },
            { name: "BMW", price: 80000 },
            { name: "Pinto", price: 10000 }
        ];

        WinJS.UI.processAll().done(function () {
            var tmplProduct = document.getElementById("tmplProduct");
            WinJS.Utilities.id("conProducts").template(tmplProduct, products);
        });
    }

    document.addEventListener("DOMContentLoaded", initialize);

})();
```

Notice that you do not need to call `forEach()` when you use the query collection `template()` method. This method performs the `forEach()` internally.

Creating External Templates

If you want to use the same template in multiple pages, then it makes sense to create an external template. In other words, you can place a template in a separate file than the page which contains the template.

Here's how you can declare a Template control so that it references an external template file. Notice that the following Template includes an href option which points to a file named productTemplate.html.

```
<!-- Template -->
<div id="tmplProduct"
    data-win-control="WinJS.Binding.Template"
    data-win-options="{
        href: 'productTemplate.html'
    }">
</div>
```

The productTemplate.html contains the product template and it looks like this:

```
<div class="product">
    Name: <span data-win-bind="innerText:name"></span>
    <br />
    Price: <span data-win-bind="innerText:price"></span>
</div>
```

Finally, Listing 3.24 contains the JavaScript code for rendering the external template.

LISTING 3.24 Rendering an External Template

```
(function () {
    "use strict";

    function initialize() {

        var products = [
            { name: "Tesla", price: 300000 },
            { name: "BMW", price: 80000 },
            { name: "Pinto", price: 10000 }
        ];

        // Get the template and template container
        var tmplProduct = document.getElementById("tmplProduct");
        var conProducts = document.getElementById("conProducts");

        // Render each array item using the template
        WinJS.UI.processAll().done(function () {
            tmplProduct.winControl.render({}).then(function () {

                products.forEach(function (product) {
                    tmplProduct.winControl.render(product, conProducts);
                });

            });
        });
    }

    document.addEventListener("DOMContentLoaded", initialize);

})();
```

You can refer to the very same productTemplate.html from several Template controls located in different pages.

> **NOTE**
>
> In Listing 3.24, the `render()` method is called with an empty object like this:
>
> ```
> tmplProduct.winControl.render({}).then(function () {
>     ...
> });
> ```
>
> This is done to work around a known bug in the WinJS library.

Summary

This chapter was all about displaying JavaScript objects in a page. In the first section, you learned about observables. In particular, you learned how observables enable you to detect when a property of a JavaScript object changes automatically. We also discussed how you can use the `WinJS.Binding`.List object to detect different types of changes in an array of items.

Next, you learned how to take advantage of declarative data binding with both normal JavaScript objects and observable JavaScript objects to display the values of JavaScript properties in a page.

Finally, I discussed how you can use WinJS templates to format and display an array of objects. You learned how to create templates both imperatively and declaratively.

CHAPTER 4
Using WinJS Controls

IN THIS CHAPTER

▶ Introduction to WinJS Controls
▶ Using the `Tooltip` Control
▶ Using the `ToggleSwitch` Control
▶ Using the `Rating` Control
▶ Using the `DatePicker` Control
▶ Using the `TimePicker` Control
▶ Using the `FlipView` Control

My goal in this chapter is to provide you with an overview of the controls included in the WinJS library. I start by explaining how you can add controls to your pages. You learn how to create WinJS controls both declaratively and imperatively and set control options.

The bulk of this chapter is devoted to descriptions and samples of how you can use the basic controls included in the WinJS library. In this chapter, I focus on describing how you can use the following controls:

▶ `Tooltip`—Used to display a popup tooltip.

▶ `ToggleSwitch`—Used to display a toggle switch which can be used in the same scenarios as a checkbox.

▶ `Rating`—Used to display and enter a user rating.

▶ `DatePicker`—Used to enter a date.

▶ `TimePicker`—Used to enter a time.

▶ `FlipView`—Used to display details for one item from a collection of items.

Introduction to WinJS Controls

You declare a WinJS control in a page by using the `data-win-control` attribute. For example, you can declare the WinJS `DatePicker` control by adding the following DIV element to a page:

```
<div id="dateBirthday"
    data-win-control="WinJS.UI.DatePicker"></div>
```

The DIV element isn't really doing anything. It is just acting as a placeholder for the control. It is a "host" for the `DatePicker` control. The `data-win-control` attribute is used to indicate the type of control that will be associated with the element.

A WinJS control does not actually become a control until you call the `WinJS.UI.processAll()` method. This method parses an HTML document, identifies any and all elements which include a `data-win-control` attribute, and generates a control for those elements.

There is one other important requirement for using WinJS controls: you must include references to the right JavaScript and Cascading Style Sheet files. In order to use any of the controls, you must add the following three references to the top of your HTML page:

```
<link href="//Microsoft.WinJS.1.0/css/ui-dark.css" rel="stylesheet" />
<script src="//Microsoft.WinJS.1.0/js/base.js"></script>
<script src="//Microsoft.WinJS.1.0/js/ui.js"></script>
```

The first reference is a reference to a Cascading Style Sheet file named ui-dark.css. The WinJS library includes two style sheets: ui-dark.css and ui-light.css. If you substitute the ui-light.css reference for the ui-dark.css reference, then you can use a light theme for all of your controls.

Figure 4.1 illustrates the appearance of the `DatePicker` control when the dark theme is used and Figure 4.2 illustrates the appearance of the `DatePicker` control when the light theme is used.

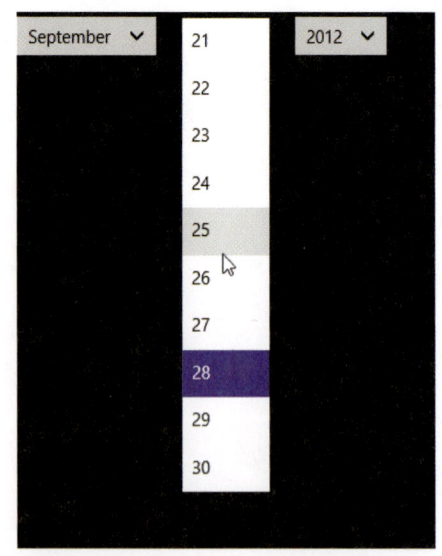

FIGURE 4.1   Using the dark theme

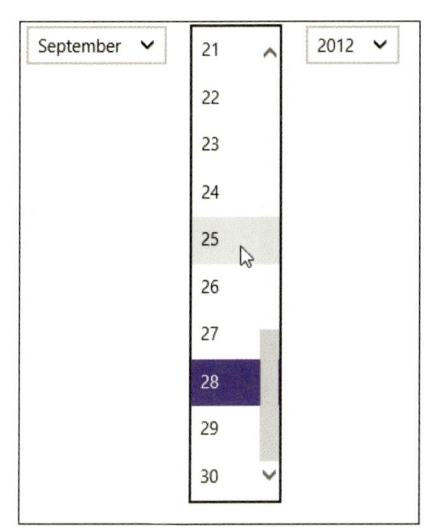

FIGURE 4.2 Using the light theme

The next two references are for the base.js and ui.js JavaScript files. You need references to both of these JavaScript libraries to use the WinJS controls.

All of the JavaScript source code for the WinJS controls is included in the ui.js file. For example, this file contains the source code for the `DatePicker` and `FlipView` controls.

You can view the source of all three of these files by expanding the References folder in the Visual Studio Solution Explorer window (see Figure 4.3). If you double-click any of the files, then you can view the contents of the files.

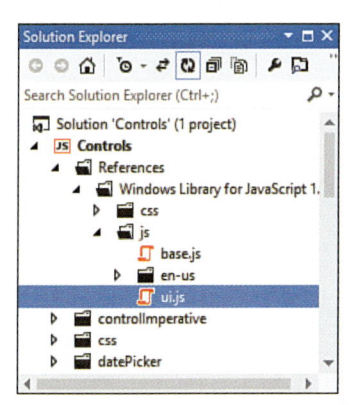

FIGURE 4.3 Viewing the WinJS files in the Solution Explorer window

Creating a WinJS Control Declaratively

There are two ways that you can create a WinJS control: declaratively and imperatively. The HTML page in Listing 4.1 illustrates how you can create a WinJS control declaratively:

LISTING 4.1 Declaring a WinJS Control (declarative\declarative.html)

```html
<!DOCTYPE html>
<html>
<head>
    <meta charset="utf-8" />
    <title>Chapter04</title>

    <!-- WinJS references -->
    <link href="//Microsoft.WinJS.1.0/css/ui-dark.css" rel="stylesheet" />
    <script src="//Microsoft.WinJS.1.0/js/base.js"></script>
    <script src="//Microsoft.WinJS.1.0/js/ui.js"></script>

    <!-- Chapter04 references -->
    <link href="/css/default.css" rel="stylesheet" />
    <script src="declarative.js"></script>
</head>
<body>

    <div id="dateBirthday"
        data-win-control="WinJS.UI.DatePicker"></div>

</body>
</html>
```

In Listing 4.1, a `DatePicker` control is declared in the body of the HTML page. Notice that the page includes references to the ui-dark.css, base.js, and ui.js files: All of the file references required to use WinJS control.

The page also includes a reference to a file named declarative.js. This file contains the custom JavaScript code associated with the page. The contents of the declarative.js file are contained in Listing 4.2.

LISTING 4.2 Declaring a WinJS Control (declarative\declarative.js)

```javascript
(function () {
    "use strict";

    function initialize() {
        WinJS.UI.processAll();
    }

    document.addEventListener("DOMContentLoaded", initialize);
})();
```

Listing 4.2 includes a call to the `WinJS.UI.processAll()` method. If you forget to call this method (which is very easy to do) then the controls declared in the HTML page are never converted into controls.

Notice that the call to `WinJS.UI.processAll()` happens within an initialize() method which is not called until the DOMContentLoaded event is raised. The `DOMContentLoaded` event happens after an HTML document is loaded. You must wait until after the document is loaded before calling `WinJS.UI.processAll()` or there won't be anything yet to process.

Creating Controls Imperatively

In the previous section, I created an instance of the `DatePicker` control declaratively. I declared the control in the HTML markup of the page.

As an alternative to creating a WinJS control declaratively, you can also create a control imperatively. In other words, you can create the control entirely in your JavaScript code.

Consider the page in Listing 4.3. It contains a DIV element with an id of dateBirthday. This DIV element does not have a `data-win-control` attribute.

LISTING 4.3 Creating a WinJS Control Imperatively (controlImperative\controlImperative.html)

```
<!DOCTYPE html>
<html>
<head>
    <meta charset="utf-8" />
    <title>Chapter04</title>

    <!-- WinJS references -->
    <link href="//Microsoft.WinJS.1.0/css/ui-dark.css" rel="stylesheet" />
    <script src="//Microsoft.WinJS.1.0/js/base.js"></script>
    <script src="//Microsoft.WinJS.1.0/js/ui.js"></script>

    <!-- Chapter04 references -->
    <link href="/css/default.css" rel="stylesheet" />
    <script src="controlImperative.js"></script>
</head>
<body>

    <div id="dateBirthday"></div>

</body>
</html>
```

The code in Listing 4.4 creates a `DatePicker` control and associates the new control with the `dateBirthday` DIV element.

114   CHAPTER 4   Using WinJS Controls

LISTING 4.4 Creating a WinJS Control Imperatively (controlImperative\controlImperative.js)

```
(function () {
    "use strict";

    function initialize() {
        var dateBirthday = document.getElementById("dateBirthday");
        var ctlBirthday = new WinJS.UI.DatePicker(dateBirthday);
    }

    document.addEventListener("DOMContentLoaded", initialize);
})();
```

The code in Listing 4.4 creates a new instance of the JavaScript `WinJS.UI.DatePicker()` class. The `DatePicker` class is created by passing the `dateBirthday` DIV element to the constructor for the `DatePicker` class. Notice that you do not need to call `WinJS.UI.processAll()` because you do not need to parse the document when creating WinJS controls imperatively.

The code in Listing 4.4 articulates the fact that a WinJS control is really just a JavaScript class. You can create this class declaratively with the data-win-control attribute or imperatively by instantiating the class in code. But, at the end of the day, it is a JavaScript class either way.

In this book, I take the declarative approach instead of the imperative approach to creating controls. There is nothing wrong with either approach. However, because the Microsoft samples favor the declarative approach, I will follow Microsoft's lead and use the declarative approach also.

Setting Control Options

Most controls support options. For example, when creating a `TimePicker` control, you want to be able to set the default time or the clock format (24-hour or 12-hour).

You can specify control options declaratively by taking advantage of the data-win-options attribute. For example, the following HTML fragment demonstrates how you can set the current time displayed by the `TimePicker` control to the time 3:04pm and the clock format to a 24-hour clock:

```
<div id="timeLunch"
    data-win-control="WinJS.UI.TimePicker"
    data-win-options="{
        current: '3:04pm',
        clock: '24HourClock'
    }"></div>
```

The options object passed to a control is a JavaScript object—hence the curly braces around the property names and values.

Introduction to WinJS Controls   115

If you prefer, you can set these options imperatively. Here's how you can create an instance of the `TimePicker` control in code and set its current and clock options:

```
(function () {
    "use strict";

    function initialize() {
        var divLunch = document.getElementById("timeLunch");
        var ctrlLunch = new WinJS.UI.TimePicker(timeLunch, {
            current: '3:04pm',
            clock: '24HourClock'
        });
    }

    document.addEventListener("DOMContentLoaded", initialize);
})();
```

The options are passed to the `TimePicker` constructor as the second parameter. The current time and clock options are set.

> **NOTE**
> You can also take advantage of the `WinJS.UI.setOptions()` method to set control options imperatively. You can call the `setOptions()` method after the control is constructed.

Retrieving Controls from an HTML Document

When a control gets created, it is always associated with a DOM element. The DOM element is the "host" for the control.

You can retrieve a control from its associated DOM element by using the `winControl` property. Every DOM element which has an associated control has a `winControl` property which represents the control.

For example, if you declare a `DatePicker` control like this:

```
<div id="dateBirthday"
    data-win-control="WinJS.UI.DatePicker"></div>
```

Then you can retrieve the `DatePicker` control in your JavaScript code like this:

```
(function () {
    "use strict";

    function initialize() {
        WinJS.UI.processAll().done(function () {
```

```
        var ctlBirthday = document.getElementById("dateBirthday").winControl;
        ctlBirthday.current = "12/25/1966";
    });
}

document.addEventListener("DOMContentLoaded", initialize);
})();
```

When you call `document.getElementById()`, you retrieve a DOM element and not a control. However, after retrieving a DOM element with `document.getElementById()`, you can use the `winControl` property to get the associated WinJS control.

The WinJS.UI.processAll() method returns a promise. You should wait until all the controls created declaratively in a document are parsed and created before attempting to interact with the controls. In the code above, the `DatePicker` is retrieved when the promise returned by the `processAll()` method is done.

Using the `Tooltip` Control

You can use the WinJS `Tooltip` control to display a customizable tooltip over any HTML element (see Figure 4.4). When you hover over the element, the tooltip appears for a certain number of seconds. When you move your cursor away from the element, the tooltip disappears.

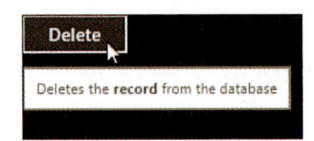

FIGURE 4.4   Displaying a tooltip with the `Tooltip` control (tooltip\tooltip.html)

You declare the `Tooltip` control in a page like this:

```
<button id="btnDelete"
    data-win-control="WinJS.UI.Tooltip"
    data-win-options="{
        innerHTML: 'Deletes the <b>record</b> from the database'
    }">Delete</button>
```

> **WARNING**
>
> Remember to call the `WinJS.UI.processAll()` method or the `Tooltip` control, just like any other WinJS control, won't appear.

Notice that you use the `innerHTML` option to set the text of the tooltip and this text can contain HTML such as B and IMG tags.

Using the `contentElement` Property

If you have a lot of HTML content to display (see Figure 4.5) then you can place the tooltip HTML content in a separate element like this:

```
<button id="btnDelete"
    data-win-control="WinJS.UI.Tooltip"
    data-win-options="{
        contentElement: select('#btnDeleteTooltip')
    }">Delete</button>

<div style="display:none">
    <div id="btnDeleteTooltip">
        Deletes the <b>record</b> from the database. Do you
        <i>really, really</i> want to do this? The record will
        be gone forever and you might weep.
    </div>
</div>
```

You use the `contentElement` option to specify a separate element which contains the HTML content for the tooltip. In the code above, the content for the tooltip is contained in a DIV element with the ID `btnDeleteTooltip`.

Notice that the `btnDeleteTooltip` is surrounded by a DIV element which has a `style="display:none"` attribute. This outer DIV element is used to prevent the contents of the `btnDeleteTooltip` from being displayed in the page. You want the contents of the `contentElement` to appear only within the tooltip.

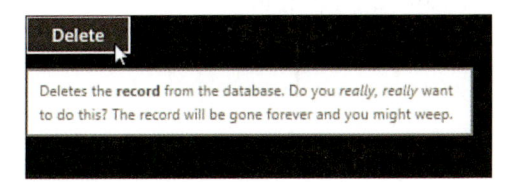

FIGURE 4.5 Showing a long tooltip

Styling a Tooltip

Because HTML already includes a tooltip attribute, you might be wondering why Microsoft introduced a WinJS Tooltip control. It is all about customization. Using the WinJS Tooltip control, you can create tooltips which match the style of your Windows Store app.

You can customize the appearance of the Tooltip control by modifying the win-tooltip Cascading Style Sheet class. For example, Figure 4.6 illustrates the appearance of the Tooltip control when you define the following win-tooltip style:

```css
.win-tooltip {
    background-color: #ffd800;
    border: solid 2px red;
    border-radius: 15px;
}
```

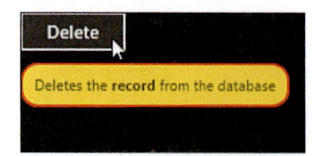

FIGURE 4.6   Customizing the appearance of the tooltip

Using the `ToggleSwitch` Control

You can use the WinJS `ToggleSwitch` control in the same situations as you would use a standard HTML checkbox (<input type="checkbox">). The difference between a `ToggleSwitch` control and a checkbox control is a `ToggleSwitch` is more finger friendly: You can swipe your finger across the `ToggleSwitch` to check or uncheck the `ToggleSwitch` (see Figure 4.7 and Figure 4.8).

FIGURE 4.7   A `ToggleSwitch` that is checked

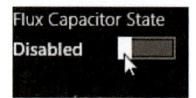

FIGURE 4.8   A `ToggleSwitch` that is unchecked

Here's how you can declare a ToggleSwitch control in a page:

```html
<div
    data-win-control="WinJS.UI.ToggleSwitch"
    data-win-options="{
        title: 'Flux Capacitor State',
        labelOff: 'Disabled',
        labelOn: 'Enabled',
        checked: true
    }"></div>
```

Determining the State of a `ToggleSwitch`

You can detect whether a `ToggleSwitch` control is in a checked or unchecked state by reading the `ToggleSwitch` control's checked property. For example, the page in Listing

4.5 contains a `ToggleSwitch` control and a DIV element which displays different messages depending on the state of the ToggleSwitch control (see Figure 4.9).

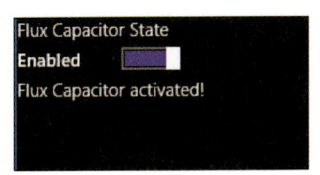

FIGURE 4.9   Displaying a message depending on the state of a `ToggleSwitch`

LISTING 4.5   Using a `ToggleSwitch` Control (toggleSwitchChecked\toggleSwitchChecked.html)

```
<div id="togFlux"
    data-win-control="WinJS.UI.ToggleSwitch"
    data-win-options="{
        title: 'Flux Capacitor State',
        labelOff: 'Disabled',
        labelOn: 'Enabled',
        checked: true
    }"></div>

<div id="divMessage"></div>
```

The code in Listing 4.6 wires up a change event handler for the `ToggleSwitch` control. When you change the state of the `ToggleSwitch` control, the change event handler is invoked. This handler displays one of two messages in a DIV element.

LISTING 4.6   Using a `ToggleSwitch` control (toggleSwitchChecked\toggleSwitchChecked.js)

```
(function () {
    "use strict";

    function initialize() {
        WinJS.UI.processAll().done(function () {

            var togFlux = document.getElementById("togFlux").winControl;
            var divMessage = document.getElementById("divMessage");

            togFlux.addEventListener("change", function (evt) {
                if (togFlux.checked) {
                    divMessage.innerHTML = "Flux Capacitor activated!";
                } else {
                    divMessage.innerHTML = "Flux Capacitor de-activated.";
                };
            })
```

```
            });
    }

    document.addEventListener("DOMContentLoaded", initialize);
})();
```

Remember to call `processAll()` before attempting to retrieve the `ToggleSwitch` control and modifying its properties (including wiring up an event handler). The `ToggleSwitch` control must exist before you can do anything with it.

Using the `Rating` Control

You can use the WinJS `Rating` control to collect and display user ratings. By default, the `Rating` control enables you to select between 1 and 5 stars to rate something (see Figure 4.10). You can change the rating by using your mouse, fingers, or by moving focus to the control and using your up/down or left/right arrow buttons.

FIGURE 4.10 Collecting a user rating

Here's how you declare a `Rating` control:

```
<div id="ratingProduct"
    data-win-control="WinJS.UI.Rating"></div>
```

There are a couple of options that you can set when declaring a `Rating` control: you can set the default rating (`averageRating`) and you can set whether a user is allowed to clear a rating (the default value is true).

```
<div id="ratingProduct"
    data-win-control="WinJS.UI.Rating"
    data-win-options="{
        averageRating:3,
        enableClear:false
    }"></div>
```

You clear a rating by swiping from right to left across the `Rating` control. This results in no stars being selected.

> **WARNING**
>
> Remember to call `WinJS.UI.processAll()` or the `Rating` control will never become a `Rating` control.

Customizing the Ratings

You can control the number of ratings which are displayed and the tooltip displayed for each rating by setting the `maxRating` and `tooltipStrings` properties. For example, the following `Rating` control only displays three stars and the stars have the tooltips "bad", "okay", and "great!" (see Figure 4.11).

```
<div id="ratingProduct"
    data-win-control="WinJS.UI.Rating"
    data-win-options="{
        averageRating:2,
        maxRating:3,
        tooltipStrings: ['bad', 'okay', 'great!']
    }"></div>
```

FIGURE 4.11 Customizing `Rating` control ratings

Notice that the `tooltipStrings` property accepts a JavaScript array. Each item in the array corresponds to a star.

Submitting a Rating

The `Rating` control raises three events: preview, cancel, and change. The preview event is raised when you hover over a star. The cancel event is raised when you don't select a star after hovering over it. Finally, if you click a star, the change event is raised.

The page in Listing 4.7 contains a `Rating` control and a DIV element. When you change the product rating, or even when you are considering changing the rating for the product, the message displayed in the DIV element is updated.

FIGURE 4.12 Handling the `Rating` control's `previewchange`, `cancel`, and `change` events

LISTING 4.7 Handling `Rating` Control Events (ratingSubmit\ratingSubmit.html)

```
<h1>Rate our Store!</h1>

<div id="ratingStore"
    data-win-control="WinJS.UI.Rating"
    data-win-options="{
```

CHAPTER 4 Using WinJS Controls

```
        maxRating: 3
    }"></div>

<div id="divMessage"></div>
```

The code in Listing 4.8 contains event handlers for the `Rating` controls `previewchange`, `cancel`, and `change` events.

LISTING 4.8 Handling `Rating` Control Events (ratingSubmit\ratingSubmit.js)

```
(function () {
    "use strict";

    function initialize() {

        WinJS.UI.processAll().done(function () {
            var ratingStore = document.getElementById("ratingStore").winControl;
            var divMessage = document.getElementById("divMessage");

            ratingStore.addEventListener("previewchange", function (evt) {
                var tentativeRating = evt.detail.tentativeRating;

                switch (tentativeRating) {
                    case 1: divMessage.innerHTML = "Don't do it! That's just mean!";
                        break;
                    case 2: divMessage.innerHTML = "Okay, you sure? We'll try
➥harder!";
                        break;
                    case 3: divMessage.innerHTML = "Thanks!";
                        break;
                }
            });

            ratingStore.addEventListener("cancel", function (evt) {
                divMessage.innerHTML = "";
            });

            ratingStore.addEventListener("change", function (evt) {
                var userRating = ratingStore.userRating;

                switch (userRating) {
                    case 1: divMessage.innerHTML = "You gave us the worst rating.";
                        break;
                    case 2: divMessage.innerHTML = "You gave us an okay rating.";
                        break;
                    case 3: divMessage.innerHTML = "You gave us a good rating.";
```

```
                        break;
                }
        });

    });
}

document.addEventListener("DOMContentLoaded", initialize);
})();
```

As you hover your mouse over the rating stars, different messages are displayed by the `previewchange` event handler. When you click a star, the change event is raised and the change handler displays a message.

Using the `DatePicker` Control

The WinJS `DatePicker` control—and, I hope you don't find this shocking—enables you to pick a date. It displays three select lists: month, day, and year (see Figure 4.13).

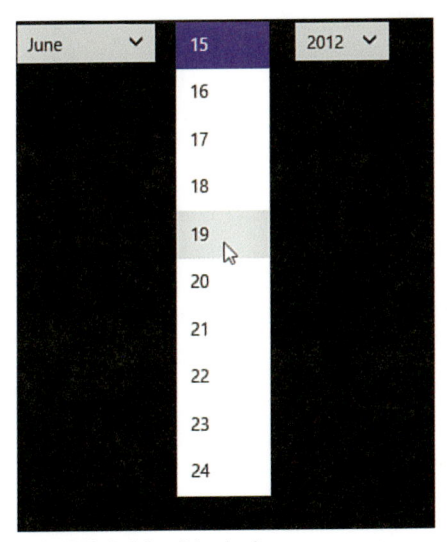

FIGURE 4.13 Displaying a `DatePicker` control

You declare a `DatePicker` like this:

```
<div id="dateBirthday"
    data-win-control="WinJS.UI.DatePicker"></div>
```

> **WARNING**
>
> Don't forget to call `WinJS.UI.processAll()` or your `DatePicker` will never become a `DatePicker`.

124   CHAPTER 4   Using WinJS Controls

By default, the `DatePicker` control has today's date selected. You can assign a particular date to the `DatePicker` control by setting the control's current property like this:

```
<div id="dateBirthday"
    data-win-control="WinJS.UI.DatePicker"
    data-win-options="{
        current: '12/25/1966'
    }"></div>
```

The code above causes the date '12/25/1966' to be selected as the default date in the `DatePicker` control.

Formatting the Year, Month, and Date

You can assign format strings to the `DatePicker yearPattern`, `monthPattern`, and `datePattern` properties to control the appearance of the year, month, and date. A format string can contain any characters. Within the format string, you can use one or more date format specifiers. A date format specifier is a magic string which displays part of a date using a particular format.

The `yearPattern` property accepts the following date format specifiers:

- {year.full}
- {year.full(n)}
- {year.abbreviated}
- {year.abbreviated(n)}
- {era.abbreviated}
- {era.abbreviated(n)}

The `monthPattern` property accepts the following date format specifiers:

- {month.full}
- {month.abbreviated}
- {month.abbreviated(n)}
- {month.solo.full}
- {month.solo.abbreviated}
- {month.solo.abbreviated(n)}
- {month.integer}
- {month.integer(n)}

Finally the `datePattern` property accepts the following date format specifiers:

- ▶ {day.integer}
- ▶ {day.integer*(n)*}
- ▶ {dayofweek.full}
- ▶ {dayofweek.abbeviated}
- ▶ {dayofweek.abbreviated*(n)*}
- ▶ {dayofweek.solo.full}
- ▶ {dayofweek.solo.abbeviated}
- ▶ {dayofweek.solo.abbreviated*(n)*}

The *(n)* refers to a number. For example, if you always want to display the day of the month using two digits (possibly including a leading zero) then you would use the date format specifier {day.integer(2)}.

Here's how you can display an integer for the year, month, and day:

```
<div id="dateBirthday"
    data-win-control="WinJS.UI.DatePicker"
    data-win-options="{
        monthPattern: '{month.integer(2)}',
        datePattern: '{day.integer(2)}',
        yearPattern: '{year.abbreviated}'
    }"></div>
```

Because the `datePattern` is set to the value {day.integer(2)}, a leading zero is displayed for single digit dates (see Figure 4.14).

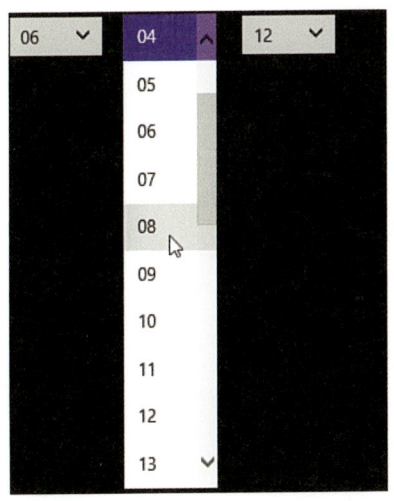

FIGURE 4.14 Formatting the year, month, and day

You can combine multiple format specifiers in a single format string. For example, if you want to display not only the day of the month but the day of the month and the day of the week, and not only the year but the year and the era, then you can declare the `DatePicker` like this:

```
<div id="dateBirthday"
    data-win-control="WinJS.UI.DatePicker"
    data-win-options="{
        monthPattern: '{month.integer(2)} - {month.full}',
        datePattern: '{day.integer(2)} {dayofweek.abbreviated}',
        yearPattern: '{year.full} {era.abbreviated}'
    }"></div>
```

Notice that the format string for the `monthPattern` includes a dash (-). You can throw in any extra characters that you need within a format string (see Figure 4.15).

FIGURE 4.15   Combining date format strings

> **NOTE**
>
> Under the covers, the `DatePicker` leverages the WinRT `Windows.Globalization.DateTimeFormatter` class to format dates. It uses the template strings used by that class.

Displaying Only Years, Months, or Days

Sometimes, you only want to enable a user to pick a month and not pick a year or a date. For example, you are creating a private jet reservation service and customers must reserve a jet for an entire month.

Listing 4.9 demonstrates how you can hide years and days and enable only months to be selected when using the `DatePicker` control.

LISTING 4.9   Displaying Only Months (datePickerMonthOnly\datePickerMonthOnly.html)

```
<!DOCTYPE html>
<html>
<head>
    <meta charset="utf-8" />
    <title>Chapter04</title>

    <!-- WinJS references -->
    <link href="//Microsoft.WinJS.1.0/css/ui-dark.css" rel="stylesheet" />
    <script src="//Microsoft.WinJS.1.0/js/base.js"></script>
    <script src="//Microsoft.WinJS.1.0/js/ui.js"></script>
```

```html
    <!-- Chapter04 references -->
    <link href="/css/default.css" rel="stylesheet" />
    <script src="datePickerMonthOnly.js"></script>

    <style type="text/css">
        #dateBirthday .win-datepicker-date {
            display:none;
        }

        #dateBirthday .win-datepicker-year {
            display:none;
        }
    </style>
</head>
<body>

<div id="dateBirthday"
    data-win-control="WinJS.UI.DatePicker"
    data-win-options="{
        monthPattern: '{month.solo.full}'
    }"></div>


</body>
</html>
```

The page in Listing 4.9 includes two Cascading Style Sheet rules which hide the `DatePicker` control's date and year select lists (see Figure 4.16).

FIGURE 4.16 Displaying only the month select list

Capturing the Selected Date

The `DatePicker` control raises the same event when you change the month, day, or year: the change event. You can retrieve the currently selected date by handling this event.

For example, the HTML page in Listing 4.10 contains a `DatePicker` control and a DIV element which displays the selected date (see Figure 4.17).

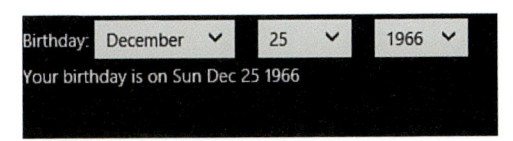

FIGURE 4.17 Displaying the `DatePicker` current date

128   CHAPTER 4   Using WinJS Controls

LISTING 4.10   Capturing the Selected Date (datePickerChange\datePickerChange.html)

```
<label>Birthday:</label>
<div id="dateBirthday"
    data-win-control="WinJS.UI.DatePicker"></div>

<div id="divMessage"></div>
```

The JavaScript file in Listing 4.11 illustrates how you can handle the change event so you can retrieve the selected date.

LISTING 4.11   Capturing the Selected Date (datePickerChange\datePickerChange.js)

```
(function () {
    "use strict";

    function initialize() {
        WinJS.UI.processAll().done(function () {
            var dateBirthday = document.getElementById("dateBirthday").winControl;
            var divMessage = document.getElementById("divMessage");

            dateBirthday.addEventListener("change", function (evt) {
                divMessage.innerHTML = "Your birthday is on "
                    + dateBirthday.current.toDateString();
            });

        });
    }


    document.addEventListener("DOMContentLoaded", initialize);
})();
```

Using the `TimePicker` Control

The WinJS `TimePicker` control enables you to select a time. By default, the `TimePicker` displays three select lists which enable you to select the hour, minute, and period (AM/PM).

FIGURE 4.18   Using the `TimePicker` control

Using the TimePicker Control

You declare a `TimePicker` control like this:

```
<div id="timeLunch"
    data-win-control="WinJS.UI.TimePicker"></div>
```

> **WARNING**
> Don't forget to call `WinJS.UI.processAll()` or the declaration of the `TimePicker` control will never get parsed and turned into a `TimePicker` control.

If you prefer military time (a 24-hour clock) then you can modify the `TimePicker`'s clock property like this:

```
<div id="timeLunch"
    data-win-control="WinJS.UI.TimePicker"
    data-win-options="{
    clock: '24HourClock'
}"></div>
```

Finally, if you want to display minutes in 15 minute increments (see Figure 4.19) instead of the default 1 minute increment, then you can set the `minuteIncrement` property like this:

```
<div id="timeLunch"
    data-win-control="WinJS.UI.TimePicker"
    data-win-options="{
        minuteIncrement: 15
    }"></div>
```

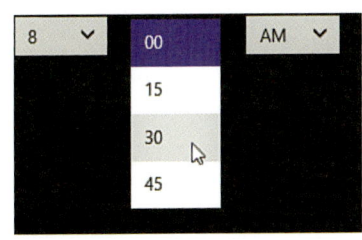

FIGURE 4.19 Changing the `TimePicker` control's minute increment

> **NOTE**
> If you have changed your computer's regional settings to display a 24-hour clock instead of a 12-hour clock, then the `TimePicker` will default to displaying a 24-hour clock.

Getting and Setting the Current Time

By default, the `TimePicker` control displays the current time. You use the current property to get or set the time displayed by the `TimePicker` control.

For example, the page in Listing 4.12 contains a `TimePicker` control and a DIV element which displays a message (see Figure 4.20). The `TimePicker` control is declared so that it displays the time 12:00pm by default.

FIGURE 4.20 Displaying lunch time with the `TimePicker` control

LISTING 4.12 Setting the Current Time with the `TimePicker` Control (timePickerSet\timePickerSet.html)

```html
<label>Select a Lunch Time:</label>
<div id="timeLunch"
    data-win-control="WinJS.UI.TimePicker"
    data-win-options="{
        current: '12:00pm'
    }"></div>

<div id="divMessage"></div>
```

The JavaScript code in Listing 4.13 illustrates how you can capture a new time selected with the `TimePicker` control. When a new time is selected, the message displayed by the DIV element is updated.

LISTING 4.13 Setting the Current Time with the `TimePicker` Control (timePickerSet\timePickerSet.html)

```javascript
(function () {
    "use strict";

    function initialize() {
        WinJS.UI.processAll().done(function () {
            var timeLunch = document.getElementById("timeLunch").winControl;
            var divMessage = document.getElementById("divMessage");

            timeLunch.addEventListener("change", function (evt) {
                divMessage.innerHTML = "Lunch time is "
                    + timeLunch.current.toTimeString();
            });

        });
```

```
    }
    document.addEventListener("DOMContentLoaded", initialize);
})();
```

Because the JavaScript language does not have a separate Time data type, the `TimePicker` control's current property returns both a date and a time. The current property represents the current date and the selected time. In the code in Listing 4.13, the time portion is extracted with the help of the JavaScript `toTimeString()` method.

> **NOTE**
>
> I looked this up on Wikipedia (http://en.wikipedia.org/wiki/Noon). Apparently, noon is neither 12:00am nor 12:00pm, but just 12 noon. Weird.

Formatting the Hour, Minute, and Period

You can use template strings to format the appearance of the items which appear in the hour, minute, and period select lists. The template string can contain any characters that you want, but there are special format specifiers which you can use when displaying the different portions of a time.

You can use the following format specifiers with the `TimePicker` `hourPattern` property:

- {hour.integer}
- {hour.integer*(n)*}

You can use the following format specifiers with the `TimePicker` `minutePattern` property:

- {minute.integer}
- {minute.integer*(n)*}

You can use the following format specifiers with the `TimePicker` `periodPattern` property:

- {period.abbreviated}
- {period.abbreviated*(n)*}

The n refers to a number. For example, if you use hour.integer(2) then a leading 0 will appear for single digit hours.

The following declaration of a `TimePicker` control illustrates how you can customize the appearance of the hour, minute, and period select lists (see Figure 4.21).

```
<div id="timeLunch"
    data-win-control="WinJS.UI.TimePicker"
    data-win-options="{
```

```
        hourPattern: 'hour: {hour.integer(2)}',
        minutePattern: 'minute: {minute.integer(2)}',
        periodPattern: 'period: {period.abbreviated}'
}"></div>
```

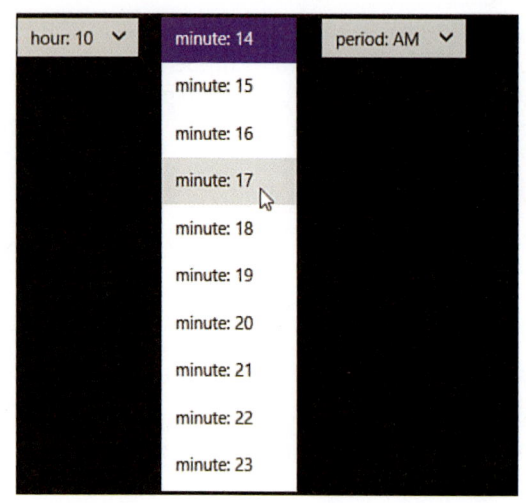

FIGURE 4.21   Formatting the hour, minute, and period

Using the `FlipView` Control

The `FlipView` control can be used to display a collection of items. Unlike the `ListView` control (which I describe in Chapter 7, "Using the `ListView` Control") the `FlipView` only displays a single item from a collection at a time.

The `FlipView` control is ideal for displaying a photo gallery: one picture at a time. It can also be used for swiping through a list of magazine or newspaper articles.

When you use a `FlipView`, only a single item from a data source is displayed. However, arrows are displayed so you can move to the next or previous item in the data source.

For example, the JavaScript file in Listing 4.14 includes a collection of three articles. Each article has a title, author, and `articleText` property.

LISTING 4.14   A List of Articles

```
(function () {
    "use strict";

    // Create List of articles
    var listArticles = new WinJS.Binding.List([
        {
            title: "Why Dogs are Better than Cats",
            author: "Arnold Wiggles",
```

```
            articleText: "Pellentesque habitant morbi tristique senectus et netus \
    et malesuada fames ac turpis egestas. Proin pharetra nonummy pede. Mauris et \
    orci."
        },
        {
            title: "Why Dogs are Better than Fish",
            author: "Jane Rubble",
            articleText: "Lorem ipsum dolor sit amet, consectetuer adipiscing elit. \
    Maecenas porttitor congue massa. Fusce posuere, magna sed pulvinar \
    ultricies, purus lectus malesuada libero, sit amet commodo magna \
    eros quis urna."
        },
        {
            title: "Why Dogs are Better than Mice",
            author: "Eric Alexander",
            articleText: "Lorem ipsum dolor sit amet, consectetuer adipiscing elit. \
    Maecenas porttitor congue massa. Fusce posuere, magna sed pulvinar \
    ultricies, purus lectus malesuada libero, sit amet commodo magna \
    eros quis urna."
        }
    ]);




    WinJS.Namespace.define("MyData",
    {
        listArticles: listArticles
    });


})();
```

Now imagine that you want to display the articles, one article at a time, in your Windows Store app. The page in Listing 4.15 illustrates how you can use a `FlipView` control to display individual articles from a list of articles (see Figure 4.22).

Notice that the page in Listing 4.15 includes a reference to the articles.js file from Listing 4.14 which contains the data for the `FlipView`.

134 CHAPTER 4 Using WinJS Controls

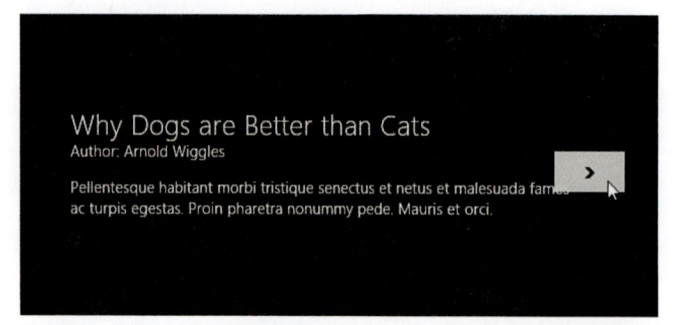

FIGURE 4.22 Displaying articles with a `FlipView` control

LISTING 4.15 Displaying an Article with a `FlipView` (flipView\flipView.html)

```html
<!DOCTYPE html>
<html>
<head>
    <meta charset="utf-8" />
    <title>Chapter04</title>

    <!-- WinJS references -->
    <link href="//Microsoft.WinJS.1.0/css/ui-dark.css" rel="stylesheet" />
    <script src="//Microsoft.WinJS.1.0/js/base.js"></script>
    <script src="//Microsoft.WinJS.1.0/js/ui.js"></script>

    <!-- Chapter04 references -->
    <link rel="stylesheet" type="text/css" href="flipView.css" />
    <script src="articles.js"></script>
    <script src="flipView.js"></script>
</head>
<body>

    <div id="tmplArticle"
        data-win-control="WinJS.Binding.Template">
        <div class="articleItem">
            <h2 data-win-bind="innerText:title"></h2>
            Author: <span data-win-bind="innerText:author"></span>
            <p data-win-bind="innerText:articleText"></p>
        </div>
    </div>



    <div id="fvArticles"
        data-win-control="WinJS.UI.FlipView"
        data-win-options="{
```

```
            itemDataSource: MyData.listArticles.dataSource,
            itemTemplate: select('#tmplArticle')
    }"></div>

</body>
</html>
```

The `FlipView` control is declared with the following HTML:

```
<div id="fvArticles"
    data-win-control="WinJS.UI.FlipView"
    data-win-options="{
        itemDataSource: MyData.listArticles.dataSource,
        itemTemplate: select('#tmplArticle')
    }"></div>
```

The `FlipView` is bound to the list of articles with the help of the `itemDataSource` property. You can bind a `FlipView` to any data source which implements the `IListDataSource` interface. There are only two objects in the WinJS library which implement this interface: the `WinJS.Binding.List` object and the `WinJS.UI.StorageDataSource` object.

In the markup above, the `FlipView` is bound to the list of articles which is a `WinJS.Binding.List`. In particular, the `FlipView` is bound to the `dataSource` property of the `listArticles` List object. The `dataSource` property returns the object which implements the `IListDataSource`.

The `FlipView` control's `itemTemplate` property points to a Template control with the id `tmplArticle` which is declared earlier in the page. The Template control contains the template used to format the article displayed by the `FlipView`.

> **WARNING**
> Make sure that you declare the Template control before the `FlipView` control and not after in the page or you will get a mysterious error and spend hours trying to debug it.

> **WARNING**
> As always, remember to call `WinJS.UI.processAll()` or the `FlipView` won't become a `FlipView`.

Displaying Page Numbers

When swiping through items displayed by a `FlipView`, it can be useful to know which item you are viewing out of how many items. In other words, you might want to display a page number (see Figure 4.23).

136   CHAPTER 4   Using WinJS Controls

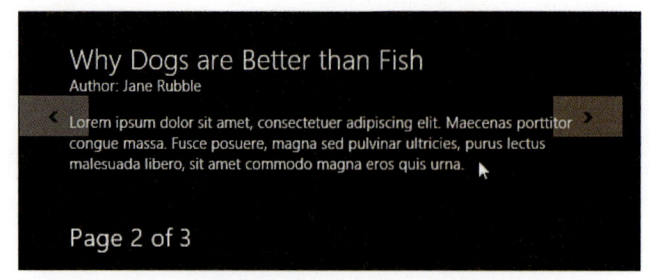

FIGURE 4.23   Displaying a page number with a FlipView

You can use the `FlipView` control's `currentPage` property to retrieve the current page (the index of the current item) displayed by the `FlipView`. You can use the `count()` method to get the total number of pages (the total number of items) contained in the data source associated with the `FlipView`.

The page in Listing 4.16 contains a `FlipView` and a DIV element. The DIV element displays both the current page and the total number of pages.

LISTING 4.16   Displaying the Current Page Number with a `FlipView` (flipViewPageNumber\flipViewPageNumber.html)

```
<div id="tmplArticle"
    data-win-control="WinJS.Binding.Template">
    <div class="articleItem">
        <h2 data-win-bind="innerText:title"></h2>
        Author: <span data-win-bind="innerText:author"></span>
        <p data-win-bind="innerText:articleText"></p>
    </div>
</div>


<div id="fvArticles"
    data-win-control="WinJS.UI.FlipView"
    data-win-options="{
        itemDataSource: MyData.listArticles.dataSource,
        itemTemplate: select('#tmplArticle')
    }"></div>


<div id="divPageNumber"></div>
```

LISTING 4.17   Displaying the Current Page Number with a `FlipView` (flipViewPageNumber\
flipViewPageNumber.js)

```
(function () {
    "use strict";

    function initialize() {
        WinJS.UI.processAll().done(function () {
            var fvArticles = document.getElementById("fvArticles").winControl;
            var divPageNumber = document.getElementById("divPageNumber");

            // Show Page Number and Page Count
            function updatePageNumber() {
                var currentPage = fvArticles.currentPage + 1;
                fvArticles.count().done(function (count) {
                    divPageNumber.innerHTML = "Page " + currentPage
                        + " of " + count;
                });
            }
            updatePageNumber();

            // Update Page Number when new page selected
            fvArticles.addEventListener("pageselected", updatePageNumber);

        });
    }

    document.addEventListener("DOMContentLoaded", initialize);
})();
```

The page number and page count displayed in the HTML page is updated with the `updatePageNumber()` function contained in Listing 4.17. This function updates the `divPageNumber` DIV element in the page.

Notice that the `FlipView count()` method does not directly return a page count. Instead, it returns a promise which returns a page count when the promise completes. This makes the `updatePageNumber()` function slightly more complicated.

Creating Custom `FlipView` Buttons

You might want to create custom buttons for navigating back and forth through the items in a `FlipView`. The default arrows which appear for navigating through a `FlipView` are subtle; they don't appear unless you hover your mouse over the control. You might want to bang the user over the head with more explicit navigation buttons.

FIGURE 4.24 Custom `FlipView` buttons

You can take advantage of two methods of the `FlipView` control to control navigation programmatically: the `previous()` and `next()` method.

For example, the page in Listing 4.18 includes two buttons named `btnPrevious` and `btnNext`.

LISTING 4.18 A `FlipView` with Custom Buttons (flipViewButtons\flipViewButtons.html)

```html
<div id="tmplArticle"
    data-win-control="WinJS.Binding.Template">
    <div class="articleItem">
        <h2 data-win-bind="innerText:title"></h2>
        Author: <span data-win-bind="innerText:author"></span>
        <p data-win-bind="innerText:articleText"></p>
    </div>
</div>

<div id="fvArticles"
    data-win-control="WinJS.UI.FlipView"
    data-win-options="{
        itemDataSource: MyData.listArticles.dataSource,
        itemTemplate: select('#tmplArticle')
    }"></div>

<div id="divNavigation">
    <button id="btnPrevious">Previous</button>
    <button id="btnNext">Next</button>
</div>
```

The JavaScript code in Listing 4.19 contains the code to wire up the `btnPrevious` and `btnNext` buttons to event handlers. When you click the `btnPrevious` button, the `previous()` method is called, and when you click the `btnNext` button, the `next()` method is called.

LISTING 4.19   A `FlipView` with Custom Buttons (flipViewButtons\flipViewButtons.js)

```javascript
(function () {
    "use strict";

    function initialize() {
        WinJS.UI.processAll().done(function () {
            var fvArticles = document.getElementById("fvArticles").winControl;
            var btnPrevious = document.getElementById("btnPrevious");
            var btnNext = document.getElementById("btnNext");

            // Setup Buttons
            btnPrevious.addEventListener("click", function () {
                fvArticles.previous();
            });
            btnNext.addEventListener("click", function () {
                fvArticles.next();
            });
        });
    }

    document.addEventListener("DOMContentLoaded", initialize);
})();
```

Summary

This chapter focused on the core controls contained in the WinJS library. I discussed the features of the `Tooltip`, `ToggleSwitch`, `Rating`, `DatePicker`, `TimePicker`, and `FlipView` controls.

You learned how to create these controls both declaratively and imperatively. You also were provided with sample code which demonstrated how you can use these controls in different scenarios.

But there are more controls to discuss! More fun to be had! In latter chapters, I introduce you to additional WinJS controls such as the menu controls and the `ListView` control. First, however, we need to talk about forms.

CHAPTER 5

Creating Forms

IN THIS CHAPTER

▶ Using HTML5 Form Validation
▶ Using HTML5 Input Elements
▶ Creating a Rich Text Editor
▶ Displaying Progress

I assume that anyone who is reading this book is already familiar with the basics of HTML, but I don't assume that you are familiar with the latest features of HTML5. In particular, I don't assume that you are familiar with the changes to HTML forms included in the HTML5 standard.

In the first section of this chapter, I describe how you can take advantage of HTML5 form validation in a Windows Store app. You learn how to use validation attributes—such as the `required` and `pattern` attribute—to enforce validation constraints.

Next, I discuss the new features of input elements included in HTML5. You learn how the new HTML5 input types enable you to control the type of data entered into a form field.

Finally, I talk about two other important new features of HTML5. I explain how you can take advantage of the `contenteditable` attribute to create input elements which accept rich text such as bold and italic text. I also discuss the new HTML5 progress element.

Using HTML5 Form Validation

In a Windows Store app, the easiest way to validate HTML form fields is to take advantage of the HTML5 validation attributes. Imagine, for example, that you want to create an HTML form which includes a form field for entering a social security number. In that case, you can use the `required` attribute to ensure that a value has been entered and you can use the `pattern` attribute to ensure that the value matches the pattern for a valid social security number.

Using the `required` Attribute

The following HTML form illustrates how you can use the `required` attribute:

```
<form>
    <div>
        <label>
            Social Security Number:
            <input id="ssn" required />
        </label>
    </div>
    <div>
        <input type="submit" />
    </div>
</form>
```

If you submit the form above, and you do not enter a value for the ssn field, then you get the error message depicted in Figure 5.1. The input field has a red border surrounding it and a callout message is displayed.

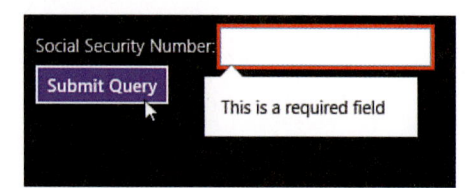

FIGURE 5.1   Using the `required` validation attribute

Using the `pattern` Attribute

You use the `pattern` attribute to validate the value entered into an input field against a regular expression pattern. For example, the following HTML form validates the social security number against a regular expression:

```
<form>
    <div>
        <label>
            Social Security Number:
            <input id="ssn"
                required
                pattern="^\d{3}-\d{2}-\d{4}$"
                title="###-##-####" />
        </label>
    </div>
    <div>
        <input type="submit" />
    </div>
</form>
```

Notice that the ssn field has both a `required` and `pattern` attribute. The `pattern` attribute is not triggered unless you enter a value.

Notice, furthermore, that the ssn field includes a `title` attribute. The `title` attribute contains the format displayed by the pattern error message.

If you enter an invalid social security number, then you get the validation error message displayed in Figure 5.2.

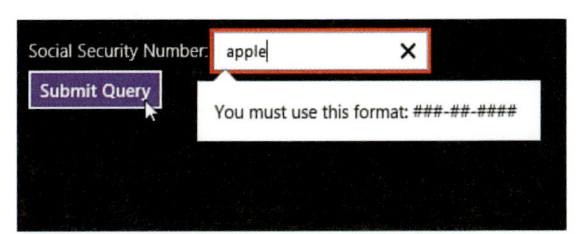

FIGURE 5.2 Using the `pattern` validation attribute

> **NOTE**
>
> My favorite site for finding regular expressions is located at http://regexlib.com.

Performing Custom Validation

If you need to add custom validation rules to a form element, then you can take advantage of the JavaScript `setCustomValidity()` method. You can use this method to associate a custom validation error message with a form field.

Imagine, for example, that you have a complex set of rules for validating a user name in a user registration form. For example, you want to ensure that the user name is a certain length, unique in the database, and does not contain special characters. This is a good candidate for custom validation.

The following HTML form includes a userName field:

```
<form>
    <div>
        <label>
            User Name:
            <input id="userName" required />
        </label>
    </div>
    <div>
        <input type="submit" />
    </div>
</form>
```

The following JavaScript code demonstrates how you can display a validation error message when the user name is too short:

```
var userName = document.getElementById("userName");

userName.addEventListener("input", function (evt) {
    // User name must be more than 3 characters
    if (userName.value.length < 4) {
        userName.setCustomValidity("User name too short!");
    } else {
        userName.setCustomValidity("");
    }
});
```

In the code above, an event listener for the input event is created. When the value of the input element is changed, then the length of the value is checked. If the user name is less than 4 characters, then the `setCustomValidity()` method is used to invalidate the input element. Otherwise, the `setCustomValidity()` method is called with an empty string to clear any previous validation errors associated with the user name element.

> **NOTE**
> The input event is raised as soon as the contents of an input element are changed. The input event differs from the change event because the change event is not raised until after the input element loses focus.

You must submit the form to see the validation error message. After you submit the form, you see the error in Figure 5.3.

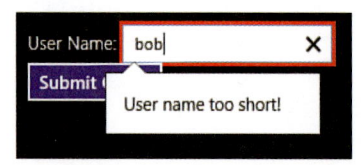

FIGURE 5.3 Using custom validation

Customizing the Validation Error Style

By default, invalid HTML fields in a form appear with a red border. For example, if you submit an HTML form without entering a value in a required field, then the field is displayed with a red border.

You can customize the appearance of form fields in different states of validity by using the following Cascading Style Sheet pseudo classes:

- `:valid`—Applies when an input element is valid.
- `:invalid`—Applies when an input element is invalid.

- **:required**—Applies when an input element is required (has the `required` attribute).
- **:optional**—Applies when an input element is not required (does not have the `required` attribute).

Imagine that you have created the following user registration form:

```html
<form>
    <div>
        <label>
            First Name:
            <input id="firstName" required />
        </label>
    </div>
    <div>
        <label>
            Last Name:
            <input id="lastName" required />
        </label>
    </div>
    <div>
        <label>
            Company:
            <input id="company" />
        </label>
    </div>
    <div>
        <input type="submit" />
    </div>
</form>
```

The form above contains required fields for the user first and last name. It also contains an optional field for the user company.

You can use the following style rules to control how the input elements are styled:

```css
:valid {
    background-color: green;
}

:invalid {
    background-color: yellow;
}

:optional {
    border: 4px solid green;
}
```

```css
:required {
    border: 4px solid red;
}
```

These rules cause valid fields to appear with a green background color and invalid fields to appear with a yellow background color. Optional fields appear with a green border and required fields appear with a red border.

Resetting a Form

After you successfully submit a form, it is a good idea to reset it so you can use the form again. For example, your app might include a form for adding new movies. Each time you add a new movie, you want the form to reset to its default state.

If you are using the validation attributes, then you cannot reset a form simply by assigning empty strings to the form fields. If you assign an empty string to a required field, then the field will be in an invalid state.

Instead, you should reset a form by calling the JavaScript `reset()` method. The `reset()` method throws a form back into its default state.

For example, here's a simple form for entering a movie title:

```html
<form id="frmAdd">
    <div>
        <label>
            Title:
            <input id="inpTitle" required />
        </label>
    </div>
    <div>
        <input type="submit" />
    </div>
</form>
```

Here's the JavaScript code which you can use for handling the form submit event:

```javascript
(function () {
    "use strict";

    function initialize() {
        var frmAdd = document.getElementById("frmAdd");
        var inpTitle = document.getElementById("inpTitle");

        frmAdd.addEventListener("submit", function (evt) {
            evt.preventDefault();
            var newMovie = {
```

```
            title: document.getElementById("inpTitle").value
        };
        addMovieToDb(newMovie).done(function () {
            frmAdd.reset();
        });
    });

    function addMovieToDb(newMovie) {
        return new WinJS.Promise(function (complete) {
            // Add to database
            complete();
        });
    }
}

document.addEventListener("DOMContentLoaded", initialize);
})();
```

The code above adds the movie title to an IndexedDB database and then resets the form so the form returns to its default state. The `reset()` method is used to return the form to its default state.

> **WARNING**
>
> If you neglect to call `evt.preventDefault()` in your form submit handler, then the page will be submitted and reloaded. You don't want to do this. In a Windows Store app, you want to avoid ever submitting back to the server.

Using HTML5 Input Elements

If you have worked with HTML, then you are most likely very familiar with the standard input element types such as `<input type="text" />` and `<input type="checkbox" />`. Different input types have different appearances and accept different types of data.

The HTML5 recommendation adds several new input types:

- search
- tel
- url
- email
- datetime
- date
- month

- week
- time
- datetime-local
- number
- range
- color

You can take advantage of these new input types to enforce validation rules. For example, an `<input type="number" />` element will accept only numerals and not other types of characters. And an `<input type="url" />` will accept only valid (absolute) URLs.

You also can take advantage of these new input types to control the user interface for entering a value into a field. For example, when using the touch keyboard, an `<input type="email" />` field displays a specialized keyboard for entering email addresses which includes specialized keys such as @ and .com (see Figure 5.4).

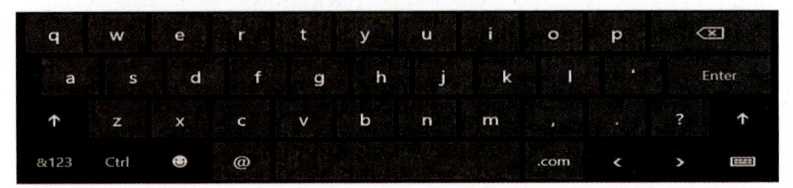

FIGURE 5.4 Specialized email touch keyboard

In this section, you learn how to take advantage of the new features of HTML5 input elements.

> **NOTE**
>
> As I write this, not all features of HTML5 forms are supported by IE10. In particular, the date, time, and color types are not supported.

Labeling Form Fields

First off, you need to know the proper way to label HTML form fields. Providing proper labels is important for making your app accessible to users with disabilities—so adding labels is the right thing to do.

There are two ways that you can use a label element to label a form element. If you want the label to appear right next to the form element, then you can include the form element inside the label's opening and closing tags like this:

```
<label>
  Title:
  <input id="inpTitle" required />
</label>
```

If the label is separated from the element being labeled in the page, then you can associate the label and the form element explicitly by using the label's `for` attribute like this.

```
<label for="inpTitle">
  Title:
</label>
... Other Content ...
<input id="inpTitle" required />
```

You should always label all of your form elements to make your apps more accessible to people with disabilities. However, if you need to provide additional hints about the appropriate input value for a form element, then you can take advantage of the new HTML5 `placeholder` attribute. When used in a Windows Store app, the `placeholder` attribute creates a watermark.

For example, the following HTML form contains a field for entering a product activation code:

```
<label>
    Activation Code:
    <input id="activationCode"
        size="10"
        placeholder="##-####-##" />
</label>
```

The form above includes a `placeholder` attribute which displays the text "##-####-##" (see Figure 5.5). As soon as you start typing a value into the field, the placeholder text disappears.

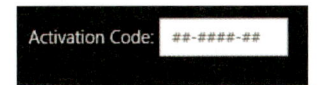

FIGURE 5.5 Using the `placeholder` attribute

> **NOTE**
> You can use the Cascading Style Sheet `:-ms-input-placeholder` pseudo class to style the text displayed by a `placeholder` attribute.

Entering a Number

If you want to prevent a user from entering anything except a number into an input field, then you should use the `type="number"` attribute like this:

```
<label>
    Favorite Number:
    <input id="inpFavNumber"
```

```
        type="number"
        placeholder="###" />
</label>
```

When the input type has the value number, and you enter anything which is not a number, then the value disappears as soon as the field loses focus. This can be confusing to the user. So it is a good idea to include a `placeholder` attribute or instruction text which indicates that the field only accepts numbers (no dollar signs, just numbers).

You can use the `min` and `max` attributes to specify a minimum and maximum value for the input field like this:

```
<label>
    Quantity:
    <input id="inpQuantity"
        type="number"
        placeholder="###"
        min="1"
        max="10" />
</label>
```

If you enter a number which does not fall into the specified range, then a validation error message is displayed (see Figure 5.6).

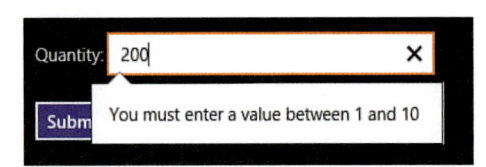

FIGURE 5.6 A number out of range

By default, you can only enter an integer value into an `<input type="number" />` field. If you want to enter a non-integer value, such as 1.5, then you need to modify the `step` attribute like this:

```
<input id="inpFavNumber"
    type="number"
    step="0.5"
    placeholder="###" />
```

The `step` attribute determines the allowable increment between numbers.

When you use a number field in a Windows Store app, and you are using the touch keyboard, you get a special keyboard for entering numbers automatically (see Figure 5.7).

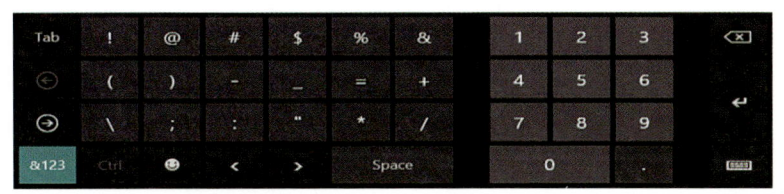

FIGURE 5.7   Entering a number with the touch keyboard

Entering a Value from a Range of Values

If you want to display a slider, then you can create an `<input type="range" />` element. For example, the following HTML form displays a slider which enables you to select a quantity of candy to buy:

```
<label>
    Quantity of Candy:
    <input id="quantity"
        type="range"
        min="10"
        max="100"
        step="5"
        value="30"/>
</label>
```

The slider displays a range of values between 10 and 100 with 5 unit increments. The default value is set to 30 (see Figure 5.8).

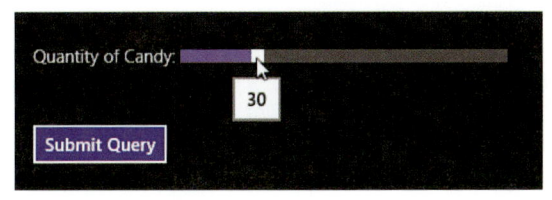

FIGURE 5.8   Displaying a slider

Entering Email Addresses, URLs, Telephone Numbers, and Search Terms

You can use the input types email, url, tel, and search to enable users to enter URLs, email addresses, telephone numbers, and search terms.

If you use `<input type="email" />`, and you are using the touch keyboard, then you get the specialized keyboard which includes @ and .com keys in Figure 5.9.

152 CHAPTER 5 Creating Forms

FIGURE 5.9 Touch keyboard for email

Using `<input type="email" />` also gives you automatic validation. You must enter a valid email address or you get the validation error message in Figure 5.10.

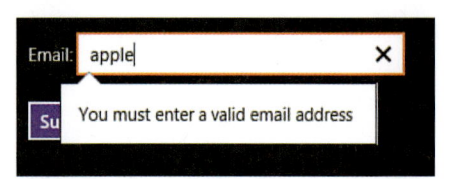

FIGURE 5.10 Validation for email

Using `<input type="url" />` creates a special input field for entering URLs. You get the touch keyboard in Figure 5.11 which includes special / and .com keys.

> **NOTE**
>
> The touch keyboard only appears when you don't have a keyboard attached to your machine or you explicitly open the touch keyboard.

FIGURE 5.11 Touch keyboard for URL

An `<input type="url" />` field requires you to enter a valid absolute URL. For example, the URL http://Superexpert.com and the URL ftp://Superexpert.com are valid, but the URL superexpert.com and the URL www.superexpert.com are not because they are not absolute URLs (see Figure 5.12).

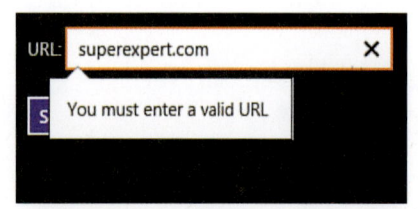

FIGURE 5.12 Validating a URL

You use the `<input type="tel" />` element to enter telephone numbers. Because there are so many different formats for telephone numbers, this input type does not perform any validation. Instead, you can use `<input type="tel" />` to display a specialized touch keyboard for telephone numbers (see Figure 5.13).

FIGURE 5.13 Entering a telephone number

Finally, there is `<input type="search" />`. There is really nothing to say about `<input type="search" />` because this input type behaves identically to `<input type="text" />`. There is no special keyboard and no special validation.

Entering a Value from a List of Values

You can use the new HTML5 list attribute to provide an auto-complete experience for your users. For example, the following code provides a list of three suggestions for car make:

```
<label>
    Car Make:
    <input id="inpCarMake"
        list="dlCarMakes" />
    <datalist id="dlCarMakes">
        <option>BMW</option>
        <option>Ford</option>
        <option>Tesla</option>
    </datalist>
</label>
```

The `list` attribute points at an HTML5 `datalist` element which contains the list of suggestions. When you start entering text into the input element, you get the suggestions displayed in Figure 5.14.

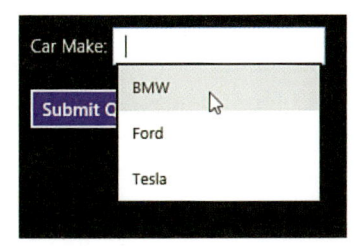

FIGURE 5.14 Getting a list of suggestions

154   CHAPTER 5   Creating Forms

You are not forced to select from the list. Using the list attribute makes an input element work more like a combo-box than a select list.

Selecting Files

You can use `<input type="file" />` to create a file picker. For example, you can use `<input type="file" />` to enable a user to select a picture file from their hard drive.

The following HTML page includes an `<input type="file" />` element and a DIV element with the ID imgPicture. After you select a picture from your hard drive, the picture appears in the img element (see Figure 5.15).

```html
<form id="frmAdd">
    <div>
        <label>
            Picture:
            <input id="inpFile" type="file" accept="image/*" />
        </label>
        <input type="submit" />
    </div>
</form>

<img id="imgPicture" />
```

When you use the `<input type="file" />` element, you can use the accept attribute to restrict the type of files which can be uploaded. For example, in the markup above, the accept element has the value `"image/*"` which prevents any file except image files from being selected.

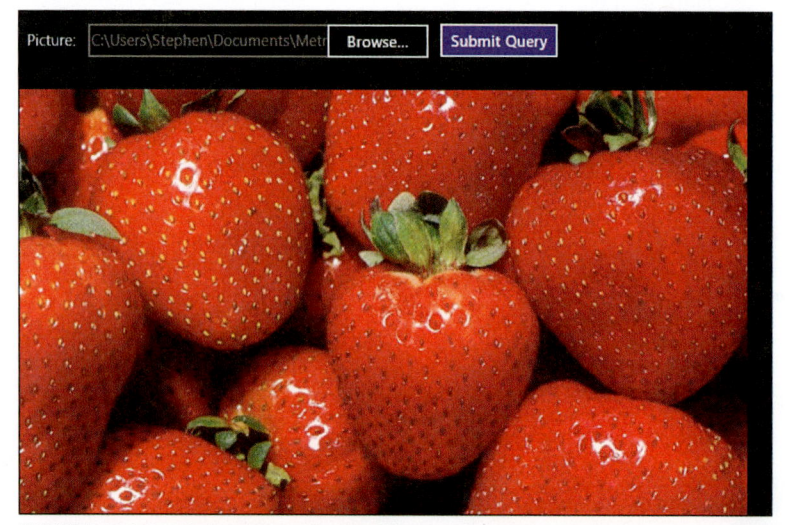

FIGURE 5.15   Selecting a picture file

The following JavaScript code is used to handle the form submit event. This code grabs the selected picture file from the input elements files collection and displays the picture in the IMG element:

```javascript
(function () {
    "use strict";

    function initialize() {
        var frmAdd = document.getElementById("frmAdd");

        frmAdd.addEventListener("submit", function (evt) {
            evt.preventDefault();

            var imgPicture = document.getElementById("imgPicture");
            var inpFile = document.getElementById("inpFile");

            if (inpFile.files.length > 0) {
                // Use HTML5 File API to create object URL to refer to the photo file
                var pictureUrl = URL.createObjectURL(inpFile.files[0]);

                // Show photo in IMG element
                imgPicture.src = pictureUrl;
            }
        });

    }

    document.addEventListener("DOMContentLoaded", initialize);
})();
```

Creating a Rich Text Editor

If you want to create a form field which accepts rich text—such as bold, italic, or underlined text—then you can use the `contenteditable` attribute. Imagine, for example, that you want to enable a user to enter a college admissions essay. In that case, you can use the following HTML form:

```html
<form>
    <label for="inpEssay">
        College Admissions Essay:
    </label>

    <div id="inpEssay" contenteditable="true" class="win-textarea richtext"></div>
```

```
    <br />
    <input type="submit" />
</form>
```

In the form above, the `contenteditable` attribute is applied to a DIV element with the id `inpEssay`. The `contenteditable` attribute makes the content of the DIV element editable (see Figure 5.16).

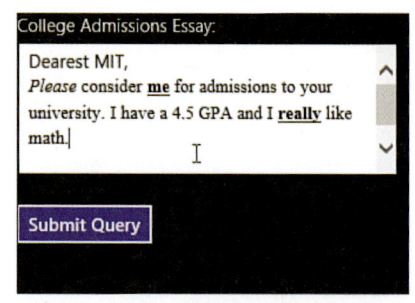

FIGURE 5.16 Creating a rich text editor

You can use CTRL-b to make the text bold, CTRL-i to make the text italic, and CTRL-u to make the text underlined.

Notice that the DIV element with the `contenteditable` attribute has two CSS classes applied to it named `win-textarea` and `richtext`. The `win-textarea` class is included as part of the WinJS library and this class applies the standard Windows Store app styles to the editor.

The `richtext` class is defined like this:

```
.richtext {
  width:300px;
  height:100px;
  white-space:pre-wrap;
}
```

The HTML5 recommendation recommends that you should always use `white-space:pre-wrap` with a `contenteditable` DIV element, and who am I to question the wisdom of the editors of the HTML5 recommendation? For this reason, I always use `white-space:pre-wrap` with a `contenteditable` DIV.

Displaying Progress

The HTML5 recommendation includes a new element named the progress element which enables you to display a progress indicator. There are two basic types of progress indicators: an indeterminate and a determinate progress indicator.

You use an indeterminate progress indicator when you want to show a busy wait indicator and you do not know how much longer a task will take. Here's how you declare an indeterminate progress indicator:

```
<progress id="progress1"></progress>
```

In a Windows Store app, the default progress indicator displays a set of animated dots moving horizontally (see Figure 5.17).

FIGURE 5.17   Displaying indeterminate progress

If you want to display a determinate progress indicator, then you need to supply values for the progress element's max and value attributes. For example, here's how you would create a progress indicator which shows progress between the values 1 and 20:

```
<progress id="progress1"
    max="20"
    value="1">
</progress>
```

And, here is JavaScript code which updates the progress every 1 second:

```
(function () {
    "use strict";

    function initialize() {
        var progress1 = document.getElementById("progress1");
        var ivlProgress = window.setInterval(updateProgress, 1000);

        function updateProgress() {
            progress1.value = ++progress1.value;
            if (progress1.value === 20) {
                window.clearInterval(ivlProgress);
            }
        }
    }
    document.addEventListener("DOMContentLoaded", initialize);
})();
```

Declaring a progress element in this way gives you a traditional progress bar (see Figure 5.18).

158 CHAPTER 5 Creating Forms

FIGURE 5.18 Displaying determinate progress

There are some style options which you can use with a progress element in a Windows Store app. When creating an indeterminate progress indicator, you can use the `win-ring` class to display an animated ring of dots instead of the default animated horizontal dots (see Figure 5.19):

```
<progress id="progress2" class="win-ring">
</progress>
```

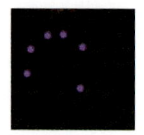

FIGURE 5.19 Displaying an animated ring of dots

If you want to control the size of an indeterminate progress indicator, then you can use the `win-medium` or `win-large` classes. For example, the following page contains three progress indicators of increasing size:

```
<progress id="progressRing1"
    class="win-ring">
</progress>

<br /><br />
<progress id="progressRing2"
    class="win-ring win-medium">
</progress>

<br /><br />
<progress id="progressRing3"
    class="win-ring win-large">
</progress>
```

Summary

The focus of this chapter was on creating HTML5 forms for Windows Store apps. In the first section, I explained how you can take advantage of the new form validation features included in HTML5. You learned how to use the `required` and `pattern` attributes to perform basic validation and the `setCustomValidity()` method to perform advanced validation.

Next, I described how you can take advantage of the new HTML5 input types. You learned how to accept numbers by using the number and range types. You also learned how to accept email addresses, URLs, telephone numbers, and search terms. I also demonstrated how you can select files from your computer hard drive by using `<input type="file" />`.

Finally, I demonstrated how you can create a rich text editor with the `contenteditable` attribute and a progress indicator with the new HTML5 progress element.

CHAPTER 6
Menus and Flyouts

IN THIS CHAPTER

▶ Using the `Flyout` Control
▶ Using the `Menu` Control
▶ Using the `AppBar` Control
▶ Configuring App Settings
▶ Displaying Windows Dialogs

This chapter focuses on the topics of flyouts, menus, toolbars, settings, and dialogs. You learn how to throw options at users and get their response.

I start by explaining how you can use the `Flyout` and `Menu` controls to display options within the body of a page. You learn how to display buttons, toggles, flyouts, and separators with a `Menu` control.

Next, I discuss the app bar. The app bar is the standard location for placing application commands in a Windows Store app. You learn how to create both global and selection commands.

You also learn how to configure your app settings. You learn how to take advantage of the `SettingsFlyout` control to extend the standard settings displayed by the Settings charm.

Finally, I show you how you can create modal dialogs with the `MessageDialog` class. You learn how to create warning dialogs and Yes/No dialogs.

Using the `Flyout` Control

You use a `Flyout` control to display a popup in a page. The popup disappears just as soon as you click outside of the popup (or press the ESC key). You can use the `Flyout` control to display information, display warnings, or gather input.

> **NOTE**
>
> The `Flyout` control supports *light dismiss*. When you click outside the `Flyout` control, the control disappears automatically.

A common use for flyouts is to display warnings. For example, if your app happens to include a "Delete All Data Forever" button, then it would be a good idea to use a flyout to warn the user before all of the user data is deleted.

Another common use for flyouts is for displaying forms which appear inline in a page. For example, the page in Listing 6.1 contains a `Flyout` control which enables you to select a typeface (see Figure 6.1).

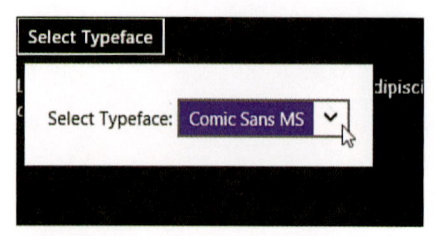

FIGURE 6.1 Displaying a flyout

LISTING 6.1 Displaying a Flyout (flyout\flyout.html)

```html
<!-- Flyout Control -->
<div id="flyTypeface"
    data-win-control="WinJS.UI.Flyout">
    <label>Select Typeface:</label>
    <select id="selectTypeface">
        <option>Arial</option>
        <option>Impact</option>
        <option>Comic Sans MS</option>
    </select>
</div>

<!-- Button which opens FlyOut -->
<button id="btnTypeface">Select Typeface</button>


<!-- The text to style -->
<p id="pText">
    Lorem ipsum dolor sit amet, consectetuer adipiscing elite
    Maecenas porttitor congue massa. Fusce posuere, magna sed
    pulvinar ultricies, purus lectus malesuada libero, sit amet
    commodo magna eros quis urna.
</p>
```

The page in Listing 6.1 contains a button that opens a flyout. The flyout displays a select list of typefaces. When you select a typeface, the lorem ipsum text is modified to appear with the selected typeface.

The JavaScript code in Listing 6.2 demonstrates how you can wire-up a button so it opens a flyout. The button click handler calls the `Flyout` control's `show()` method to display the flyout.

When you call the `show()` method, you should pass an anchor element. The anchor element determines where the `Flyout` will appear in the page. In Listing 6.2, the `Flyout` is anchored to the button.

LISTING 6.2 Displaying a Flyout (flyout\flyout.js)

```
(function () {
    "use strict";

    function initialize() {
        WinJS.UI.processAll().done(function () {
            var btnTypeface = document.getElementById("btnTypeface");
            var flyTypeface = document.getElementById("flyTypeface").winControl;
            var selectTypeface = document.getElementById("selectTypeface");
            var pText = document.getElementById("pText");

            // Wire-up handler to show FlyOut
            btnTypeface.addEventListener("click", function () {
                flyTypeface.show(btnTypeface);
            });

            // Wire-up handler for typeface select
            selectTypeface.addEventListener("change", function () {
                pText.style.fontFamily = selectTypeface.value;
            });

        });
    }

    document.addEventListener("DOMContentLoaded", initialize);
})();
```

WARNING

Remember to call `WinJS.UI.processAll()` when using the `Flyout` control or the `Flyout` control will never fly out.

Using the Menu Control

The WinJS `Menu` control is derived from the `Flyout` control—so it has a lot of features in common. Like the `Flyout` control, the `Menu` control appears in a popup and the menu disappears automatically when you click outside of the menu area.

However, unlike the `Flyout` control, the `Menu` control is specifically designed to display menu commands. You can place only menu commands in a `Menu` control and not other types of controls or HTML elements. The `Menu` control supports the following types of menu commands:

- `button`—You click the menu item to do something.
- `toggle`—You toggle the menu item.
- `flyout`—Clicking the menu item displays a flyout.
- `separator`—A separator between different groups of menu commands.

Listing 6.3 illustrates how you can declare the `Menu` control so it uses each of these menu commands.

LISTING 6.3 Displaying a Menu (menu\menu.html)

```html
<!-- Clicking this button shows the Menu -->
<button id="btnEdit">Edit</button>

<!-- The Menu control -->
<div id="menuEdit"
    data-win-control="WinJS.UI.Menu">
    <button
        data-win-control="WinJS.UI.MenuCommand"
        data-win-options="{
            id:'menuCommandDelete',
            label:'Delete',
            type: 'button'
        }"></button>
    <hr
        data-win-control="WinJS.UI.MenuCommand"
        data-win-options="{
            type: 'separator'
        }" />
    <button
        data-win-control="WinJS.UI.MenuCommand"
        data-win-options="{
            id:'menuCommandBold',
            label:'Bold',
            type: 'toggle'
        }"></button>
    <button
        data-win-control="WinJS.UI.MenuCommand"
        data-win-options="{
            id:'menuCommandItalic',
            label:'Italic',
```

```
                type: 'toggle'
            }"></button>
        <button
            data-win-control="WinJS.UI.MenuCommand"
            data-win-options="{
                id:'menuCommandTypeface',
                label:'Typeface',
                type: 'flyout',
                flyout: select('#flyTypeface')
            }"></button>

</div>

<!-- Flyout Control -->
<div id="flyTypeface"
    data-win-control="WinJS.UI.Flyout">
    <label>Select Typeface:</label>
    <select id="selectTypeface">
        <option>Arial</option>
        <option>Impact</option>
        <option>Comic Sans MS</option>
    </select>
</div>

<!-- The text to style -->
<p id="pText">
    Lorem ipsum dolor sit amet, consectetuer adipiscing elite
    Maecenas porttitor congue massa. Fusce posuere, magna sed
    pulvinar ultricies, purus lectus malesuada libero, sit amet
    commodo magna eros quis urna.
</p>
```

The page in Listing 6.3 contains a chunk of lorem ipsum text. You use the menu control to modify the appearance of the text (see Figure 6.2).

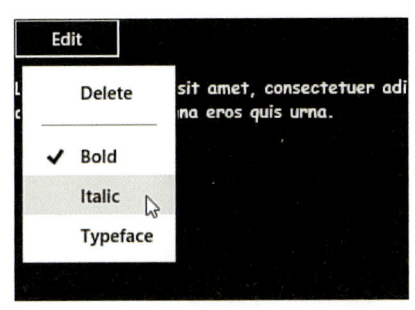

FIGURE 6.2 Using a `Menu` control

This menu contains five menu commands (instances of the `WinJS.UI.MenuCommand` class). It contains a button, separator, two toggles, and a flyout command.

The button command deletes all of the text. This command is wired-up to a click event handler in the JavaScript file in Listing 6.4.

The separator command does absolutely nothing at all. It just displays a separator between different groups of commands on the menu (a horizontal line).

The two toggle commands enable you to toggle the text between bold/normal and italic/normal. Click handlers for these commands are included in Listing 6.4.

Finally, the flyout command displays a `Flyout` control. The `Flyout` control is included in the HTML page in Listing 6.3 with the name flyTypeface. The Flyout enables you to select a typeface for the text (see Figure 6.3). When the Flyout appears, the menu disappears.

LISTING 6.4 Displaying a Menu (menu\menu.js)

```javascript
(function () {
    "use strict";

    function initialize() {
        WinJS.UI.processAll().done(function () {
            var btnEdit = document.getElementById("btnEdit");
            var menuEdit = document.getElementById("menuEdit").winControl;
            var selectTypeface = document.getElementById("selectTypeface");
            var pText = document.getElementById("pText");

            // When you click Edit then show the Menu
            btnEdit.addEventListener("click", function () {
                menuEdit.show(btnEdit);
            });

            // Wire-up menu commands
            document.getElementById("menuCommandDelete").addEventListener("click",
➥ function (evt) {
                pText.innerHTML = "[deleted]";
            });
            document.getElementById("menuCommandBold").addEventListener("click",
➥ function (evt) {
                var toggleState = document.getElementById("menuCommandBold").
➥winControl.selected;
                if (toggleState) {
                    pText.style.fontWeight = 'bold'
                } else {
                    pText.style.fontWeight = 'normal'
                }
            });
```

```
            document.getElementById("menuCommandItalic").addEventListener("click",
➥ function (evt) {
            var toggleState = document.getElementById("menuCommandItalic").
➥winControl.selected;
                if (toggleState) {
                    pText.style.fontStyle = 'italic'
                } else {
                    pText.style.fontStyle = 'normal'
                }
            });
            selectTypeface.addEventListener("change", function () {
                pText.style.fontFamily = selectTypeface.value;
            });

        });
    }

    document.addEventListener("DOMContentLoaded", initialize);
})();
```

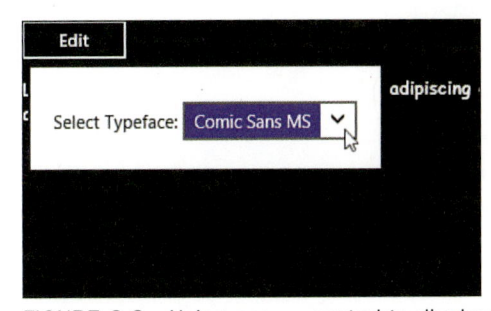

FIGURE 6.3 Using a `Menu` control to display a flyout

Using the `AppBar` Control

Windows Store apps have a standard location for application commands: the app bar. The app bar typically appears at the bottom of an app. However, you also can display an app bar at both the bottom and top of an app. The app bar does not appear until you swipe from either the bottom or top of the page or right-click when using a mouse.

For example, Figure 6.4 illustrates the appearance of the two app bars in the Windows 8 version of Internet Explorer. The bottom app bar contains the address bar for navigating to websites and the top app bar contains the active tabs. If you click on the page, both app bars disappear and you get a full screen experience.

168 CHAPTER 6 Menus and Flyouts

> **NOTE**
> Because the top app bar is typically used for navigating to different pages in an app, the top app bar is also called the nav bar.

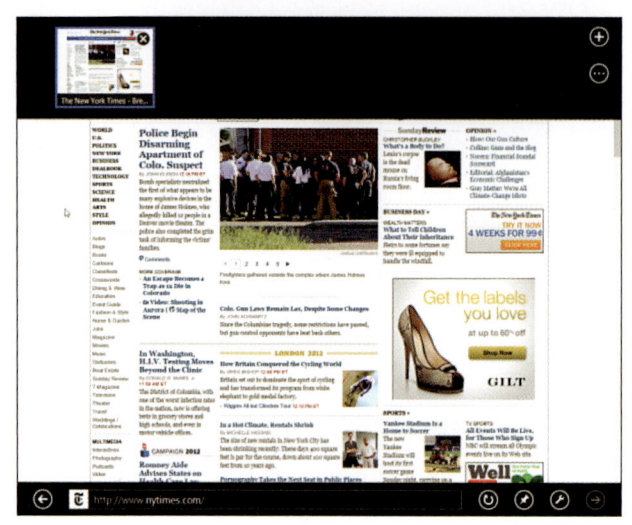

FIGURE 6.4   Internet Explorer app bar

Creating a Simple App Bar

You use the WinJS `AppBar` control to add app bars to your Windows Store app. For example, here is how you would declare an app bar which appears on the bottom of your app:

```
<div id="appBar1"
    data-win-control="WinJS.UI.AppBar">

    <button data-win-control="WinJS.UI.AppBarCommand"
        data-win-options="{
            id:'cmdPlay',
            label:'Play',
            icon:'play',
            tooltip:'Play Song'
        }">
    </button>
    <button data-win-control="WinJS.UI.AppBarCommand"
        data-win-options="{
            id:'cmdPause',
            label:'Pause',
            icon:'pause',
            tooltip:'Pause Song'
        }">
```

```
        </button>

</div>
```

> **NOTE**
> The `AppBar` control is included in the default.html page by default—but commented out.

This app bar contains two buttons: a Play Song and a Pause Song button. Each button has both a label and an icon (see Figure 6.5).

FIGURE 6.5 A simple app bar

If you want to create an app bar which appears on the top of your app (a nav bar), then you need to set the `AppBar` placement property like this:

```
<div id="appBar1"
    data-win-control="WinJS.UI.AppBar"
    data-win-options="{
        placement:'top'
    }">

    <button data-win-control="WinJS.UI.AppBarCommand"
        data-win-options="{
            id:'cmdSave',
            label:'Save',
            icon:'save',
            tooltip:'Save Song List'
        }">
    </button>

</div>
```

The placement property defaults to the value `"bottom"`. Above, I set the property to the value `"top"` so the app bar appears at the top of the app (see Figure 6.6).

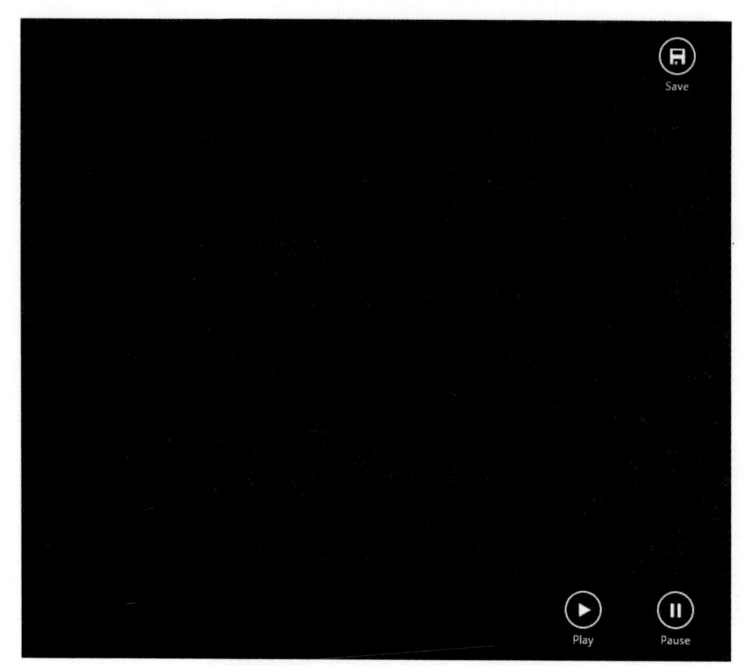

FIGURE 6.6 Creating both bottom and top app bars

Using App Bar Commands

There are four types of app bar commands:

- button—Creates a button that performs some action.
- toggle—Creates a toggle button that switches between two states.
- flyout—Creates a flyout that you can use to display a form.
- separator—Creates a separator (vertical line) between other commands.

Listing 6.5 contains a sample of an app bar which contains all four of these commands:

LISTING 6.5 Using Different Types of App Bar Commands

```
<!-- AppBar Control -->
<div id="appBar1"
    data-win-control="WinJS.UI.AppBar">

    <!-- AppBar Commands -->
    <button data-win-control="WinJS.UI.AppBarCommand"
        data-win-options="{
            id:'cmdPlay',
            label:'Play',
            icon:'play',
```

```
                    tooltip:'Play Song'
                }">
            </button>
            <button data-win-control="WinJS.UI.AppBarCommand"
                data-win-options="{
                    id:'cmdMute',
                    type: 'toggle',
                    label:'Mute',
                    icon:'mute',
                    tooltip:'Mute Song'
                }">
            </button>
            <hr data-win-control="WinJS.UI.AppBarCommand"
                data-win-options="{
                    type: 'separator'
                }" />
            <button data-win-control="WinJS.UI.AppBarCommand"
                data-win-options="{
                    id:'cmdAddSong',
                    type: 'flyout',
                    label:'Add',
                    icon:'add',
                    tooltip:'Add Song',
                    flyout: select('#flyAddSong')
                }">
            </button>


</div>

<!-- Add Song Flyout -->
<div id="flyAddSong"
    data-win-control="WinJS.UI.Flyout">
    <form>
        <input id="inpNewSong" required />
        <input type="submit" value="Add" />
    </form>
</div>
```

When you swipe or right-click, then you get the app bar depicted in Figure 6.7.

172 CHAPTER 6 Menus and Flyouts

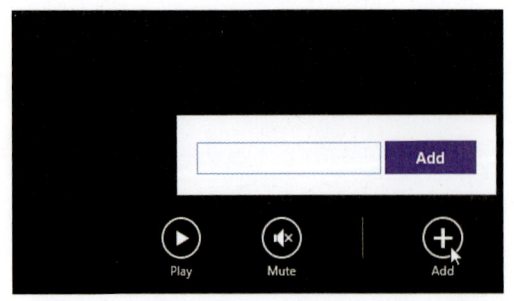

FIGURE 6.7 An app bar with different types of commands

The most common app bar command is the button command. You can create a click handler for a button command and do some action in response to clicking the button. For example, here is how you would create a click handler for the cmdPlay button:

```
(function () {
    "use strict";

    function initialize() {
        WinJS.UI.processAll().done(function () {
            var cmdPlay = document.getElementById("cmdPlay");
            cmdPlay.addEventListener("click ", function () {
                console.log("Play song");
            });
        });
    }

    document.addEventListener("DOMContentLoaded", initialize);
})();
```

The button command includes both a label and icon property which you can use to control the appearance of the button in the app bar. You can either point the icon property to a custom PNG image or you can use one of the over 100 built-in icons.

> **NOTE**
>
> There is a complete list of the built-in icons in the WinJS UI.js library. Just open the UI.js file in the Solution Explorer window by expanding the References folder and do a search for "glyphs."

The toggle command displays a button which looks just like a button command. However, when you click the button, the button toggles between a highlighted and not highlighted state.

Here's how you can use the selected property to determine whether a toggle button is selected:

```
(function () {
    "use strict";

    function initialize() {
        WinJS.UI.processAll().done(function () {

            var cmdMute = document.getElementById("cmdMute");
            cmdMute.addEventListener("click", function () {
                console.log(cmdMute.winControl.selected);
            });

        });
    }

    document.addEventListener("DOMContentLoaded", initialize);
})();
```

The separator command creates a vertical bar between commands so you can group them. Use an HR element instead of a BUTTON element when creating a separator command.

Finally, the flyout command displays a `Flyout` control. In Listing 6.5, the cmdAdd command displays a `Flyout` that contains a form for entering the title of a new song.

Showing Contextual Commands

Some app bar commands apply to the entire app. Other app bar commands apply only when an item is selected. For example, it might make sense to always display an Add button in the app bar. Displaying a Delete or Edit button, on the other hand, makes sense only when an item is selected.

The app bar has two built-in sections named "global" and "selection." By default, when you add commands to the app bar, the commands appear in the global section. These commands appear on the right-hand side of the app bar.

You also have the option of adding commands to the selection section. These commands appear on the left-hand side of the app bar. Commands in the selection section should appear only when something is selected.

Imagine that you want to display a list of tasks by using a `ListView` control. You want users to be able to add new tasks and delete existing tasks. In that case, it makes sense to place the Add button in the app bar global section and the Delete button in the app bar selection section (see Figure 6.8).

174 CHAPTER 6 Menus and Flyouts

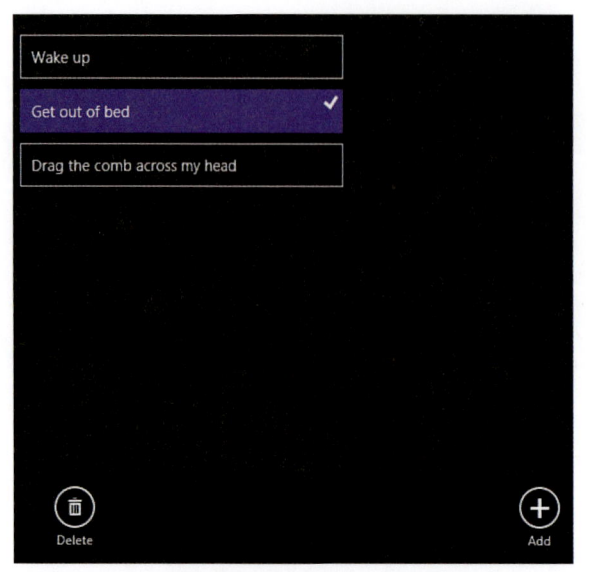

FIGURE 6.8 Global versus selection app bar sections

Here's how you can declare your app bar so it contains an `Add` and `Delete` command:

```
<div id="appBar1"
    data-win-control="WinJS.UI.AppBar">
    <button data-win-control="WinJS.UI.AppBarCommand"
        data-win-options="{
            id:'cmdAdd',
            label:'Add',
            icon:'add',
            tooltip:'Add Task',
            type: 'flyout',
            flyout: select('#flyAdd'),
            section: 'global'
        }">
    </button>
    <button data-win-control="WinJS.UI.AppBarCommand"
        data-win-options="{
            id:'cmdDelete',
            label:'Delete',
            icon:'delete',
            tooltip:'Delete Task',
            section: 'selection',
            extraClass:'appBarSelection'
        }">
    </button>
</div>
```

Notice that the `Add` command is placed in the global section of the app bar. You don't really need to be explicit about this—global is the default value.

The `Delete` command is placed in the selection section. Notice, furthermore, that an additional CSS class named `appBarSelection` is associated with the `Delete` command. I'll take advantage of that class in a moment to hide and display the `Delete` command.

Here's the JavaScript code for hiding and displaying the app bar commands:

```javascript
// Hide selection commands by default
appBar1.hideCommands(document.querySelectorAll('.appBarSelection'));


// When ListView item selected, display app bar
lvTasks.addEventListener("selectionchanged", function () {
    if (lvTasks.selection.count() == 1) {
        appBar1.showCommands(document.querySelectorAll('.appBarSelection'));
        appBar1.show();
    } else {
        appBar1.hideCommands(document.querySelectorAll('.appBarSelection'));
    };
});
```

When the app first starts, you want to hide the `Delete` command because nothing is selected. In the code above, the `hideCommands()` method is used to hide every command associated with the `appBarSelection` CSS class.

Next, the code handles the `selectionchanged` event raised by the `ListView` control. When you select an item in the `ListView` (by swiping or right clicking the item) then the selection commands are displayed with the help of the `showCommands()` method.

Because the app bar is hidden by default, you might not notice the `Delete` command. For that reason, the code above calls the `show()` method to force the app bar to be displayed. That way, when you select an item in the `ListView`, the app bar is displayed automatically and you know that you can delete an item.

> **NOTE**
> You can force the app bar to always appear with the app bar control sticky property. When the sticky property has the value true, then the app bar does not disappear automatically.

Configuring App Settings

Windows Store apps have a standard location for users to configure app settings. You access app settings from the Settings charm in the charm bar which you can open by:

- ▶ Moving your mouse to the bottom right of your screen
- ▶ Swiping with your finger from the right edge of the screen
- ▶ Hitting the key Windows + i

By default, System settings—such as network and volume settings—appear at the bottom of the Settings window. Permission settings also appear automatically. Finally, if you did in fact get your Windows Store app from the Windows Store, then the Settings window will also include Rate and review settings.

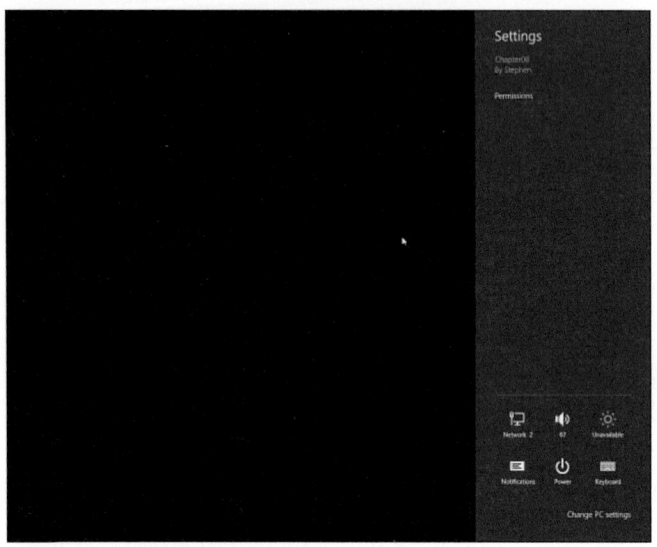

FIGURE 6.9 Default settings

You can add custom settings to the Settings window for your app. These custom settings can be configuration settings such as user preferences. The custom settings might also include information about your app, including Help and About pages.

You create custom app settings with the help of the `SettingsFlyout` control. For each app settings section that you want to create, you create a separate HTML file which contains a `SettingsFlyout`. I'll demonstrate how this works by creating both About Page settings and Personal settings.

Creating About Page Settings

Most apps include an About Page which provides information about the company who built the application. The About Page is purely informational (see Figure 6.10).

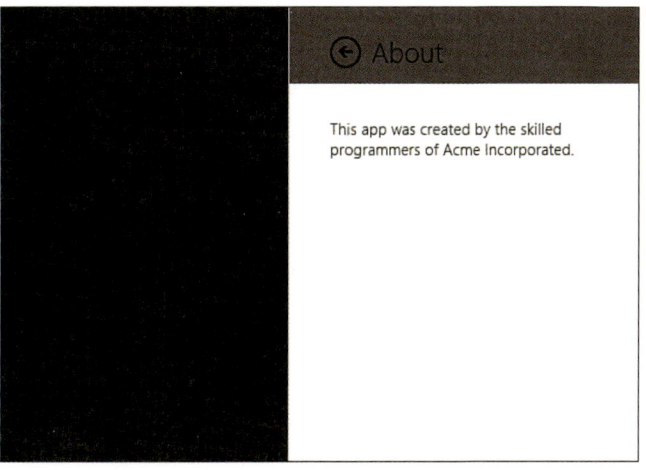

FIGURE 6.10 Creating About settings

If you want to create an About setting in your Settings window, then you first need to create a new HTML file which contains a `SettingsFlyout` control. The HTML page in Listing 6.6 illustrates how you can create an About setting.

LISTING 6.6 About Settings

```html
<!DOCTYPE html>
<html>
    <head>
        <title>About</title>
    </head>
    <body>
        <div id="divAbout"
            data-win-control="WinJS.UI.SettingsFlyout"
            data-win-options="{
                width:'narrow'
            }">
            <div class="win-header"
                style="background-color:#464646">
                <button
                    onclick="WinJS.UI.SettingsFlyout.show()"
                    class="win-backbutton"></button>
                <div class="win-label">About</div>
            </div>
            <div class="win-content">
                This app was created by the skilled programmers of Acme
                Incorporated.
            </div>
        </div>
    </body>
</html>
```

The page in Listing 6.6 contains a single `WinJS SettingsFlyout` control. Notice that the `SettingsFlyout` control is declared with a "narrow" width. When you open settings with a narrow width, the settings take up the same size as the Settings window. Alternatively, you can set the width to the value "wide" to create a larger space for displaying settings.

You can place whatever content that you please within the `Flyout` and the content will appear when you open the settings. However, there are some guidelines from Microsoft. The `SettingsFlyout` control in Listing 6.6 contains a back button so you can get back to the Settings window. The control also takes advantage of several standard WinJS style classes such as `win-label` and `win-content`.

Before you can use the About settings, you must register the settings by handling the WinJS.Application settings event like this:

```
(function () {
    "use strict";
    WinJS.Application.onsettings = function (e) {
        e.detail.applicationcommands = {
            "divAbout": { href: "aboutSettings.html", title: "About" }
        };
        WinJS.UI.SettingsFlyout.populateSettings(e);
    }
    WinJS.Application.start();
})();
```

You assign a collection of settings commands to the `e.details.applicationcommands` object. In the code above, the path and title of the About settings are assigned to the collection of application commands.

> **WARNING**
>
> When creating settings, you must call `WinJS.Application.start()` or the settings event will never be raised.

Creating Personal Settings

Imagine that you want to enable users to enter their first and last names in the app settings for a Windows Store app (see Figure 6.11). You are building a friendly app and you want to address the user by name.

Configuring App Settings   179

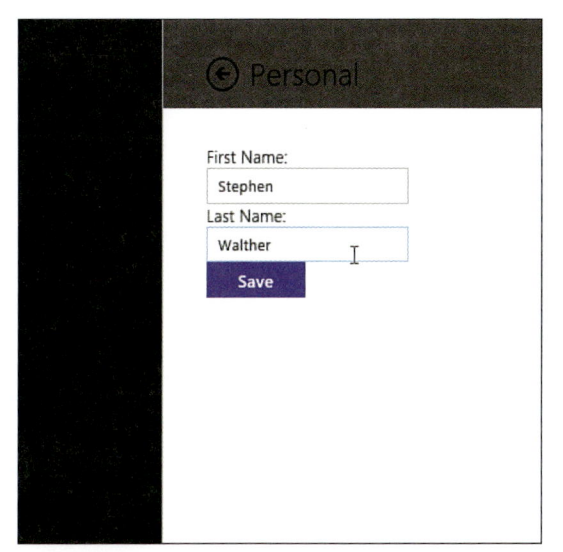

FIGURE 6.11   Collecting Personal settings

The HTML page in Listing 6.7—named personalSettings.html—contains a SettingsFlyout that contains an HTML form. The form has two form fields named inpFirstName and inpLastName and both form fields are required.

LISTING 6.7   `SettingsFlyout` for Personal Settings

```html
<!DOCTYPE html>
<html>
    <head>
        <title>Security</title>
        <script type="text/javascript" src="personalSettings.js"></script>
    </head>
    <body>
        <div id="divPersonal"
            data-win-control="WinJS.UI.SettingsFlyout"
            data-win-options="{
                width:'narrow'
            }">
            <div class="win-header"
                style="background-color:#464646">
                <button
                    onclick="WinJS.UI.SettingsFlyout.show()"
                    class="win-backbutton"></button>
                <div class="win-label">Personal</div>
            </div>
            <div class="win-content">
                <form id="frmPersonal">
```

```
            <div>
                <label>
                    First Name: <br />
                    <input id="inpFirstName" required />
                </label>
            </div>
            <div>
                <label>
                    Last Name: <br />
                    <input id="inpLastName" required />
                </label>
            </div>
            <div>
                <input type="submit" value="Save" />
            </div>
        </form>
        </div>
    </div>
    </body>
</html>
```

Notice that the page in Listing 6.7 refers to a JavaScript file named personalSettings.js. The personalSettings.js file is contained in Listing 6.8. This JavaScript file is responsible for both loading and saving the user first and last names.

LISTING 6.8 Loading and Saving Personal Settings

```
(function () {
    'use strict';

    WinJS.UI.Pages.define("personalSettings.html",
    {
        processed: function (element, options) {
            var roamingSettings =
➥ Windows.Storage.ApplicationData.current.roamingSettings;
            var divPersonal = document.getElementById("divPersonal").winControl;
            var frmSecurity = document.getElementById("frmPersonal");
            var inpFirstName = document.getElementById("inpFirstName");
            var inpLastName = document.getElementById("inpLastName");

            // Read the first and last name
            divPersonal.addEventListener("beforeshow", function () {
                inpFirstName.value = roamingSettings.values["firstName"] || "";
                inpLastName.value = roamingSettings.values["lastName"] || "";
            });
```

```
            // Save first and last names
            frmSecurity.addEventListener("submit", function () {
                roamingSettings.values["firstName"] = inpFirstName.value;
                roamingSettings.values["lastName"] = inpLastName.value;
            });

        }
    });
}());
```

The JavaScript code in Listing 6.8 includes an event handler for the `SettingsFlyout` `beforeshow` event. This event is raised right before the `SettingsFlyout` is displayed. In Listing 6.8, the user's first and last name is loaded from roaming settings and assigned to the two form fields.

The code in Listing 6.8 also includes an event handler for the form submit event. This handler saves the user's first and last name to roaming settings. The first and last name is saved permanently on the computer so the settings are available whenever the user runs the app again in the future. Because the settings are stored in roaming storage, the settings are also available across different computers.

> **NOTE**
>
> Roaming settings are stored in the computer registry and synchronized across devices. Currently, Microsoft limits you to storing 100KB in roaming storage (use the `ApplicationDate.RoamingStorageQuota` property to view the limit).

To use the Personal settings in a page, you must register the settings in the JavaScript file associated with the page. The following code registers both the About Page settings (from the previous section) and the Personal settings:

```
(function () {
    "use strict";
    WinJS.Application.onsettings = function (e) {
        e.detail.applicationcommands = {
            "divPersonal": { href: "personalSettings.html", title: "Personal" },
            "divAbout": { href: "aboutSettings.html", title: "About" }
        };
        WinJS.UI.SettingsFlyout.populateSettings(e);
    }
    WinJS.Application.start();
})();
```

Displaying Windows Dialogs

Sometimes, nothing beats a good old-fashioned modal dialog. A modal dialog blocks all user interaction with your app until the modal dialog gets its answer.

Modal dialogs are necessary when your app will not work without some crucial information. For example, a Weather app cannot display the weather without knowing your location. So it makes sense to use a modal dialog to ask for the user's location when the app first runs.

You also can use modal dialogs in the same situations in which you would use JavaScript alerts: when you really need to get in a user's face to convey critical warnings or information. You should use modal dialogs sparingly.

> **NOTE**
>
> JavaScript alerts do not work in Windows Store apps written with JavaScript. Because I consider JavaScript alerts to be closely related to the (deprecated) HTML blink tag, this is a good thing.

You create modal dialogs by using the `MessageDialog` class. Here's how you can open a dialog with the message "Did you know that your fly is unzipped?" (see Figure 6.12).

```
var message = new Windows.UI.Popups.MessageDialog(
    "Did you know that your fly is unzipped?"
);
message.showAsync();
```

FIGURE 6.12 Using a message dialog

You can customize the appearance of the dialog by supplying commands. For example, here is how you would create a Yes/No dialog:

```
// Create dialog
var message = new Windows.UI.Popups.MessageDialog(
    "Did you know that your fly is unzipped?",
    "Warning!!!"
);

// Add commands
message.commands.append(new Windows.UI.Popups.UICommand("&Yes"));
message.commands.append(new Windows.UI.Popups.UICommand("&No"));

// Show dialog
message.showAsync().done(function (answer) {
    if (answer.label === "&Yes") {
        console.log("You picked yes");
    } else {
        console.log("You picked no");
    }
});
```

The code above appends two `UICommand` objects to the message dialog which are labeled Yes and No (see Figure 6.13). You can use the promise returned by the `showAsync()` method to determine which of the two buttons was clicked.

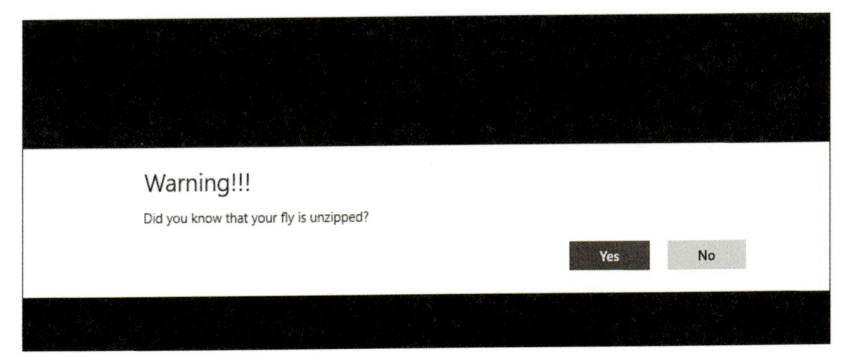

FIGURE 6.13   A yes/no dialog

> **NOTE**
>
> Notice that the buttons labels are "&Yes" and "&No". The & is used to specify the keyboard shortcut for invoking the button. You can press ALT-Y to invoke the Yes button and ALT-N to invoke the No button. When you hold down the ALT key, the shortcuts appear with underlines.

Summary

The chapter was all about flyouts, menus, settings, toolbars, and dialogs. I started by discussing how you can use the `Flyout` control to make simple ephemeral popups which can contain any HTML content at all.

Next, I explained how you can use the `Menu` control to display menu commands. You learned how to include buttons, flyouts, toggles, and separators in a menu.

I also discussed the app bar. You learned how the app bar is the standard location in a Windows Store app for placing commands. I demonstrated how you can add both global commands and selection commands to the app bar.

You also learned how to take advantage of the `SettingsFlyout` control to extend the settings displayed in your Windows Store app's Settings window. You learned how to store and retrieve settings from roaming settings.

Finally, I showed you how you can create modal dialogs by taking advantage of the `MessageDialog` class. We created warning dialogs and Yes/No dialogs.

Stay tuned. In the next chapter, we discuss the most important control in the WinJS library: the `ListView` control.

CHAPTER 7

Using the `ListView` Control

This entire chapter is devoted to one control: the `ListView` control. This is the single most important control included in the WinJS library. If you need to display a list of items—for example, a list of products, a list of movies, a list of files, a list of photos—then the `ListView` control is the control to use.

In this chapter, I explain how you can take advantage of all of the most important features of the `ListView` control. You learn the basics including how to select, sort, filter, and group items in a `ListView`.

I also discuss more advanced features of the `ListView` control. In particular, you learn how to use the `ListView` control with semantic zoom to generate different representations of the same data. You also learn how to use the `ListView` control to display huge sets of data efficiently by enabling incremental loading of `ListView` items.

Introduction to the `ListView` Control

Let's start with the basics. You can bind a `ListView` control to any data source which implements the JavaScript `IListDataSource` interface. The WinJS library includes two objects which implement this data source:

- ▶ `WinJS.Binding.List`—Enables you to represent a JavaScript array as a data source.

- ▶ `WinJS.UI.Storage`—Enables you to represent files from your computer hard drive as a data source. For example, you can use the `WinJS.UI.Storage` data source with the `ListView` control to display a list of pictures retrieved from your computer's Pictures library.

IN THIS CHAPTER

- ▶ Introduction to the `ListView` Control
- ▶ Selecting Items in a `ListView` Control
- ▶ Sorting Items in a `ListView` Control
- ▶ Filtering Items in a `ListView` Control
- ▶ Grouping Items in a `ListView` Control
- ▶ Switching Views with Semantic Zoom
- ▶ Switching a `ListView` Template Dynamically
- ▶ Loading `ListView` Items Incrementally

In this chapter, we focus on using the `WinJS.Binding.List` data source because this is the most flexible data source. You can create an instance of the `WinJS.Binding.List` data source from any JavaScript array.

For example, you can perform an Ajax request against a remote server and retrieve an array of products. You can then display the array of products by using the List data source with the `ListView` control.

> **NOTE**
>
> Instead of using either the `WinJS.Binding.List` or `WinJS.UI.Storage` data sources, you can create a custom data source and use it with the ListView control. You might want to create a custom data source, for example, if you need to display data from an `IndexedDB` database with a `ListView` control. We create several custom data sources—including an `IndexedDB` data source—in the next chapter.

Let's look at how you can use the `ListView` control with a `WinJS.Binding.List` data source. The page in Listing 7.1 contains a `ListView` control which displays a set of products (see Figure 7.1).

LISTING 7.1 Binding to a List Data Source (simple\simple.html)

```html
<!DOCTYPE html>
<html>
<head>
    <meta charset="utf-8" />
    <title>Chapter05</title>

    <!-- WinJS references -->
    <link href="//Microsoft.WinJS.1.0.RC/css/ui-dark.css" rel="stylesheet" />
    <script src="//Microsoft.WinJS.1.0.RC/js/base.js"></script>
    <script src="//Microsoft.WinJS.1.0.RC/js/ui.js"></script>

    <!-- Chapter05 references -->
    <link href="simple.css" rel="stylesheet" />
    <script src="simple.js"></script>
</head>
<body>

    <div id="tmplProduct"
        data-win-control="WinJS.Binding.Template">
        <div>
            <h2 data-win-bind="innerText:name"></h2>
            Price: <span data-win-bind="innerText:price"></span>
        </div>
    </div>
```

Introduction to the `ListView` Control

```
    <div id="lvProducts"
        data-win-control="WinJS.UI.ListView"
        data-win-options="{
            itemTemplate: select('#tmplProduct')
        }"></div>

</body>
</html>
```

The `ListView` control in Listing 7.1 uses a template to render each product. The template is contained in a Template control with the id `tmplProduct`.

> **WARNING**
> Make sure that you declare the Template control in the page before the `ListView` control or you will get a mysterious and hard to debug exception.

The JavaScript file in Listing 7.2 contains the array of products. A `WinJS.Binding.List` object is created from the array of products and the List object is bound to the `ListView` control with the help of the `itemDataSource` property. When you view the page, you see the list of products from the JavaScript array.

LISTING 7.2   Binding to a List Data Source (simple\simple.js)

```
(function () {
    "use strict";

    function initialize() {
        WinJS.UI.processAll().done(function () {
            // Get reference to ListView control
            var lvProducts = document.getElementById("lvProducts").winControl;

            // Create a List of products
            var listProducts = new WinJS.Binding.List([
                { name: "Bread", price: 2.20 },
                { name: "Cheese", price: 1.19 },
                { name: "Milk", price: 2.33 },
                { name: "Apples", price: 5.20 },
                { name: "Steak", price: 12.99 }
            ]);

            // Bind the list of products to the ListView
            lvProducts.itemDataSource = listProducts.dataSource;
```

188   CHAPTER 7   Using the `ListView` Control

```
        });
    }

    document.addEventListener("DOMContentLoaded", initialize);
})();
```

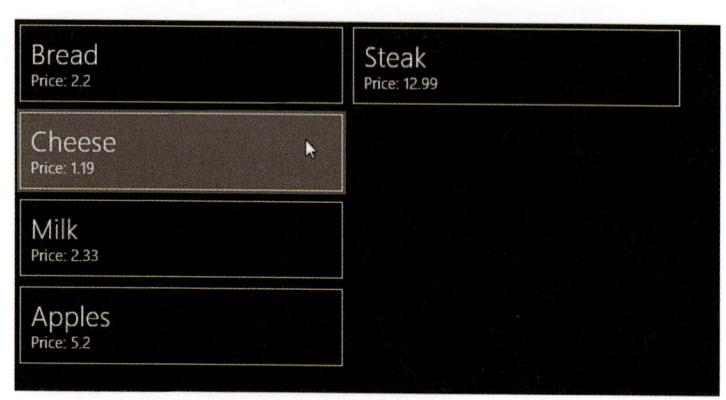

FIGURE 7.1   Displaying a list of products

You can stick just about anything in a JavaScript array: the results of a database query, the results of an Ajax call, the Fibonacci series. For this reason, when you bind a `ListView` control to a List, you can bind to almost any type of data.

For example, the `ListView` in Listing 7.3 displays a list of blog posts retrieved from a blog feed.

LISTING 7.3   Binding to a Blog Feed (blog\blog.html)

```
<div id="tmplBlog"
    data-win-control="WinJS.Binding.Template">
    <div>
        <span data-win-bind="innerHTML: title.text WinJS.Binding.oneTime"></span>
    </div>
</div>

<div id="lvBlog"
    data-win-control="WinJS.UI.ListView"
    data-win-options="{
        itemTemplate: select('#tmplBlog')
    }"></div>
```

The list of blog posts is retrieved from an RSS feed located at http://StephenWalther.com (hey, that's my blog) with the help of the WinRT `SyndicationClient` class. Listing 7.4 contains the code which grabs the feed and binds it to the `ListView` control.

LISTING 7.4 Binding to a Blog Feed (blog\blog.html)

```
(function () {
    "use strict";

    function initialize() {
        WinJS.UI.processAll().done(function () {
            // Get reference to ListView control
            var lvBlog = document.getElementById("lvBlog").winControl;

            // Use WinRT SyndicationClient to get blog feed
            var client = new Windows.Web.Syndication.SyndicationClient();
            var feedURI = new Windows.Foundation.Uri("http://stephenwalther.com/
➥blog/feed");
            client.retrieveFeedAsync(feedURI).done(function (feed) {

                // Convert feed items to a List
                var listItems = new WinJS.Binding.List(feed.items);

                // Bind list to ListView
                lvBlog.itemDataSource = listItems.dataSource;
            });

        });
    }

    document.addEventListener("DOMContentLoaded", initialize);
})();
```

The `SyndicationClient` returns an instance of the `SyndicationFeed` class. The `SyndicationFeed` class has an items property which contains the blog entries.

The blog entries are passed to the constructor for the `WinJS.Binding.List` class and the List class is bound to the `ListView` control. Figure 7.2 illustrates how the blog entries are displayed by the `ListView`.

190 CHAPTER 7 Using the `ListView` Control

> **WARNING**
>
> By default, a `ListView` control will try to make each of its list items into an observable by calling the `WinJS.Binding.as()` method. Unfortunately, this does not work on WinRT objects such as the items returned by the `SyndicationClient` class. You'll get an exception if you try to bind WinRT objects to a `ListView` control.
>
> There are two ways to get around this problem. If you look closely at the template in Listing 7.3, you will notice that the blog title is bound using the `WinJS.Binding.oneTime()` binding converter. When you use the `WinJS.Binding.oneTime()` converter, the `ListView` control does not attempt to convert the items bound to it into observables.
>
> Another solution to this problem would be to copy the array of WinRT objects into a new JavaScript array of JavaScript objects before binding to the `ListView` control. JavaScript objects, unlike WinRT objects, are happy to be made into observables.

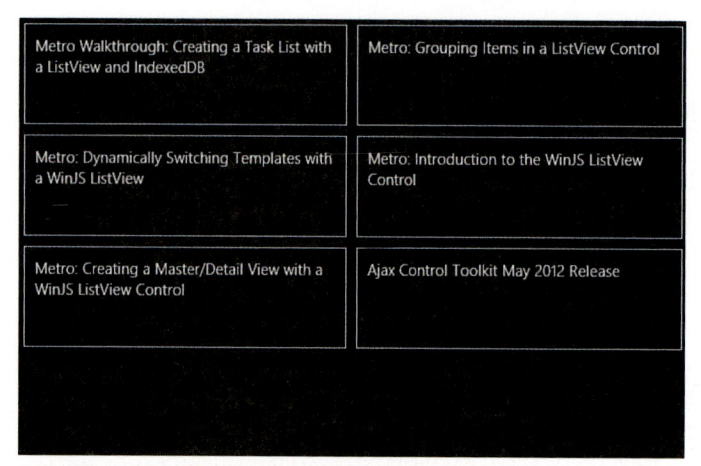

FIGURE 7.2 Displaying a list of blog posts

Using List Layout versus Grid Layout

The `ListView` control supports two layouts: grid layout and list layout. The default layout is grid layout. When a `ListView` displays items in grid layout, the items are displayed in multiple columns. If there are too many items to fit in the `ListView` then you scroll to the right to view the additional items (see Figure 7.3).

> **NOTE**
>
> Under the covers, grid layout uses the W3C CSS 3 Grid Layout recommendation. You can read the details here: http://dev.w3.org/csswg/css3-grid-layout/.

Introduction to the `ListView` Control   191

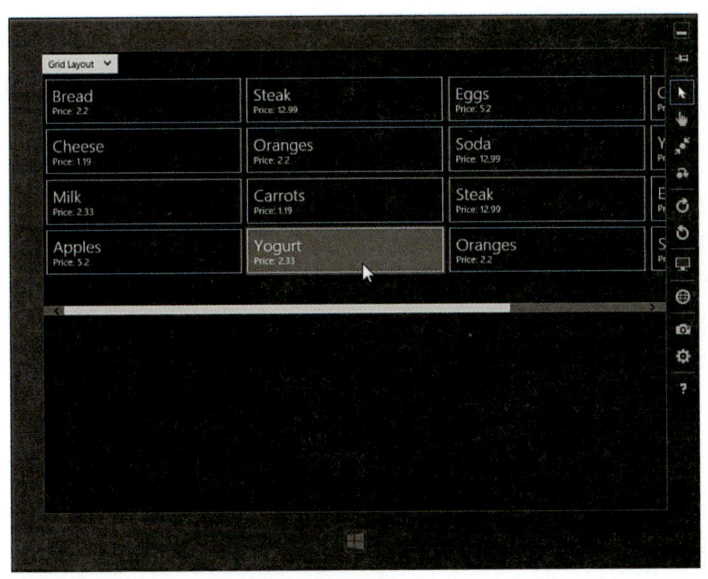

FIGURE 7.3 `ListView` in grid layout

When the `ListView` uses grid layout, you can set the `maxRows` property to set the maximum number of grid rows that should be displayed. Here's how you would set the `maxRows` so a `ListView` displays only one row (see Figure 7.4):

```
<div id="lvProducts"
    data-win-control="WinJS.UI.ListView"
    data-win-options="{
        itemTemplate: select('#tmplProduct'),
        layout: {type:WinJS.UI.GridLayout, maxRows:1}
    }"></div>
```

192   CHAPTER 7   Using the `ListView` Control

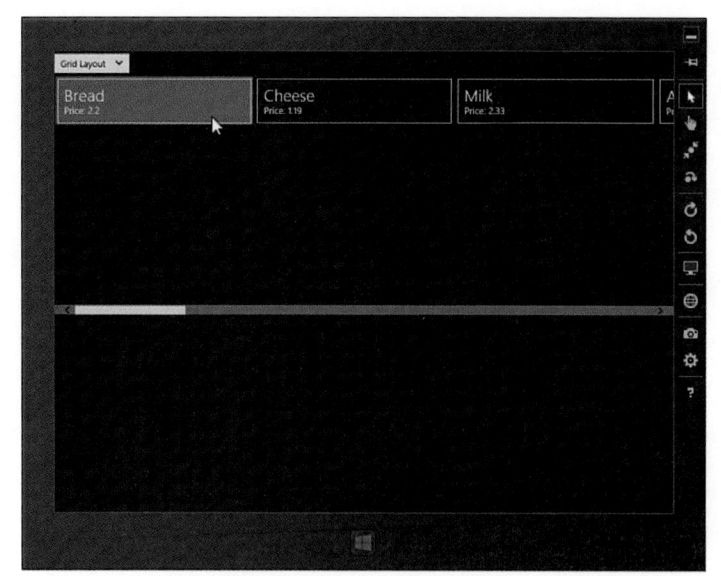

FIGURE 7.4   Setting the `GridLayout maxRows` property

The other layout mode that you can use with a `ListView` control is list layout. In list layout mode, the items are displayed vertically. If all of the items do not fit in the `ListView` then you can scroll the `ListView` vertically (see Figure 7.5).

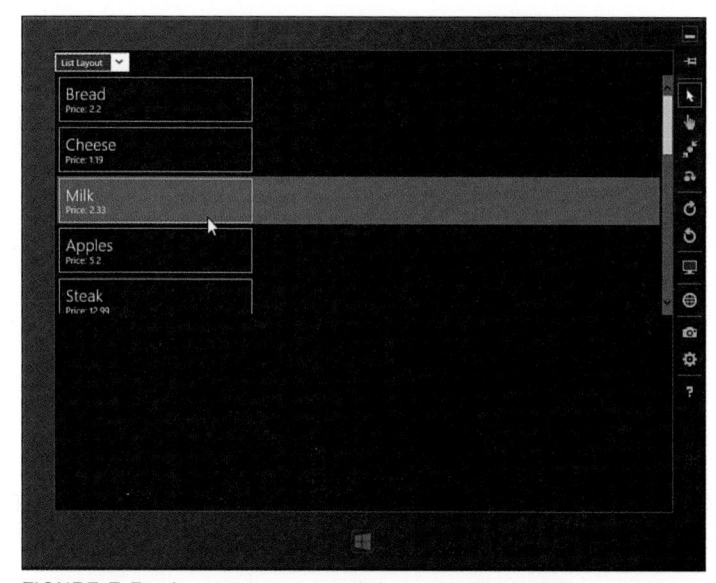

FIGURE 7.5   A `ListView` control that uses list layout

Here's how you can declare a `ListView` so it uses list layout:

Introduction to the `ListView` Control   193

```
<div id="lvProducts"
    data-win-control="WinJS.UI.ListView"
    data-win-options="{
        itemTemplate: select('#tmplProduct'),
        layout: {type:WinJS.UI.ListLayout}
    }"></div>
```

When `ListView` items are rendered with list layout, then the items are not actually displayed using HTML UL and LI elements. Instead, DIV elements are rendered for each item.

Preventing Overlapping `ListView` Items

Displaying items in a `ListView` control in grid layout mode can be frustrating unless you understand the trick the `ListView` control uses to display each item.

Consider the `ListView` displayed in Figure 7.6. This `ListView` displays 7 items:

AA

BBBBBBBB

CC

DD

EE

FF

GG

However, the BBBBBBBB item overlaps the FF list item in the next column. The wide B item messes up the rendering of the `ListView`. This doesn't look very nice!

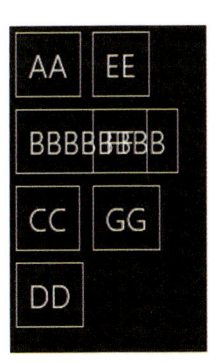

FIGURE 7.6   Overlapping `ListView` items

If you move the BBBBBBBB item to the top of the list, then the overlapping problem goes away (see Figure 7.7). All of the items are rendered with the width of the BBBBBBBB item. However, now the problem is every item in the ListView is the same width as the BBBBBBBB and that looks weird.

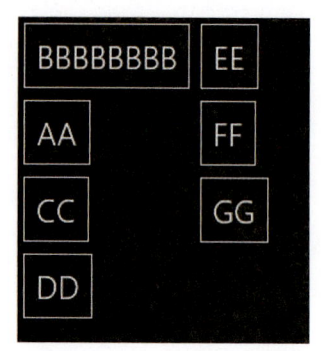

FIGURE 7.7 Non-overlapping but super wide `ListView` items

Here's the trick that the `ListView` uses to calculate the width and height of each list item. The `ListView` simply calculates the width and height of the first item and uses that width and height for every other item.

Because of the way that the `ListView` control calculates the width and height of list items, I recommend that you always be explicit about item width and height. Otherwise, depending on the width and height of the first item, you might either get overlapping or unnecessarily wide or tall list items.

So how can you be explicit about the width and height of your list items? When a `ListView` renders its items, the items are rendered in DIV elements that look something like this:

```html
<div class="win-listview">
   <div class="win-container" style="width:142px;height:54px">
      <div class="win-item">
         AAAA
      </div>
   </div>
   <div class="win-container" style="width:142px;height:54px">
      <div class="win-item">
         BBBB
      </div>
   </div>
   <div class="win-container" style="width:142px;height:54px">
      <div class="win-item">
         CCCC
      </div>
   </div>
   ... and so on ...
</div>
```

To simplify things, I've left out several levels of nested DIVs. But the basic idea is that a `ListView` renders a win-container DIV element which contains a win-item DIV element for each list item.

Introduction to the `ListView` Control 195

Notice that each win-container DIV element has a style attribute with an explicit width and height. All of the win-container DIV elements have the exact same width and height. The `ListView` control assigns a width and height based on the size of the first list item.

Because the style attribute takes precedence over the win-container class attribute, any width and height that you try to assign with the win-container class will be ignored.

In grid layout mode, you could use the win-item class to provide an explicit width and height for each list item. However, using the win-item class in list layout mode causes other problems. Notice that the gray background in Figure 7.8 does not stretch all of the way across.

FIGURE 7.8 Gray selection background is not wide enough

Here's the solution that I recommend. This solution works for both grid and list layout modes. I recommend that you always provide a DIV element in the `ListView` control's item template with an associated class. For example, the following template contains a `productItem` DIV element:

```
<div id="tmplProduct"
    data-win-control="WinJS.Binding.Template">
    <div class="productItem">
        <h2 data-win-bind="innerText:name"></h2>
    </div>
</div>
```

When using grid layout, you should always provide the `productItem` with an explicit width and height. For example, the following `productItem` class—applied to a `ListView` control with the ID `lvProducts`—causes each list item to be 50 pixels wide and tall and to appear with a border and padding.

```
#lvProducts .productItem {
    width: 50px;
    height: 50px;
    border: solid 1px white;
    padding: 10px;
}
```

Figure 7.9 illustrates the result of using this `productItem` class. All of the items are displayed with the same width and height.

196 CHAPTER 7 Using the `ListView` Control

Notice that the first item—the BBBBBBBB—is cut off. The default style sheet ui-dark.css and ui-light.css both set overflow:hidden. This is good because it prevents some DIV elements from being wider or taller than others, which looks bad.

FIGURE 7.9 Providing an explicit width and height

When using list layout mode, I also recommend that you create a container DIV element in the template. However, in list layout mode unlike grid layout mode, you should not supply an explicit width or height. Let the items expand to the full width of the `ListView`.

The following CSS classes—applied in list layout mode—result in a border and padding for each list item, as illustrated in Figure 7.10.

```css
#lvProducts .productItem {
    border: solid 1px white;
    padding: 10px;
}

#lvProducts.win-listview {
    width: 300px;
}
```

> **WARNING**
>
> There is a space between `#lvProducts` and `.productItem` (because it is a child selector) but there is no space between `#lvProducts.win-listview` (because it is not a child selector).

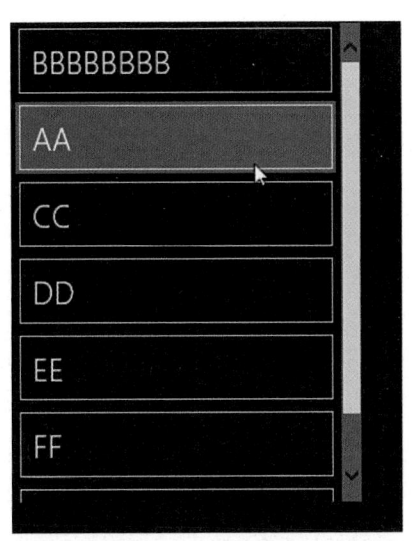

FIGURE 7.10 `ListView` items displayed in list layout mode.

Selecting Items in a `ListView` Control

The `ListView` control includes built-in support for selecting items. By default, you can select a `ListView` item by right-clicking the item or by swiping your finger up on the item.

There are three ListView events which are relevant for selecting items:

- `iteminvoked`—Occurs when a `ListView` item is tapped.
- `selectionchanging`—Occurs before the current selection changes.
- `selectionchanged`—Occurs after the current selection changes.

Invoking a list item is not the same as selecting it. When you select a list item, the `selectionchanged` event is raised and the list item appears with a checkmark. When you invoke an item, the `iteminvoked` event is raised but the item is not selected. You use the `iteminvoked` event for actions other than selecting.

There are several `ListView` properties which are relevant for selecting items:

- `selection`—Gets a `WinJS.UI.ISelection` object which has methods for setting and retrieving the selected items in a `ListView`.
- `selectionMode`—Gets or sets the selection mode. Possible values are `'none'`, `'single'`, or `'multi'`. The value `'multi'` is the default.
- `swipeBehavior`—Gets or sets a value which determines what happens when you swipe your finger up on a `ListView` item. Possible values are `'select'` and `'none'`.
- `tapBehavior`—Gets or sets a value which determines what happens when you click/tap on an item. Possible values are `'directSelect'`, `'toggleSelect'`, `'invokeOnly'`, or `'none'`.

198   CHAPTER 7   Using the `ListView` Control

The `tapBehavior` property has confusing names for its values. Depending on the value of `tapBehavior`, different combinations of the `selectionchanged` and `iteminvoked` events are raised (see Table 7.1).

TABLE 7.1   Setting the `tapBehavior` Property

	selectionchanged	iteminvoked
`'directSelect'`	yes	yes
`'toggleSelect'`	yes	yes
`'invokeOnly'`	no	yes
`'none'`	no	no

Notice that both `'directSelect'` and `'toggleSelect'` raise the `selectionchanged` and `iteminvoked` events. The difference between these values is that `'toggleSelect'` toggles the selected item and `'directSelect'` does not.

Creating a Master/Detail View

Imagine, for example, that you want to create a master/detail view with two `ListView` controls. The master `ListView` displays product categories and the details `ListView` displays products (see Figure 7.11).

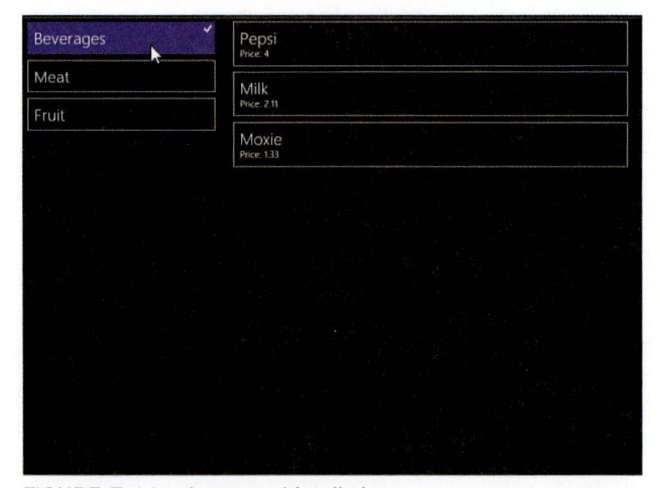

FIGURE 7.11   A master/detail view

The page in Listing 7.5 contains the necessary Template and `ListView` controls.

LISTING 7.5   Creating a Master/Detail Form (masterDetail\masterDetail.html)

```
<!-- Templates -->
<div id="tmplCategory"
    data-win-control="WinJS.Binding.Template">
```

```
    <div class="categoryItem">
        <h2 data-win-bind="innerText:categoryName"></h2>
    </div>
</div>

<div id="tmplProduct"
    data-win-control="WinJS.Binding.Template">
    <div class="productItem">
        <h2 data-win-bind="innerText:productName"></h2>
        Price: <span data-win-bind="innerText:price"></span>
    </div>
</div>

<div id="container">

    <!-- Master ListView for Categories -->
    <div id="lvCategories"
        data-win-control="WinJS.UI.ListView"
        data-win-options="{
            itemTemplate: select('#tmplCategory'),
            selectionMode: 'single',
            tapBehavior: 'directSelect',
            swipeBehavior: 'select',
            layout: {type: WinJS.UI.ListLayout}
        }"></div>

    <!-- Details ListView for Products -->
    <div id="lvProducts"
        data-win-control="WinJS.UI.ListView"
        data-win-options="{
            itemTemplate: select('#tmplProduct'),
            selectionMode: 'none',
            layout: {type: WinJS.UI.ListLayout}
        }"></div>
</div>
```

Notice that the categories ListView—the ListView with the ID lvCategories—has its selectionMode, tapBehavior, and swipeBehavior properties set. You can select categories by tapping or swiping.

The JavaScript file in Listing 7.6 contains the code for displaying the right products when a category is selected.

LISTING 7.6 Creating a Master/Detail Form (masterDetail\masterDetail.js)

```javascript
(function () {
    "use strict";

    function initialize() {
        WinJS.UI.processAll().done(function () {
            // Get references to ListView controls
            var lvProducts = document.getElementById("lvProducts").winControl;
            var lvCategories = document.getElementById("lvCategories").winControl;

            // Create array of categories and products
            var products = [
                {
                    categoryName: "Beverages",
                    products: [
                        { productName: "Pepsi", price: 4.00 },
                        { productName: "Milk", price: 2.11 },
                        { productName: "Moxie", price: 1.33 }
                    ]
                },
                {
                    categoryName: "Meat",
                    products: [
                        { productName: "Steak", price: 34.33 },
                        { productName: "Chicken", price: 2.01 }
                    ]
                },
                {
                    categoryName: "Fruit",
                    products: [
                        { productName: "Apples", price: 2.88 },
                        { productName: "Oranges", price: 7.01 }
                    ]
                }
            ];

            // Create a List of categories and products
            var listProducts = new WinJS.Binding.List(products);

            // Bind the list to the Categories ListView
            lvCategories.itemDataSource = listProducts.dataSource;

            // Handle the selectionchanged event
            lvCategories.addEventListener("selectionchanged", function () {
                if (lvCategories.selection.count() > 0) {
```

```
                lvCategories.selection.getItems().done(function (items) {
                    // Get products for first selected item
                    var selectedProducts = items[0].data.products;

                    // Convert to list
                    var listSelectedProducts = new WinJS.Binding.
➡List(selectedProducts);

                    // Bind to Products ListView
                    lvProducts.itemDataSource = listSelectedProducts.dataSource;
                });
            }
        });


    });
    }

    document.addEventListener("DOMContentLoaded", initialize);
})();
```

Both the categories and associated products are contained in a single JavaScript array named products. After being converted into a `WinJS.Binding.List`, this array is bound to the categories `ListView`.

When you select a category—by either tapping or swiping—the `ListView` `selectionchanged` event is raised. The code in Listing 7.6 contains a handler for this event:

```
// Handle the selectionchanged event
lvCategories.addEventListener("selectionchanged", function () {
    if (lvCategories.selection.count() > 0) {
        lvCategories.selection.getItems().done(function (items) {
            // Get products for first selected item
            var selectedProducts = items[0].data.products;

            // Convert to list
            var listSelectedProducts = new WinJS.Binding.List(selectedProducts);

            // Bind to Products ListView
            lvProducts.itemDataSource = listSelectedProducts.dataSource;
        });
    }
});
```

The `ListView` control's `selection.getItems()` method is called to retrieve the selected category. This method returns a promise. In the done handler for the promise, the products associated with the selected category are retrieved and converted into a `WinJS.Binding.List` object. The List is bound to the products `ListView` and the matching products are displayed.

Selecting Multiple Items

If you set the `ListView` control's `selectionMode` property to the value 'multi' then you can select more than one `ListView` item at a time.

Imagine that you want to display a list of products and enable a customer to add multiple products to a shopping cart (see Figure 7.12). In that case, you can display the products and the shopping cart with two `ListView` controls (see Listing 7.7).

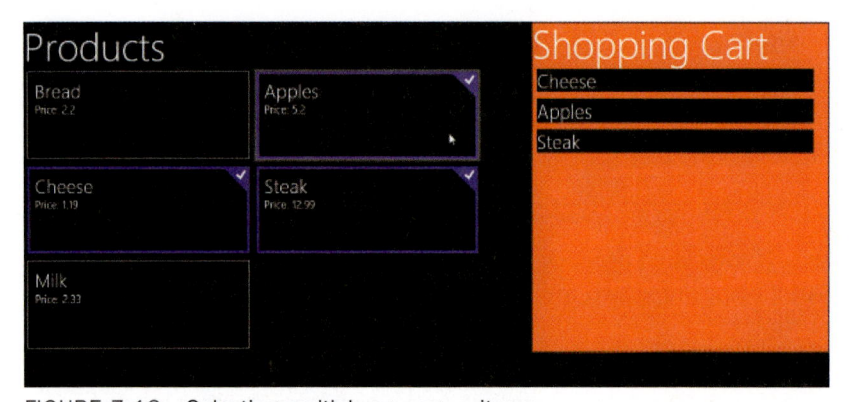

FIGURE 7.12 Selecting multiple `ListView` items

LISTING 7.7   Selecting Multiple Items (selectMultiple\selectMultiple.html)

```html
<!-- Templates -->

<div id="tmplProduct"
    data-win-control="WinJS.Binding.Template">
    <div class="productItem">
        <h2 data-win-bind="innerText:productName"></h2>
        Price: <span data-win-bind="innerText:price"></span>
    </div>
</div>

<div id="tmplShoppingCart"
    data-win-control="WinJS.Binding.Template">
    <div class="shoppingCartItem">
        <h2 data-win-bind="innerText:productName"></h2>
    </div>
</div>
```

Selecting Items in a `ListView` Control

```html
<div id="container">
    <div id="containerProducts">
        <h1>Products</h1>
        <!-- Products ListView -->
        <div id="lvProducts"
            data-win-control="WinJS.UI.ListView"
            data-win-options="{
                itemTemplate: select('#tmplProduct'),
                selectionMode: 'multi',
                tapBehavior: 'toggleSelect',
                swipeBehavior: 'select'
            }"></div>
    </div>
    <div id="containerShoppingCart">
        <h1>Shopping Cart</h1>
        <!-- Shopping Cart ListView -->
        <div id="lvShoppingCart"
            data-win-control="WinJS.UI.ListView"
            data-win-options="{
                itemTemplate: select('#tmplShoppingCart'),
                selectionMode: 'none',
                layout: {type: WinJS.UI.ListLayout}
            }"></div>
    </div>
</div>
```

Notice that the products `ListView`—the `ListView` with the ID `lvProducts`—has its `selectionMode` property set to the value `'multi'` and its `tapBehavior` property set to the value `'toggleSelect'`. The value `'toggleSelect'` causes the `ListView` item to toggle between selected and unselected when you tap it.

The JavaScript file in Listing 7.8 contains the code for copying selected items to the shopping cart. When you select an item, the `selectionchanged` event is raised and the selected items are copied into a new JavaScript array. This array is converted into a `WinJS.Binding.List` and bound to the shopping cart `ListView`.

LISTING 7.8 Selecting Multiple Items (selectMultiple\selectMultiple.js)

```javascript
(function () {
    "use strict";

    function initialize() {
        WinJS.UI.processAll().done(function () {
            // Get references to ListView controls
            var lvProducts = document.getElementById("lvProducts").winControl;
            var lvShoppingCart = document.getElementById("lvShoppingCart")
➥winControl;
```

```js
        // Create List of products
        var listProducts = new WinJS.Binding.List([
            { productName: "Bread", price: 2.20 },
            { productName: "Cheese", price: 1.19 },
            { productName: "Milk", price: 2.33 },
            { productName: "Apples", price: 5.20 },
            { productName: "Steak", price: 12.99 }
        ]);

        // Bind the list to the Products ListView
        lvProducts.itemDataSource = listProducts.dataSource;

        // Handle the selectionchanged event
        lvProducts.addEventListener("selectionchanged", function () {
            lvProducts.selection.getItems().done(function (items) {
                // Copy selected items into new array
                var selectedProducts = [];
                items.forEach(function (item) {
                    selectedProducts.push(item.data);
                });

                // Convert selected products into List
                var listProducts = new WinJS.Binding.List(selectedProducts);

                // Bind the list to the shopping cart
                lvShoppingCart.itemDataSource = listProducts.dataSource;
            });
        });


    });
    }

    document.addEventListener("DOMContentLoaded", initialize);
})();
```

Sorting Items in a ListView Control

You can sort the items displayed with a ListView control by sorting the items in the ListView control's data source. For example, you might want to sort a list of products in order of the product name or price.

The WinJS.Binding.List object supports the createSorted() method. This method accepts a sort function which returns a new WinJS.Binding.List sorted according to the function.

For example, the following code sorts a list of products in order of the product name:

```
// Create a List of products
var listProducts = new WinJS.Binding.List([
    { name: "Bread", price: 2.20 },
    { name: "Cheese", price: 1.19 },
    { name: "Milk", price: 2.33 },
    { name: "Apples", price: 5.20 },
    { name: "Steak", price: 12.99 }
]);

// Sort the products
var sortedListProducts = listProducts.createSorted(function (item1, item2) {
    return item1.name > item2.name ? 1 : -1;
});

// Bind the list of products to the ListView
lvProducts.itemDataSource = sortedListProducts.dataSource;
```

The code above uses the `createSorted()` method to create a new sorted data source based on the original unsorted products data source. The `ListView` is bound to the new data source instead of the original data source.

In the code above, the products are sorted with the following sort function:

```
function (item1, item2) {
    return item1.name > item2.name ? 1 : -1;
}
```

A sort function sorts items by returning one of three possible values:

- ▶ 0—When the two items should be sorted in the same order.
- ▶ -1—When the first item should be sorted before the second item.
- ▶ 1—When the first item should be sorted after the second item.

The `sortedListProducts` data source is a live data source. If you add a new item to the `listProducts` data source, then the new item will appear in the `ListView` in the right order. Changes to the `listProducts` data source are picked up automatically.

> **NOTE**
>
> You can use the same types of sort functions with the WinJS `createSorted()` method as you would use with the standard JavaScript array `sort()` method.

Filtering Items in a `ListView` Control

You can filter the items displayed in a `ListView` by filtering the items in the data source associated with the `ListView`. For example, when browsing through a large set of products, you might want to enable a user to filter the products by only showing products which match a filter string (see Figure 7.13).

FIGURE 7.13   Filtering a list of products

You can take an existing `WinJS.Binding.List` and create a new filtered `WinJS.Binding.List` by calling the `createFiltered()` method. This method accepts a filter function which returns either the value true or false depending on whether an item from the original list should be included in the new list.

The code in Listings 7.9 and 7.10 illustrates how you can use the `createFiltered()` method to create a `keyup` search form. The page in Listing 7.9 contains an input box and a `ListView` control.

LISTING 7.9   Filtering a List of Products (filtering\filtering.html)

```
<div>
    <input id="inputFilter" />
</div>
<div id="tmplProduct"
    data-win-control="WinJS.Binding.Template">
    <div class="productItem">
        <h2 data-win-bind="innerText:name"></h2>
        Price: <span data-win-bind="innerText:price"></span>
    </div>
</div>

<div id="lvProducts"
    data-win-control="WinJS.UI.ListView"
    data-win-options="{
        itemTemplate: select('#tmplProduct')
    }"></div>
```

Filtering Items in a `ListView` Control   207

The JavaScript code in Listing 7.10 and filters the `ListView` so it only displays products which match the filter string.

LISTING 7.10   Filtering a List of Products (filtering\filtering.js)

```javascript
(function () {
    "use strict";

    // Create a List of products
    var listProducts = new WinJS.Binding.List([
        { name: "Bread", price: 2.20 },
        { name: "Broccoli", price: 1.19 },
        { name: "Bananas", price: 2.33 },
        { name: "Apples", price: 5.20 },
        { name: "Apple Sauce", price: 12.99 }
    ]);

    function initialize() {

        WinJS.UI.processAll().done(function () {
            // Get references to DOM elements and Controls
            var lvProducts = document.getElementById("lvProducts").winControl;
            var inputFilter = document.getElementById("inputFilter");

            // Bind the unfiltered list of products to the ListView
            lvProducts.itemDataSource = listProducts.dataSource;

            inputFilter.addEventListener("keyup", function () {
                // Filter the data source
                var filteredListProducts = listProducts.createFiltered(function (item) {
                    return item.name.toLowerCase().indexOf(inputFilter.value) == 0;
                });

                // Bind the list of products to the ListView
                lvProducts.itemDataSource = filteredListProducts.dataSource;
            });

        });
    }

    document.addEventListener("DOMContentLoaded", initialize);
})();
```

208　CHAPTER 7　Using the `ListView` Control

Here's the section of code that uses the `createFiltered()` method:

```
// Filter the data source
var filteredListProducts = listProducts.createFiltered(function (item) {
    return item.name.toLowerCase().indexOf(inputFilter.value) == 0;
});

// Bind the list of products to the ListView
lvProducts.itemDataSource = filteredListProducts.dataSource;
```

The function passed to the `createFiltered()` method determines the items included in the filtered list of products. This function matches only those items in the data source which start with the text entered into the input box. So if you type "br" into the input box, then "Bread" and "Broccoli" are matched but not "Bananas".

Grouping Items in a `ListView` Control

You can group the items which appear in a `ListView` control. For example, instead of displaying a flat list of products, you can group products by product category (see Figure 7.14).

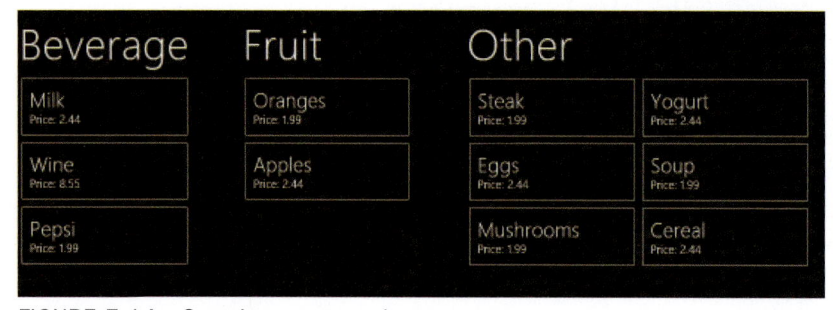

FIGURE 7.14　Grouping `ListView` items

If you want to take advantage of groups, then you need to create a grouped data source. You create a grouped data source by calling the `WinJS.Binding.List createGrouped()` method.

The code in Listing 7.11 and Listing 7.12 illustrates how you can use the `createGrouped()` method to group products by categories.

LISTING 7.11　Grouping `ListView` Items (grouped\grouped.html)

```
<!-- Templates -->
<div id="tmplProductGroupHeader" data-win-control="WinJS.Binding.Template">
    <div class="productGroupHeader">
        <h1 data-win-bind="innerText: title"></h1>
    </div>
</div>
```

```
<div id="tmplProduct"
    data-win-control="WinJS.Binding.Template">
    <div class="productItem">
        <h2 data-win-bind="innerText:name"></h2>
        Price: <span data-win-bind="innerText:price"></span>
    </div>
</div>

<!-- Products ListView -->
<div id="lvProducts"
    data-win-control="WinJS.UI.ListView"
    data-win-options="{
        itemTemplate: select('#tmplProduct'),
        groupHeaderTemplate: select('#tmplProductGroupHeader')
    }"></div>
```

The HTML page in Listing 7.11 contains two templates: one template for the group header and one template for the individual items shown in each group. The group header template is associated with the `ListView` control declaratively with the `ListView` control's `groupHeaderTemplate` property.

> **WARNING**
>
> The `ListView` control only supports groups when using grid layout mode.

LISTING 7.12 Grouping `ListView` Items (grouped\grouped.js)

```
(function () {
    "use strict";

    function initialize() {
        WinJS.UI.processAll().done(function () {
            // Get reference to ListView control
            var lvProducts = document.getElementById("lvProducts").winControl;

            // Create a List of products
            var listProducts = new WinJS.Binding.List([
                        { name: "Milk", price: 2.44, category: "Beverages" },
                        { name: "Oranges", price: 1.99, category: "Fruit" },
                        { name: "Wine", price: 8.55, category: "Beverages" },
                        { name: "Apples", price: 2.44, category: "Fruit" },
                        { name: "Steak", price: 1.99, category: "Other" },
                        { name: "Eggs", price: 2.44, category: "Other" },
                        { name: "Mushrooms", price: 1.99, category: "Other" },
                        { name: "Yogurt", price: 2.44, category: "Other" },
```

CHAPTER 7 Using the ListView Control

```
            { name: "Soup", price: 1.99, category: "Other" },
            { name: "Cereal", price: 2.44, category: "Other" },
            { name: "Pepsi", price: 1.99, category: "Beverages" }
        ]);

        // Create grouped data source
        var groupListProducts = listProducts.createGrouped(
            function (dataItem) {
                return dataItem.category;
            },
            function (dataItem) {
                return { title: dataItem.category };
            },
            function (group1, group2) {
                return group1 > group2 ? 1 : -1;
            }
        );

        // Bind the list of products to the ListView
        lvProducts.groupDataSource = groupListProducts.groups.dataSource;
        lvProducts.itemDataSource = groupListProducts.dataSource;

    });
}

document.addEventListener("DOMContentLoaded", initialize);
})();
```

The JavaScript code in Listing 7.12 is used to create both the grouped data source and the item data source. The grouped data source is created by calling the `createGrouped()` method.

Notice that the `createGrouped()` method requires three functions as arguments:

- **groupKey**—This function associates each list item with a group. The function accepts a data item and returns a key which represents a group. In the code above, we return the value of the category property for each product.

- **groupData**—This function returns the data item displayed by the group header template. For example, in the code above, the function returns a title for the group which is displayed in the group header template.

- **groupSorter**—This function determines the order in which the groups are displayed. The code above displays the groups in alphabetical order: Beverages, Fruit, Other.

The two data sources—the grouped and the item data sources—are bound to the `ListView` control with the following two lines of code:

```
// Bind the list of products to the ListView
lvProducts.groupDataSource = groupListProducts.groups.dataSource;
lvProducts.itemDataSource = groupListProducts.dataSource;
```

The grouped data source is a live data source—so the groups displayed by the `ListView` change when you change the data source. Furthermore, you can use the grouped data source with a filtered data source.

Switching Views with Semantic Zoom

Semantic Zoom is a feature of Windows 8 which enables you to view data at two different zoom levels. For example, the Windows 8 Start screen takes advantage of Semantic Zoom. By default, when you open the Start screen, you view a close up view of your apps (see Figure 7.15). However, you can zoom out to see a more far away view of your apps (see Figure 7.16).

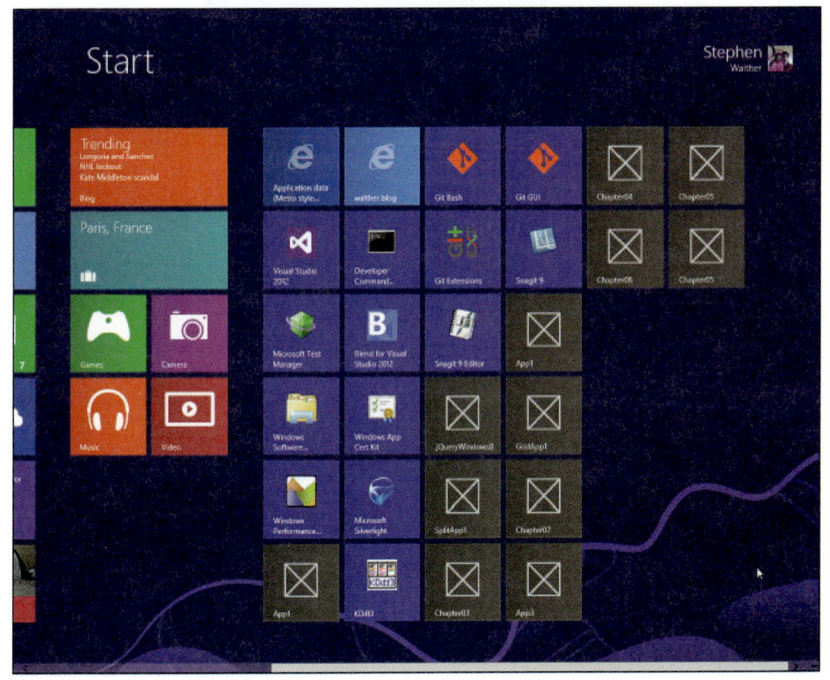

FIGURE 7.15   Default Start Screen

212   CHAPTER 7   Using the `ListView` Control

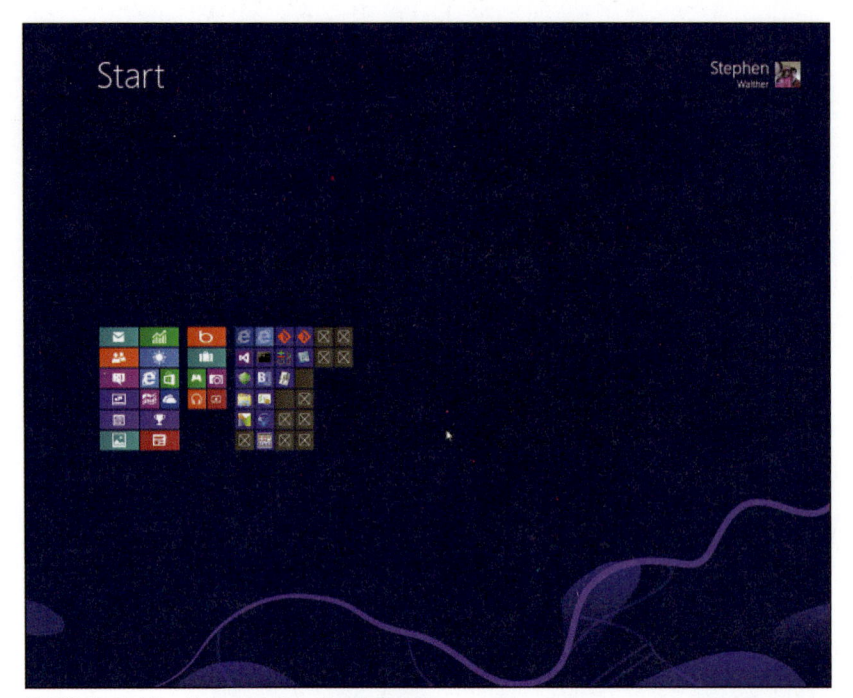

FIGURE 7.16   Zoomed Out Start Screen

When using the mouse, you can zoom out by clicking the – button which appears at the bottom right of the screen. When using touch, you can zoom in and out by using pinch and stretch gestures.

You can implement Semantic Zoom in your Windows Store app by taking advantage of the WinJS `SemanticZoom` control. When used with the `ListView` control, the `SemanticZoom` control enables you to provide two different views of the same data: the hundred foot view and the ten foot view.

Imagine that you are working with a lot of products and the products can be grouped by category. To make it easier for a user to navigate to different categories, you can take advantage of Semantic Zoom. By default, you see the products grouped into categories (Figure 7.17). However, if you zoom out, then you can see a list of categories (Figure 7.18).

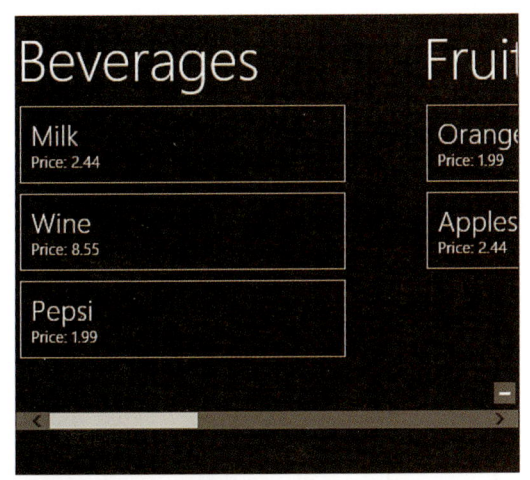

FIGURE 7.17 Using Semantic Zoom (ten foot view)

FIGURE 7.18 Using Semantic Zoom (hundred foot view)

The HTML page in Listing 7.13 illustrates how you can implement Semantic Zoom. The page contains a `SemanticZoom` control which has two child `ListView` controls. The different `ListViews` are displayed at different zoom levels.

LISTING 7.13 Zooming with Semantic Zoom (semanticZoom\semanticZoom.html)

```
<!-- Zoom In Template -->
<div id="tmplProductGroupHeader" data-win-control="WinJS.Binding.Template">
    <div class="productGroupHeader">
        <h1 data-win-bind="innerText: title"></h1>
    </div>
</div>

<div id="tmplProduct"
    data-win-control="WinJS.Binding.Template">
    <div class="productItem">
        <h2 data-win-bind="innerText:name"></h2>
        Price: <span data-win-bind="innerText:price"></span>
    </div>
```

214   CHAPTER 7   Using the `ListView` Control

```html
</div>

<!-- Zoom Out Template -->
<div id="tmplCategory"
    data-win-control="WinJS.Binding.Template">
    <div class="categoryItem">
        <h2 data-win-bind="innerText:title"></h2>
    </div>
</div>


<!-- SemanticZoom and ListViews -->
<div id="divSemanticZoom" data-win-control="WinJS.UI.SemanticZoom">
    <!-- Zoom In ListView (Products) -->
    <div id="lvProducts"
        data-win-control="WinJS.UI.ListView"
        data-win-options="{
            itemTemplate: select('#tmplProduct'),
            groupHeaderTemplate: select('#tmplProductGroupHeader')
        }"></div>

    <!-- Zoom Out ListView (Categories) -->
    <div id="lvCategories"
        data-win-control="WinJS.UI.ListView"
        data-win-options="{
            itemTemplate: select('#tmplCategory')
        }"></div>
</div>
```

Here are the lines of code from Listing 7.13 where the `SemanticZoom` control is used:

```html
<div id="divSemanticZoom" data-win-control="WinJS.UI.SemanticZoom">
    <!-- Zoom In ListView (Products) -->
    <div id="lvProducts"
        data-win-control="WinJS.UI.ListView"
        data-win-options="{
            itemTemplate: select('#tmplProduct'),
            groupHeaderTemplate: select('#tmplProductGroupHeader')
        }"></div>

    <!-- Zoom Out ListView (Categories) -->
    <div id="lvCategories"
        data-win-control="WinJS.UI.ListView"
        data-win-options="{
            itemTemplate: select('#tmplCategory')
        }"></div>
</div>
```

Switching Views with Semantic Zoom   215

The `SemanticZoom` control contains the two `ListView` controls with the different zoom levels. The `SemanticZoom` control switches between these two `ListView` controls displaying one zoom level or the other.

The JavaScript file in Listing 7.14 contains the code for implementing Semantic Zoom. A data source representing a list of products is bound to the zoomed in `ListView` control. Additionally, a grouped data source is bound to both the zoomed in and zoomed out `ListView` controls.

LISTING 7.14   Zooming with Semantic Zoom (semanticZoom\semanticZoom.js)

```javascript
(function () {
    "use strict";

    function initialize() {
        WinJS.UI.processAll().done(function () {
            // Get reference to ListView control
            var lvProducts = document.getElementById("lvProducts").winControl;

            // Create a List of products
            var listProducts = new WinJS.Binding.List([
                { name: "Milk", price: 2.44, category: "Beverages" },
                { name: "Oranges", price: 1.99, category: "Fruit" },
                { name: "Wine", price: 8.55, category: "Beverages" },
                { name: "Apples", price: 2.44, category: "Fruit" },
                { name: "Steak", price: 1.99, category: "Other" },
                { name: "Eggs", price: 2.44, category: "Other" },
                { name: "Mushrooms", price: 1.99, category: "Other" },
                { name: "Yogurt", price: 2.44, category: "Other" },
                { name: "Soup", price: 1.99, category: "Other" },
                { name: "Cereal", price: 2.44, category: "Other" },
                { name: "Pepsi", price: 1.99, category: "Beverages" }
            ]);

            // Create grouped data source
            var groupListProducts = listProducts.createGrouped(
                function (dataItem) {
                    return dataItem.category;
                },
                function (dataItem) {
                    return { title: dataItem.category };
                },
                function (group1, group2) {
                    return group1 > group2 ? 1 : -1;
                }
            );
```

216   CHAPTER 7   Using the `ListView` Control

```
        // Bind the list of products to the Zoom In ListView
        lvProducts.itemDataSource = groupListProducts.dataSource;
        lvProducts.groupDataSource = groupListProducts.groups.dataSource;

        // Bind the list of categories to the Zoom Out ListView
        lvCategories.itemDataSource = groupListProducts.groups.dataSource;
    });


    }

    document.addEventListener("DOMContentLoaded", initialize);
})();
```

Switching a `ListView` Template Dynamically

You can assign a function to the `ListView` control's `itemTemplate` property. This is great, because it means that you can switch the template used to render a `ListView` item at runtime.

Imagine, for example, that you want to display products using two templates: one template for normal products and one template for on sale products (see Figure 7.19). The HTML page in Listing 7.15 includes the two templates.

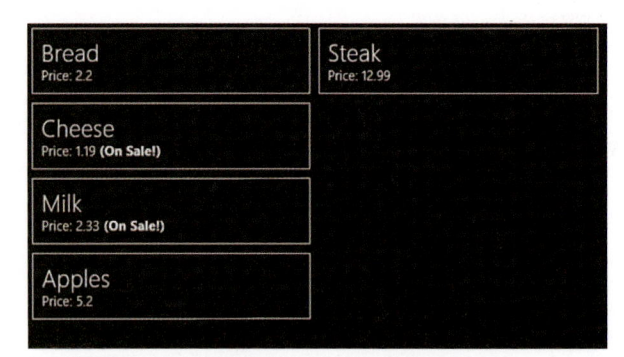

FIGURE 7.19   Switching templates dynamically

LISTING 7.15   Switching Templates Dynamically (dynamicTemplate\dynamicTemplate.js)

```html
<div id="tmplProduct"
    data-win-control="WinJS.Binding.Template">
    <div class="productItem">
        <h2 data-win-bind="innerText:name"></h2>
        Price: <span data-win-bind="innerText:price"></span>
```

```
        </div>
    </div>

    <div id="tmplProductOnSale"
        data-win-control="WinJS.Binding.Template">
        <div class="productItem">
            <h2 data-win-bind="innerText:name"></h2>
            Price: <span data-win-bind="innerText:price"></span>
            <b>(On Sale!)</b>
        </div>
    </div>


    <div id="lvProducts"
        data-win-control="WinJS.UI.ListView"></div>
```

The only difference between the normal product template and the on sale template is that the on sale template includes the message "On Sale!"

Notice that the item template used by the `ListView` control is not set declaratively. Instead, we set the template imperatively in the JavaScript file in Listing 7.16.

LISTING 7.16 Switching Templates Dynamically (dynamicTemplate\dynamicTemplate.js)

```
(function () {
    "use strict";

    function initialize() {
        WinJS.UI.processAll().done(function () {
            // Get reference to ListView control
            var lvProducts = document.getElementById("lvProducts").winControl;

            // Create a List of products
            var listProducts = new WinJS.Binding.List([
                { name: "Bread", price: 2.20 },
                { name: "Cheese", price: 1.19, onSale: true },
                { name: "Milk", price: 2.33, onSale: true },
                { name: "Apples", price: 5.20 },
                { name: "Steak", price: 12.99 }
            ]);


            // Assign an item template function
            lvProducts.itemTemplate = function (itemPromise) {
                return itemPromise.then(function (item) {
                    // Select either normal product template or on sale template
```

218 CHAPTER 7 Using the `ListView` Control

```
                    var itemTemplate = document.getElementById("tmplProduct");
                    if (item.data.onSale) {
                        itemTemplate = document.getElementById("tmplProductOnSale");
                    };

                    // Render selected template to DIV container
                    var container = document.createElement("div");
                    itemTemplate.winControl.render(item.data, container);
                    return container;
                });
            };

            // Bind the list of products to the ListView
            lvProducts.itemDataSource = listProducts.dataSource;
        });
    }

    document.addEventListener("DOMContentLoaded", initialize);
})();
```

The dynamic template switching happens in the following chunk of code, which requires some explanation:

```
lvProducts.itemTemplate = function (itemPromise) {
    return itemPromise.then(function (item) {
        // Select either normal product template or on sale template
        var itemTemplate = document.getElementById("tmplProduct");
        if (item.data.onSale) {
            itemTemplate = document.getElementById("tmplProductOnSale");
        };

        // Render selected template to DIV container
        var container = document.createElement("div");
        itemTemplate.winControl.render(item.data, container);
        return container;
    });
};
```

When each `ListView` item is rendered, a promise is passed to the function. The data item associated with the `ListView` item is not available until the promise completes. Notice that the item parameter passed to the function includes a data property which represents the data item associated with the `ListView` item. You can use the `item.data.onSale` property to determine whether a product is on sale.

When the promise completes, you can return the HTML fragment which will be rendered for the `ListView` item. In the code above, the HTML fragment is rendered with the help of either the `tmplProduct` template (for a normal product) or the `tmplProductOnSale` template (for an on sale product). The template is rendered to a DOM element named container which is returned from the function.

Loading `ListView` Items Incrementally

Imagine that you want to use the `ListView` control to scroll through a huge catalog of products. For example, a product catalog which contains thousands of products. How can you scroll through such a large catalog of products efficiently?

The `ListView` control automatically supports random access loading of data items. If you bind a `ListView` to a data source with thousands of items, the `ListView` will load and render only the subset of items required to display the current page and the previous and next pages. So, instead of rendering thousands of items, the `ListView` might only need to load and render a small number of items.

This works great when the data items can be loaded quickly. However, this approach does not work as well when the data items need to be loaded across a network (from an Ajax call). In that case, in order to create a smooth user experience, you need to incrementally load the items displayed by a `ListView` control.

The following properties are used to control how a `ListView` control loads items from its data source:

- ▶ `automaticallyLoadPages`—Gets or sets a Boolean value which determines whether the `ListView` control will load additional pages automatically. Additional pages are loaded automatically when the user scrolls beyond the number of pages specified by the `pagesToLoadThreshold` property.

- ▶ `loadingBehavior`—Gets or sets the `ListView` strategy for loading additional items. The two possible values are "`randomaccess`" and "`incremental`".

- ▶ `loadingState`—Gets a string value which represents the loading state of the `ListView`. The two possible values are "`complete`" and "`loading`".

- ▶ `pagesToLoad`—Gets or sets an integer which determines the number of new pages to load. This property is used when `automaticallyLoadPages` is enabled or the `loadMorePages()` method is called.

- ▶ `pagesToLoadThreshold`—Gets or sets an integer value which determines when a new set of pages are loaded. When `automaticallyLoadPages` is enabled, and the user scrolls beyond the `pagesToLoadThreshold`, then new pages are loaded automatically.

And you can use the following method to cause the `ListView` control to load more items manually:

- ▶ `loadMorePages`—When `loadingBehavior` has the value incremental, it causes the `ListView` control to load more pages of items. The number of items loaded is determined by the `pagesToLoad` property.

Finally, the `ListView` control raises the following event while it is in the process of loading items:

▶ `loadingstatechanged`—Raised when a `ListView` control finishes loading.

The `ListView` control's `loadingBehavior` property determines whether the `ListView` control loads items incrementally. When incremental loading is enabled, you can choose to load additional pages automatically or manually by setting the `automaticallyLoadPages` property.

For example, the JavaScript file in Listing 7.17 creates an array of products which contains 10,000 products (a really big catalog of products).

LISTING 7.17   Loading `ListView` Items Incrementally (incremental\incremental.js)

```
(function () {
    "use strict";

    function initialize() {
        WinJS.UI.processAll().done(function () {
            // Get reference to ListView control
            var lvProducts = document.getElementById("lvProducts").winControl;

            // Create an array of products
            var products = [];
            for (var i = 0; i < 10000; i++) {
                products.push({
                    name: "Product " + i,
                    price: Math.floor((Math.random() * 5000) + 1)
                });
            }

            // Create a List of products
            var listProducts = new WinJS.Binding.List(products);

            // Enable incremental loading
            lvProducts.loadingBehavior = "incremental";
            lvProducts.automaticallyLoadPages = true;
            lvProducts.pagesToLoad = 10;

            // Bind the list of products to the ListView
            lvProducts.itemDataSource = listProducts.dataSource;
        });
    }

    document.addEventListener("DOMContentLoaded", initialize);
})();
```

In Listing 7.17, incremental loading is enabled with the following lines of code:

```
lvProducts.loadingBehavior = "incremental";
lvProducts.automaticallyLoadPages = true;
lvProducts.pagesToLoad = 10;
```

When the `ListView` is first rendered, the `ListView` displays only the first 152 `ListView` items. When you scroll the `ListView` close to the end of the `ListView` items, then the next batch of 152 `ListView` items are retrieved and displayed. The items are added to the `ListView` incrementally.

> **NOTE**
>
> The exact number of items loaded by the `ListView` depends on the number of items that can be displayed in a page. Notice that you use the `ListView` pagesToLoad property to specify the number of *pages* to load and not the number of *items* to load. The exact number of items loaded by the `ListView` depends on the width and height of the `ListView` and the width and the height of the `ListView` items.
>
> The `ListView` will calculate the number of items that it can show on the screen at a time (the page size). For example, if 10 items can be shown on the screen at a time, and the `ListView` pagesToLoad property is set to the value 5, then the `ListView` will load 70 items at a time (the extra 20 is for the previous and next page).

Summary

This chapter was all about the `ListView` control. You learned how to take advantage of this control to display a collection of items in either a list or a grid.

First, I explained the basic features of this control. You learned how to select, sort, filter, and group items in a `ListView`. I also discussed several advanced features of the control, including how to switch `ListView` item templates dynamically and how to load `ListView` items incrementally.

In the next chapter, I show you how you can use a `ListView` control with different types of custom data sources including an `IndexedDB` data source and a Web Service data source.

CHAPTER 8
Creating Data Sources

IN THIS CHAPTER

- ▶ Creating Custom Data Sources
- ▶ Creating a File Data Source
- ▶ Creating a Web Service Data Source
- ▶ Creating an `IndexedDB` Data Source

The WinJS library includes two objects which you can use as data sources—the List and the `StorageDataSource` objects. If you need to use a `ListView` or `FlipView` with other types of data, then you need to write a custom data source.

The goal of this chapter is to explain how you can write custom data sources. In this chapter, I explain how you can create three custom data sources:

- ▶ `FileDataSource`—The file data source stores data on the local file system.
- ▶ `WebServiceDataSource`—The web service data source enables you to use a remote web service to retrieve and store data.
- ▶ `IndexedDBDataSource`—The `IndexedDB` data source enables you to retrieve and store data using an `IndexedDB` database.

The full source of these data sources is contained in the GitHub project for this book (https://github.com/StephenWalther/Windows8AppsUnleashed).

Creating Custom Data Sources

Let me start by giving you an overview of how you can create a custom data source. In this section, I'll explain how you can implement the methods of a custom data source which uses a JavaScript array to store data. I'll walk through creating the constructor for this data source as well as the most important methods for this data source. After discussing this (overly simple) data source in this section, we'll dive into building more practical data sources in later sections such as the web service data source and `IndexedDB` data source.

Creating the Data Source Class

The easiest way to create a custom data source is to derive a new class from the base `VirtualizedDataSource` class. For example, you can use the following code to create a new data source named `MyDataSource`:

```
var MyDataSource = WinJS.Class.derive(
    WinJS.UI.VirtualizedDataSource,
    // Constructor
    function () {
        this._adapter = new MyDataAdapter();
        this._baseDataSourceConstructor(this._adapter);
    }
);
```

In the code above, two arguments are passed to the `WinJS.Class.derive()` method to create the new `MyDataSource` class: a base class (`WinJS.UI.VirtualizedDataSource`) and a constructor for the new class.

In the constructor for your derived `VirtualizedDataSource` class, you call the `_baseDataSourceContructor()` method with a data adapter. The bulk of the work which goes into building a custom data source goes into creating this data adapter class.

Creating a Data Adapter

You create a data adapter by implementing the `IListDataAdapter` interface. This interface has the following methods:

- ▶ change()
- ▶ getCount()
- ▶ insertAfter()
- ▶ insertAtEnd()
- ▶ insertAtStart()
- ▶ insertBefore()
- ▶ itemsFromDescription()
- ▶ itemsFromEnd()
- ▶ itemsFromIndex()
- ▶ itemsFromKey()
- ▶ itemsFromStart()
- ▶ itemSignature()
- ▶ moveAfter()

- `moveBefore()`
- `moveToEnd()`
- `moveToStart()`
- `remove()`
- `setNotificationHandler()`

The interface also includes the following property:

- `compareByIdentity`

Fortunately, you don't need to actually implement all of these methods and properties. You can implement only the methods that you actually need.

For example, if you want to create a simple, read-only, data source, then you only need to implement the `getCount()` and `itemsFromIndex()` methods. If you want to create a more complicated, read-write, data source, then you need to also implement the `change()`, `insertAtEnd()`, and `remove()` methods.

In the following sections, I describe how you can implement several of these methods such as the `getCount()` and `itemsFromIndex()` methods.

Implementing the `getCount()` Method

The `getCount()` method should return the total number of records represented by the data source. For example, if you are storing items in a JavaScript array, then the `getCount()` method should return the length of the array:

```
getCount: function () {
    return WinJS.Promise.wrap(this._arrayData.length);
}
```

The `getCount()` method must return a Promise. Therefore, you either need to wrap the value in a Promise using `WinJS.Promise.wrap()` or you need to create a new Promise object.

Implementing the `itemsFromIndex()` Method

The `itemsFromIndex()` method returns a set of items from the data source. Three arguments are passed to this method:

- `requestIndex`—The index of the first item to retrieve from the data source.
- `countBefore`—The number of items before the requested index to retrieve from the data source.
- `countAfter`—The number of items after the requested index to retrieve from the data source.

The `countBefore` and `countAfter` parameters are intended to be interpreted as hints. You can return more than the `countBefore` or `countAfter` number of items if you wish.

Here's a simple implementation of the `itemsFromIndex()` method. This method returns a portion of JavaScript array.

```
itemsFromIndex: function (requestIndex, countBefore, countAfter) {
    var startIndex = Math.max(0, requestIndex - countBefore);
    var subItems = this._arrayData.slice(startIndex);
    return WinJS.Promise.wrap({
        items: subItems,
        offset: requestIndex - startIndex,
        totalCount: this._arrayData.length
    });
}
```

The `itemsFromIndex()` method should return an object which implements the `IFetchResult` interface. In the code above, three properties of the `IFetchResult` interface are returned: items, offset, and `totalCount`.

The items property represents the array of items returned by the `itemsFromIndex()` method. Each item in the items array must implement the `IListItem` interface. At the very minimum, each item must have a key and a data property.

The offset property represents the position of the item which corresponds to the `requestIndex` in the items array. If you return items before the requested index, then the offset will be greater than 0.

Finally, the `totalCount` property returns the total number of items represented by the data source and not just the number of items being returned.

Each item in the items array returned by `itemsFromIndex` must implement the `IListItem` interface. Here's a sample of the data returned from the `itemsFromIndex()` method:

```
{
  items: [
    {key:"1", data: {name: "wake up"}},
    {key:"3", data: {name: "get out of bed"}},
    {key:"4", data: {name: "drag the comb across my head"}}
  ]
  offset: 0,
  totalCount: 30
}
```

> **NOTE**
>
> In addition to the `itemsFromIndex()` method, you also can implement the `itemsFromDescription()`, `itemsFromEnd()`, `itemsFromKey()`, or `itemsFromStart()` methods. Implementing these additional methods for fetching data is optional.

Implementing the `insertAtEnd()` Method

If you want to support creating new items, then you should implement the `insertAtEnd()` method. Two arguments are passed to this method, the key of the new item and the actual new item.

Here is a sample which illustrates how you can use the `insertAtEnd()` method to add a new item to a JavaScript array.

```
insertAtEnd: function (key, data) {
    var newItem = {
        key: (++this._maxKey).toString(),
        data: data
    };
    this._arrayData.push(newItem);
    return WinJS.Promise.wrap(newItem);
}
```

Typically, you don't provide a key and you let the data source generate the key for you. Therefore, typically, you ignore the key argument. In the code above, the key is generated by adding one to the previously generated key and converting the result into a string.

> **WARNING**
>
> Data source keys must be strings.

Notice that the `insertAtEnd()` method returns the new item including its key. The method should return an object which implements the `IItem` interface wrapped in a promise.

Implementing the `remove()` Method

If you need the ability to delete an item from a data source, then you need to implement the `remove()` method. The key of the item being removed is passed to the method and the method returns nothing if the item is removed.

Here's some sample code which removes an item from an array:

```
remove: function (key) {
    var i = this._getIndexFromKey(key);
    this._arrayData.splice(i, 1);
    return WinJS.Promise.wrap(null);
},

_getIndexFromKey: function (key) {
    for (var i = 0; i < this._arrayData.length; i++) {
        if (this._arrayData[i].key == key) {
            return i;
```

228   CHAPTER 8   Creating Data Sources

```
            }
        }
}
```

Implementing the `change()` Method

If you need to support editing items in a data source, then you need to implement the `change()` method. Three arguments are passed to the `change()` method: the key of the item being edited, the new value of the item being edited, and the index of the item being edited.

Here's some sample code for implementing the `change()` method:

```
change: function (key, data, indexHint) {
    var newItem = {
        key: key,
        data: data
    };
    var i = this._getIndexFromKey(key);
    this._arrayData[i] = data;
    return new WinJS.Promise.wrap(null);
},

_getIndexFromKey: function (key) {
    for (var i = 0; i < this._arrayData.length; i++) {
        if (this._arrayData[i].key == key) {
            return i;
        }
    }
}
```

Notice that the `change()` method returns an empty promise. The method just completes without returning anything special.

Handling Errors

If there is an error when inserting, removing, or changing an item, then you can return an `EditError` object. You can return one of the following four values:

- ▶ `WinJS.UI.EditError.canceled`—Return this error when the edit operation, for whatever reason, is canceled.

- ▶ `WinJS.UI.EditError.noResponse`—Return this error when the edit operation times out.

- ▶ `WinJS.UI.EditError.notPermitted`—Return this error when writing to a read-only data source.

- ▶ `WinJS.UI.EditError.noLongerMeaningful`—Return this error when the item has already been changed.

For example, when creating a read-only data source, you can create the `insertAtEnd()` method like this:

```
insertAtEnd: function (unused, data) {
    return WinJS.Promise.wrapError(new
WinJS.ErrorFromName(WinJS.UI.EditError.notPermitted));
}
```

Implementing the `setNotificationHandler()` Method

The `setNotificationHandler()` method enables you to raise notifications when the status of a data source changes. You can call any of the following methods:

- `beginNotifications()`
- `changed()`
- `countChanged()`
- `endNotifications()`
- `indexChanged()`
- `inserted()`
- `invalidateAll()`
- `itemAvailable()`
- `moved()`
- `reload()`
- `removed()`

You don't need to raise these notifications when using the standard data adapter methods such as the `insertAtEnd()`, `remove()`, and `change()` methods discussed above. However, you will need to raise these notifications when you add a custom method to your data source.

Imagine, for example, that you want to add a `nuke()` method to your data source. When you call the `nuke()` method, all of the data is removed from your data source.

Here's how you would implement the `nuke()` method in the data adapter class:

```
setNotificationHandler: function (notificationHandler) {
    this._notificationHandler = notificationHandler;
},

nuke: function () {
    this._arrayData = [];
    this._notificationHandler.reload();
}
```

In the code above, the `setNotificationHandler()` method assigns the predefined `notificationHandler` method to a private variable named `_notificationHandler`. This makes this predefined `notificationHandler` method available to all of the methods in the data adapter.

The `nuke()` method, our custom method, sets the data source array to an empty array and calls the `notificationHandler reload()` method. If you don't call `reload()` then the `ListView` bound to the data source won't clear away its items.

Here's how you can expose the custom `nuke()` method from a data source:

```
var MyDataSource = WinJS.Class.derive(
    WinJS.UI.VirtualizedDataSource,
    // Constructor
    function (fileName) {
        this._adapter = new MyDataAdapter();
        this._baseDataSourceConstructor(this._adapter);
    },
    // Instance methods
    {
        nuke: function () {
            this._adapter.nuke();
        }
    }
);
```

The `MyDataSource` class in the code above includes a `nuke()` method. The `nuke()` method simply delegates to the data adapter `nuke()` method.

Creating a File Data Source

In this section, I discuss how you can create a custom file data source. The file data source stores and retrieves data from the file system.

> **NOTE**
> The complete source code for the `FileDataSource` is included in the GitHub source code in a folder named file.

The `FileDataSource` includes implementations of the `getCount()`, `itemsFromIndex()`, `insertAtEnd()`, `remove()`, and `change()` methods.

When you call either the `getCount()` or `itemsFromIndex()` methods, the `FileDataSource` loads its data from the file system and calls JSON.parse() to parse the file data into a JavaScript array. The `FileDataSource` loads data in its `_ensureData()` method:

Creating a File Data Source

```
_ensureData: function () {
    var that = this;

    // Attempt to return cached data
    if (this._cachedData) {
        return WinJS.Promise.wrap(that._cachedData);
    }

    // Otherwise, load from file
    return new WinJS.Promise(function (complete, error) {
        var local = WinJS.Application.local;
        var def = '{"maxKey":-1,"items":[]}';
        local.readText(that._fileName, def).done(function(fileContents) {
            that._cachedData = JSON.parse(fileContents);
            complete(that._cachedData);
        });
    });
}
```

The `readText()` method reads a text file from the file system. If the text file does not exist, then the `readText()` method returns the value of def instead. In either case, the result of reading the text file is converted into a JavaScript array with the help of the `JSON.parse()` method.

When you call the `insertAtEnd()`, `remove()`, or `change()` methods, the `FileDataSource` calls `JSON.stringify()` to convert the data into a string. The `FileDatasource` then saves the data to the file system. The `FileDataSource` saves the data in its `_saveData()` method:

```
_saveData: function (data) {
    this._cachedData = data;
    var local = WinJS.Application.local;
    var str = JSON.stringify(data);
    return local.writeText(this._fileName, str);
}
```

The `_saveData()` method converts the JavaScript array into a string with the help of a call to `JSON.stringify()`. Next, the string is saved to the file system by calling the `writeText()` method.

Using the File Data Source

Imagine that you want to create a simple task list app with the file data source. You want to be able to display a list of existing tasks and create new tasks (see Figure 8.1).

232 CHAPTER 8 Creating Data Sources

FIGURE 8.1 Task list created with a file data source

You also want to be able to delete individual tasks by right-clicking/swiping a task and clicking the Delete button (see Figure 8.2) or delete all of the tasks by clicking the Nuke button.

FIGURE 8.2 Deleting tasks with the file data source

The user interface for the task list app is contained in the HTML page in Listing 8.1. The HTML page includes a `ListView` control which displays the list of tasks.

LISTING 8.1 File Data Source (file\file.html)

```html
<!DOCTYPE html>
<html>
<head>
    <meta charset="utf-8" />
    <title>List Data Source</title>

    <!-- WinJS references -->
    <link href="//Microsoft.WinJS.1.0/css/ui-dark.css" rel="stylesheet" />
    <script src="//Microsoft.WinJS.1.0/js/base.js"></script>
    <script src="//Microsoft.WinJS.1.0/js/ui.js"></script>

    <!-- DataSources references -->
    <link href="file.css" rel="stylesheet" />
    <script type="text/javascript" src="fileDataSource.js"></script>
    <script src="file.js"></script>
</head>
<body>
    <div id="tmplTask" data-win-control="WinJS.Binding.Template">
        <div class="taskItem">
            <span data-win-bind="innerText:name"></span>
        </div>
    </div>

    <div id="lvTasks"
        data-win-control="WinJS.UI.ListView"
        data-win-options="{
            itemTemplate: select('#tmplTask'),
            selectionMode: 'single'
        }"></div>

    <form id="frmAdd">
        <fieldset>
            <legend>Add Task</legend>
            <label>New Task</label>
            <input id="inputTaskName" required />
            <button>Add</button>
        </fieldset>
    </form>
    <button id="btnNuke">Nuke</button>
    <button id="btnDelete">Delete</button>
    <button id="btnEdit">Edit</button>
```

CHAPTER 8 Creating Data Sources

```
</body>
</html>
```

The JavaScript file associated with the HTML page is contained in Listing 8.2. This JavaScript code contains the code which binds the `ListView` control to the `FileDataSource`.

LISTING 8.2 File Data Source (file\file.js)

```javascript
/// <reference path="//Microsoft.WinJS.1.0/js/base.js" />
/// <reference path="//Microsoft.WinJS.1.0/js/ui.js" />
function init() {

    WinJS.UI.processAll().done(function () {
        var lvTasks = document.getElementById("lvTasks").winControl;

        // Create data source and bind to ListView
        var tasksDataSource = new DataSources.FileDataSource("tasks.json");
        lvTasks.itemDataSource = tasksDataSource;


        // Wire-up frmAdd and Delete, Nuke buttons
        document.getElementById("frmAdd").addEventListener("submit", function (evt) {
            evt.preventDefault();
            tasksDataSource.beginEdits();
            tasksDataSource.insertAtEnd(null, {
                name: document.getElementById("inputTaskName").value
            }).done(function (newItem) {
                tasksDataSource.endEdits();
                document.getElementById("frmAdd").reset();
                lvTasks.ensureVisible(newItem.index);
            });
        });

        document.getElementById("btnDelete").addEventListener("click", function () {
            if (lvTasks.selection.count() == 1) {
                lvTasks.selection.getItems().done(function (items) {
                    tasksDataSource.beginEdits();
                    tasksDataSource.remove(items[0].key).done(function () {
                        tasksDataSource.endEdits();
                    });
                });
            }
        });
```

Creating a File Data Source

```
            document.getElementById("btnEdit").addEventListener("click", function () {
                if (lvTasks.selection.count() == 1) {
                    lvTasks.selection.getItems().done(function (items) {
                        tasksDataSource.beginEdits();
                        tasksDataSource.change(items[0].key, { name: "Changed!"
➥ }).done(function () {
                            tasksDataSource.endEdits();
                        });
                    });
                }
            });

            document.getElementById("btnNuke").addEventListener("click", function () {
                tasksDataSource.nuke();
            });

        });

    }

    document.addEventListener("DOMContentLoaded", init);
```

The file data source is created and bound to the `ListView` with the following two lines of code:

```
var tasksDataSource = new DataSources.FileDataSource("tasks.json");
lvTasks.itemDataSource = tasksDataSource;
```

The name of the file to create is passed to the constructor of the `FileDataSource`. In the code above, a file named tasks.json is used to store the list of tasks.

New tasks are created with the help of the following code:

```
document.getElementById("frmAdd").addEventListener("submit", function (evt) {
    evt.preventDefault();
    tasksDataSource.beginEdits();
    tasksDataSource.insertAtEnd(null, {
        name: document.getElementById("inputTaskName").value
    }).done(function (newItem) {
        tasksDataSource.endEdits();
        document.getElementById("frmAdd").reset();
        lvTasks.ensureVisible(newItem.index);
    });
});
```

When you submit the HTML form for adding new tasks, the file data source `insertAtEnd()` method is called to create the new task. If the new task is successfully created, then the `ListView` control's `ensureVisible()` method is called to ensure that the new task is scrolled into view.

> **WARNING**
> Always call `beginEdits()` and `endEdits()` when inserting, editing, or deleting data with a data source. If you neglect to use `beginEdits()` and `endEdits()` then you can get null reference exceptions when you edit items too fast.

Creating a Web Service Data Source

In this section, I discuss how you can build a web service data source. The web service data source enables you to bind a `ListView` control to a remote web service. You can use the data source to both retrieve and modify data.

You can use the web service data source, for example, to retrieve a list of products from a catalog of products stored in a database on a remote website. That way, when the catalog of products is updated, your Windows Store app will display the latest products.

> **NOTE**
> When working with Ajax, I strongly recommend that you take advantage of the free Fiddler2 tool to help debug failed Ajax requests. You can download Fiddler2—which works great with Windows 8—from http://fiddler2.com.

> **NOTE**
> The complete source code for the `WebServiceDataSource` is included in the GitHub source in a folder named webService.

Creating the Data Source

The web service data source uses the `WinJS.xhr()` method to make the Ajax calls to the remote web service. For example, the `getCount()` method looks like this:

```
getCount: function () {
    var that = this;

    return new WinJS.Promise(function (complete, error) {
        var options = {
            url: that._url + "/getCount"
        };
        return WinJS.xhr(options).then(function (xhr) {
            var count = JSON.parse(xhr.response);
```

```
            complete(count);
        },
        function (xhr) {
            console.log("Could not call getCount()");
        });
    });
}
```

The `getCount()` method invokes a remote web service action named `getCount()` by performing an HTTP GET request.

The `remove()` method invokes a remote web service action named `remove()` by performing an HTTP DELETE request. The `remove()` method looks like this:

```
remove: function(key) {
    var that = this;
    return new WinJS.Promise(function (complete, error) {
        var options = {
            url: that._url + "/remove/" + key,
            type: "DELETE",
            headers: {
                authenticationToken: that._authenticationToken
            }
        };
        WinJS.xhr(options).then(
            function (xhr) {
                complete();
            },
            function (xhr) {
                console.log("Could not call remove()");
            }
        );
    });
}
```

In general, each method of the web service data source delegates to a remote web service action with the same name.

Creating the Web Service

There are several ways that you can create a web service. Even if you restrict yourself to Microsoft technologies, you have several options. You can create a WCF service, a WCF Data Service, an ASMX web service, a Windows Azure Mobile Services service, or an ASP.NET Web API service.

I decided to create a web service by taking advantage of the ASP.NET Web API. You can add a Web API controller to either an ASP.NET Web Forms or an ASP.NET MVC project. I

238 CHAPTER 8 Creating Data Sources

decided to create an ASP.NET MVC 4 project. When creating the ASP.NET MVC 4 project, I selected the Web API project template (see Figure 8.3).

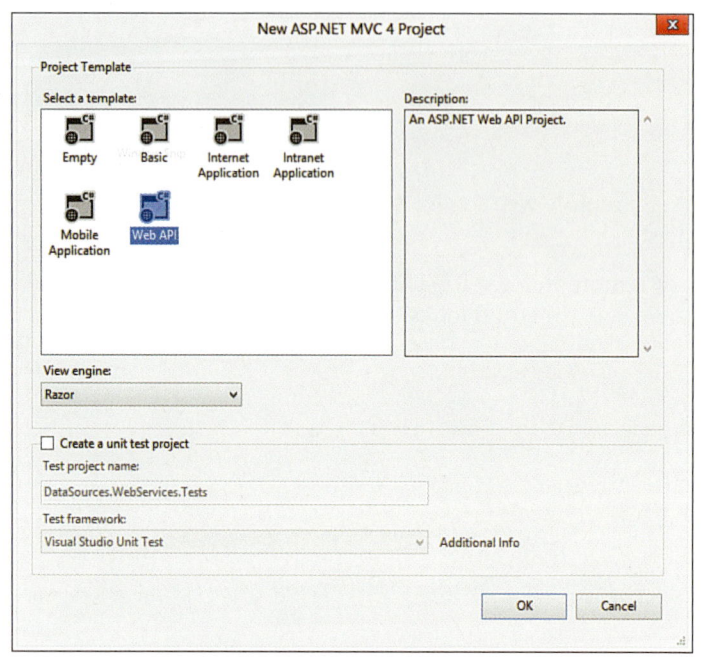

FIGURE 8.3 Creating an ASP.NET MVC 4 project using the Web API project template

To take advantage of an ASP.NET Web API service, you need to add the right routes to the App_Start\RouteConfig.cs file. These routes map incoming browser requests to the correct API controller and API controller action.

I added the following routes to the App_Start\RouteConfig.cs file:

```
routes.MapHttpRoute(
    name: "TasksGetCount",
    routeTemplate: "api/tasks/getCount",
    defaults: new { controller="tasks", action="getCount" }
);

routes.MapHttpRoute(
    name: "TasksItemsFromIndex",
    routeTemplate: "api/tasks/itemsFromIndex",
    defaults: new { controller = "tasks", action = "itemsFromIndex" }
);

routes.MapHttpRoute(
    name: "TasksInsertAtEnd",
    routeTemplate: "api/tasks/insertAtEnd",
    defaults: new { controller = "tasks", action = "insertAtEnd" }
```

```
);

routes.MapHttpRoute(
    name: "TasksRemove",
    routeTemplate: "api/tasks/remove/{key}",
    defaults: new { controller = "tasks", action = "remove" }
);

routes.MapHttpRoute(
    name: "TasksNuke",
    routeTemplate: "api/tasks/nuke",
    defaults: new { controller = "tasks", action = "nuke" }
);
```

For example, when you make an HTTP GET request for /api/tasks/getcount, then the `TasksController.GetCount()` Web API controller action is invoked.

The Web API Controller is named `TasksController`. It contains `GetCount()`, `ItemsFromIndex()`, `InsertAtEnd()`, `Remove()`, and `Nuke()` controller actions. The controller actions use the Microsoft Entity Framework to interact with a database table of tasks.

Here's what the `GetCount()` controller action looks like:

```
[HttpGet]
public int GetCount() {
    return _db.Tasks.Count();
}
```

The `GetCount()` method returns the total number of tasks stored in the Tasks database table. Notice that the `GetCount()` method is decorated with an [HttpGet] attribute. This attribute enables you to invoke the `GetCount()` method by performing an Ajax GET request.

The `Remove()` controller action looks like this:

```
[HttpDelete]
public bool Remove(string key)
{
    var id = int.Parse(key);
    _db.Tasks.Remove(_db.Tasks.Find(id));
    _db.SaveChanges();
    return true;
}
```

The `Remove()` controller action accepts a key argument which represents the item to be deleted. The key argument must be a string argument because the WinJS ListView/data source requires keys to be strings.

Notice that the `Remove()` method is decorated with an `[HttpDelete]` attribute. The `Remove()` action can be invoked only with an HTTP DELETE request.

There is one wrinkle when using non-standard HTTP methods such as the HTTP DELETE or HTTP PUT methods. You must add the following section to the ASP.NET MVC application's root Web.config file:

```
<system.webServer>
  <modules runAllManagedModulesForAllRequests="true">
  </modules>
</system.webServer>
```

If you don't add the section above to the Web.config file, then all HTTP DELETE requests return 404 status codes.

Using the Web Service Data Source

After you create and configure the remote web service, using the web service data source is straightforward. The following code illustrates how you can create an instance of the web service data source and bind it to a `ListView` control named `lvTasks`:

```
var lvTasks = document.getElementById("lvTasks").winControl;
var tasksDataSource = new
DataSources.WebServiceDataSource("http://localhost:51807/api/tasks", "id");
lvTasks.itemDataSource = tasksDataSource;
```

When you create an instance of the web service data source, you must supply two arguments to the constructor: the URL of the web service and the name of the primary key property of the data to retrieve.

The URL http://localhost:51807/api/tasks is the address of a local web service using port 51807. This port is generated randomly. You can determine the port number used by a Visual Studio project by opening the Project Properties dialog and selecting the Web tab (see Figure 8.4).

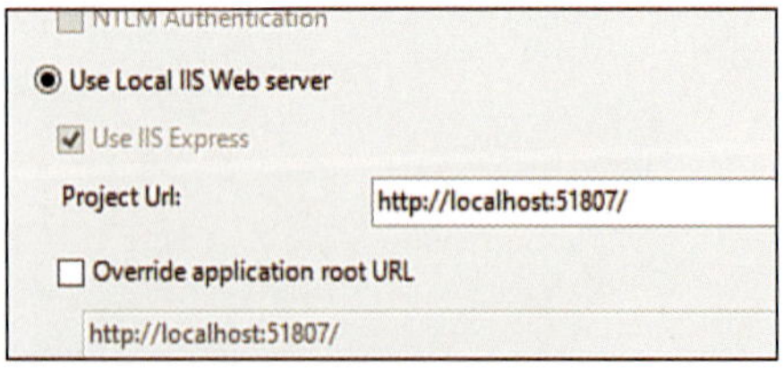

FIGURE 8.4   Determining the port number used by a Visual Studio project

> **NOTE**
>
> If you want to avoid building custom web services with the ASP.NET Web API then a great alternative is to take advantage of Windows Azure Mobile Services. Windows Azure Mobile Services enable you to easily store and retrieve data in the Windows Azure cloud. Learn more at https://www.windowsazure.com/en-us/develop/mobile/.

Creating an `IndexedDB` Data Source

The Indexed Database API (`IndexedDB`) is a W3C recommendation for exposing a database in the browser. The IndexedDB recommendation is supported by Firefox 12, Chrome 19, and IE 10. And, of course, the IndexedDB recommendation is supported by Windows Store apps.

Behind the scenes, different browsers use different databases behind the IndexedDB API. For example, Firefox uses SqlLite and IE uses SQLCE. The IndexedDB API provides a standard way to interact with these databases across browsers and across platforms.

If you need to store lots of data in a Windows Store app, and query subsets of the data, then IndexedDB is a good choice. Because IndexedDB supports indexes and cursors, you can work efficiently with large sets of data.

In this section, I discuss how you can create an IndexedDB data source. I discuss how you can build a simple app which enables you to filter a list of movies by category (see Figure 8.5).

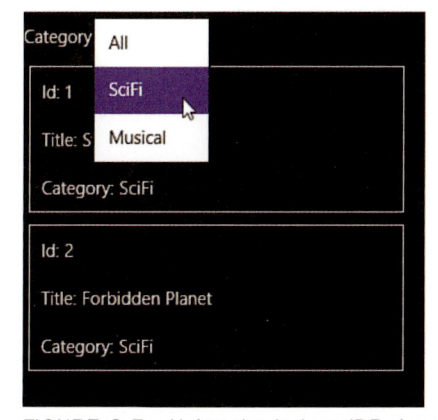

FIGURE 8.5   Using the IndexedDB data source

Overview of `IndexedDB`

An IndexedDB database might be different than the type of database that you normally use. An IndexedDB database is an object-oriented database and not a relational database. Instead of storing data in tables, you store data in object stores. An IndexedDB database contains one or more object stores which contain a collection of JavaScript objects.

The IndexedDB API includes both asynchronous and synchronous methods. Currently, only the asynchronous methods are widely supported by browsers. If you want to open a database connection, add an object to an object store, or get a count of items in an object store, then you need to perform these operations asynchronously.

Creating or Connecting to an IndexedDB Database

You don't create a new IndexedDB database upfront—instead, you create a new database when a user first connects to your database. You create new IndexedDB databases by handling the `upgradeneeded` event when attempting to open a connection to an IndexedDB database.

For example, here's how you would both open a connection to an existing database named TasksDB and create the TasksDB database when it does not already exist:

```javascript
var reqOpen = window.indexedDB.open("TasksDB", 2);
reqOpen.onupgradeneeded = function (evt) {
    var newDB = evt.target.result;
    newDB.createObjectStore("tasks", { keyPath: "id", autoIncrement: true });
};
reqOpen.onsuccess = function () {
    var db = reqOpen.result;
    // Do something with db
};
```

When you call `window.indexedDB.open()`, and the database does not already exist, then the `upgradeneeded` event is raised. In the code above, the `upgradeneeded` handler creates a new object store named tasks. The new object store has an auto-increment column named id which acts as the primary key column.

If the database already exists with the right version, and you call `window.indexedDB.open()`, then the success event is raised. At that point, you have an open connection to the existing database and you can start doing something useful with the database.

Adding Objects to an Object Store

You use asynchronous methods to interact with an `IndexedDB` database. For example, the following code illustrates how you would add a new object to the tasks object store:

```javascript
var transaction = db.transaction("tasks", "readwrite");
var store = transaction.objectStore("tasks");
var reqAdd = store.add({
    name: "Feed the dog"
});
reqAdd.onsuccess = function () {
    // Task added successfully
};
```

Creating an IndexedDB Data Source

The code above creates a new read-write database transaction, adds a new task to the tasks object store, and handles the success event. If the new task gets added successfully, then the success event is raised.

Getting a Count of Objects in an Object Store

You can get a count of the number of objects in a particular object store by taking advantage of the `count()` method. For example, you can use the following code to determine the number of items in the tasks objects store:

```javascript
var transaction = db.transaction("tasks");
var store = transaction.objectStore("tasks");
var reqCount = store.count();
reqCount.onsuccess = function (evt) {
    var count = evt.target.result;
    console.log(count);
};
```

The code above creates a new read-only database transaction and gets a count of the number of objects in the tasks object store by calling the `count()` method.

Notice that the call to the `count()` method is asynchronous. You get the count by handling the success event and reading the `target.result` property.

Retrieving Objects from an Object Store

You retrieve objects from an object store by opening a cursor and moving through the cursor one object at a time. For example, the following code opens a cursor which returns the objects from the tasks object store:

```javascript
var items = [];
var transaction = db.transaction("tasks");
var store = transaction.objectStore("tasks");
var req = store.openCursor();
req.onsuccess = function (evt) {
    var cursor = evt.target.result;
    if (cursor) {
        items.push(cursor.value);
        cursor.continue();
    } else {
        // All done!
    }
}
```

When you open a cursor, and nothing goes wrong, then the success event is raised. You can use `cursor.value` to get the current object. Calling `cursor.continue()` moves the cursor forward and raises the success event again.

When you reach the end of the cursor, then cursor will have the value null. In that case, you know that you have retrieved all of the objects from the object store.

> **NOTE**
> `cursor.continue()` advances by a single object. If you need to advance by more than one object, then you can use `cursor.advance()`.

Using Indexes and Key Ranges

When you create a database, you can create indexes on object properties. An index enables you to efficiently retrieve objects which match a value or range of values.

Here's how you would create a tasks object store which includes an index on its `dateCreated` property:

```
var reqOpen = window.indexedDB.open("TasksDB", 2);
reqOpen.onupgradeneeded = function (evt) {
    var newDB = evt.target.result;
    var store=newDB.createObjectStore("tasks", { keyPath: "id", autoIncrement: true
➥});
    store.createIndex("dateCreatedIndex", "dateCreated");
};
```

After you create an index, you can retrieve objects from an object store by using the index with a key range. A key range represents the criteria which an index uses to match objects in a store.

When creating a key range, you can specify the following properties:

- `only`—Enables you to retrieve only the objects which match the supplied value.
- `lowerBound`—Enables you to retrieve all objects which have a value greater than the supplied value.
- `upperBound`—Enables you to retrieve all objects which have a value less than the supplied value.
- `bound`—Enables you to retrieve all objects which have a value greater than or less than the supplied values.

For example, here is how you would retrieve all of the tasks from the tasks object store which were created before 1999:

```
var items = [];
var transaction = db.transaction("tasks");
var store = transaction.objectStore("tasks");
var index = store.index("dateCreatedIndex");
var keyRange = IDBKeyRange.upperBound(new Date("1/1/1999"));
```

Creating an `IndexedDB` Data Source   245

```
var req = index.openCursor(keyRange);
req.onsuccess = function (evt) {
    var cursor = evt.target.result;
    if (cursor) {
        items.push(cursor.value);
        cursor.continue();
    } else {
        // All done!
    }
}
```

You also can use an index when getting a count of objects which match a particular key range. For example, the following code gets a count of the number of tasks which were created before 1999:

```
var transaction = db.transaction("tasks");
var store = transaction.objectStore("tasks");
var index = store.index("dateCreatedIndex");
var keyRange = IDBKeyRange.upperBound(new Date("1/1/1999"));
var req = index.count(keyRange);
req.onsuccess = function (evt) {
    var count = evt.target.result;
}
```

Using the `IndexedDB` Data Source

The `IndexedDB` data source enables you to bind a `ListView` control to a collection of JavaScript objects stored in an `IndexedDB` database. You create an `IndexedDB` data source by providing three arguments:

- ▶ `objectStoreName`—The name of the object store to represent with the data source.

- ▶ `creationOptions`—The `creationOptions` determine how the `IndexedDB` database and object store are created.

- ▶ `cursorOptions` (optional)—If you supply `cursorOptions`, then you can filter the objects in the object store using a key range.

For example, here is how you would create an instance of the `IndexedDB` data source which represents a collection of movies:

```
// Create the data source options
var createOptions = {
    databaseName: "MoviesDB",
    databaseVersion: 1,
    indexNames: ["category"]
};
```

246 CHAPTER 8 Creating Data Sources

```
// Create the IndexedDB data source
var moviesDataSource = new DataSources.IndexedDbDataSource("movies", createOptions);
```

In the code above, the `creationOptions` represent the properties of an `IndexedDB` database, object store, and indexes. If the database does not already exist, then the `IndexedDB` data source creates the database.

Here are the properties of the `creationOption` object:

- **databaseName**—The name of the `IndexedDB` database
- **databaseVersion**—The version of the `IndexedDB` database
- **indexNames**—An index is created for each property name in this array.

When you create an instance of the `IndexedDB` data source, you also have the option of supplying a `cursorOptions` object. The `cursorOptions` object filters the object store. Here are the properties of the `cursorOptions` object:

- **indexName**—Create a key range using this index.
- **only**—Create a key range and only return objects which match this value.
- **lowerBound**—Create a key range and only return objects which have a value greater than this lower bound.
- **upperBound**—Create a key range and only return objects which have a value less than this upper bound.

For example, here is how you would filter tasks so that only tasks created before 1999 are returned:

```
WinJS.UI.processAll().done(function () {
    var lvTasks = document.getElementById("lvTasks").winControl;

    var createOptions = {
        indexNames: ["dateCreated"],
        databaseVersion: 3
    };

    var cursorOptions = {
        indexName: "dateCreated",
        upperBound: new Date("1/1/1999")
    };

    var tasksDataSource = new DataSources.IndexedDbDataSource("tasks",
➥createOptions, cursorOptions);
    lvTasks.itemDataSource = tasksDataSource;
});
```

Creating an `IndexedDB` Data Source   247

In the code above, the `createOptions` object causes the tasks object store to be created with an index on its `dateCreated` property. The `cursorOptions` object uses that index to return only those tasks which have a `dateCreated` below the `upperBound` 1/1/1999.

I want to show you a more complete sample of using the `IndexedDB` data source. The Movie app contained in Listing 8.3 and Listing 8.4 enables you to select different movie categories and display only the movies in the selected category. The app also enables you to create new movies and delete existing movies (see Figure 8.6).

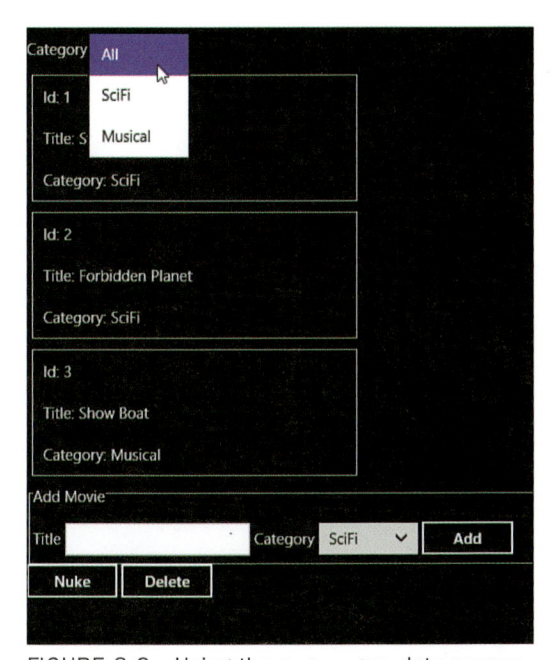

FIGURE 8.6   Using the `IndexedDB` data source

LISTING 8.3   Creating a Movie App with the `IndexedDB` Data Source (indexedDb\indexedDb.html)

```html
<!DOCTYPE html>
<html>
<head>
    <meta charset="utf-8" />
    <title>DataSources</title>

    <!-- WinJS references -->
    <link href="//Microsoft.WinJS.1.0/css/ui-dark.css" rel="stylesheet" />
    <script src="//Microsoft.WinJS.1.0/js/base.js"></script>
    <script src="//Microsoft.WinJS.1.0/js/ui.js"></script>

    <!-- DataSources references -->
    <link href="indexedDb.css" rel="stylesheet" />
```

CHAPTER 8 Creating Data Sources

```html
    <script type="text/javascript" src="indexedDbDataSource.js"></script>
    <script src="indexedDb.js"></script>
</head>
<body>

    <div id="tmplMovie" data-win-control="WinJS.Binding.Template">
        <div class="movieItem">
            Id: <span data-win-bind="innerText:id"></span>
            <br /><br />
            Title: <span data-win-bind="innerText:title"></span>
            <br /><br />
            Category: <span data-win-bind="innerText:category"></span>
        </div>
    </div>

    <div>
        <label>Category</label>
        <select id="selectCategory">
            <option>All</option>
            <option>SciFi</option>
            <option>Musical</option>
        </select>
    </div>

    <div id="lvMovies"
        data-win-control="WinJS.UI.ListView"
        data-win-options="{
            itemTemplate: select('#tmplMovie'),
            selectionMode: 'single'
        }"></div>


    <form id="frmAdd">
        <fieldset>
            <legend>Add Movie</legend>
            <div>
                <label>Title</label>
                <input id="inputMovieTitle" required />

                <label>Category</label>
                <select id="selectMovieCategory">
                    <option>SciFi</option>
                    <option>Musical</option>
                </select>
                <button>Add</button>
            </div>
```

```
            </fieldset>
        </form>


        <button id="btnNuke">Nuke</button>
        <button id="btnDelete">Delete</button>

</body>
</html>
```

The HTML page in Listing 8.3 contains a select list which enables you to select a movie category (All, SciFi, Musical). When you select a particular movie category, only those movies in the category are displayed in a `ListView` control.

LISTING 8.4 Creating a Movie App with the `IndexedDB` Data Source (indexedDb\indexedDb.js)

```
/// <reference path="//Microsoft.WinJS.1.0/js/base.js" />
/// <reference path="//Microsoft.WinJS.1.0/js/ui.js" />


function init() {

    WinJS.UI.processAll().done(function () {
        var lvMovies = document.getElementById("lvMovies").winControl;

        // Create the data source options
        var createOptions = {
            databaseName: "MoviesDB",
            databaseVersion: 1,
            indexNames: ["category"]
        };

        // Create the IndexedDB data source
        var moviesDataSource = new
➥DataSources.IndexedDbDataSource("movies", createOptions);

        // Add seed data
        addSeedData().done(function () {

            // Bind data source to ListView
            lvMovies.itemDataSource = moviesDataSource;
        });


        function addSeedData() {
            return new WinJS.Promise(function (complete) {
```

CHAPTER 8 Creating Data Sources

```javascript
            moviesDataSource.getCount().then(function (count) {
                if (count > 0) {
                    complete();
                } else {
                    var seedData = [
                        { title: "Star Wars", category: "SciFi" },
                        { title: "Forbidden Planet", category: "SciFi" },
                        { title: "Show Boat", category: "Musical" }
                    ];

                    var promises = [];
                    seedData.forEach(function (data) {
                        promises.push(moviesDataSource.insertAtEnd(null,
➥data));
                    });
                    WinJS.Promise.join(promises).done(function () {
                        complete();
                    });
                }
            });
        });
    }


    // Wire-up SelectCategory, Add, Delete, Nuke buttons
    document.getElementById("selectCategory").addEventListener("change",
➥function (evt) {
        var category = document.getElementById("selectCategory").
➥value;
        if (category === "All") {
            moviesDataSource = new DataSources.IndexedDbDataSource("movies",
➥createOptions);
        } else {
            var cursorOptions = {
                indexName: "category",
                only: document.getElementById("selectCategory").value
            };
            moviesDataSource = new DataSources.IndexedDbDataSource("movies",
➥createOptions, cursorOptions);
        }
        lvMovies.itemDataSource = moviesDataSource;
    });


    document.getElementById("frmAdd").addEventListener("submit",
➥function (evt) {
```

Creating an IndexedDB Data Source 251

```javascript
                evt.preventDefault();
                moviesDataSource.beginEdits();
                moviesDataSource.insertAtEnd(null, {
                    title: document.getElementById("inputMovieTitle").value,
                    category: document.getElementById("selectMovieCategory").value
                }).done(function (newItem) {
                    moviesDataSource.endEdits();
                    document.getElementById("frmAdd").reset();
                    lvMovies.ensureVisible(newItem.index);
                });
            });

            document.getElementById("btnDelete").addEventListener("click", function () {
                if (lvMovies.selection.count() == 1) {
                    moviesDataSource.beginEdits();
                    lvMovies.selection.getItems().done(function (items) {
                        moviesDataSource.remove(items[0].key);
                        moviesDataSource.endEdits();
                    });
                }
            });

            document.getElementById("btnNuke").addEventListener("click", function () {
                moviesDataSource.nuke();
            });

        });
    }

    document.addEventListener("DOMContentLoaded", init);
```

Listing 8.4 contains the JavaScript code for the Movie app. When you first open the app, an `IndexedDB` data source is created without any `cursorOption` and all of the movies stored in the movies object store are displayed:

```javascript
// Create the IndexedDB data source
var moviesDataSource = new DataSources.IndexedDbDataSource("movies", createOptions);

// Add seed data
addSeedData().done(function () {
    // Bind data source to ListView
    lvMovies.itemDataSource = moviesDataSource;
});
```

Notice that the code above also includes a call to a method named `addSeedData()`. This method adds initial seed data to the `IndexedDB` database so the database is not empty when you first run the Movie app.

If you select a particular movie category using the select list, then the following code executes:

```
document.getElementById("selectCategory").addEventListener("change",
function (evt) {
    var category = document.getElementById("selectCategory").value;
    if (category === "All") {
        moviesDataSource = new DataSources.IndexedDbDataSource("movies",
➥createOptions);
    } else {
        var cursorOptions = {
            indexName: "category",
            only: document.getElementById("selectCategory").value
        };
        moviesDataSource = new DataSources.IndexedDbDataSource("movies",
➥createOptions, cursorOptions);
    }
    lvMovies.itemDataSource = moviesDataSource;
});
```

This code uses a `cursorOption` object to create a new `IndexedDB` data source which only represents a subset of objects from the movies store.

Summary

In this chapter, I focused on creating custom data sources which you can use with the controls in the WinJS library. You learned how to derive a new data source from the base `VirtualizedDataSource` class.

I discussed three custom data sources. First, I created a file data source which enables you to store and retrieve data from your computer's file system. Next, I created a web service data source which enables you to interact with a remote web service. Finally, I discussed how you can create a data source which works with `IndexedDB`.

CHAPTER 9

App Events and States

IN THIS CHAPTER

▶ App Events

▶ Suspending, Terminating, and Resuming an App

▶ Application View States

The goal of this chapter is to explain Windows Store app events, lifecycle, and view states. In the first part, I explain the standard sequence of events which are raised whenever you start a Windows Store app. You learn how to handle the loaded, activated, and ready events.

In the next part, I explain how you can handle application suspension, termination, and resumption. You learn how to store and retrieve the state of your application in session state so you can maintain the illusion that your app is always running.

Finally, I discuss application view states. You learn how to switch among snapped, filled, and full-screen view states and how to detect different view states using media queries from both CSS and JavaScript.

App Events

Whenever you launch a Windows Store app, the following WinJS application events are fired in the following order:

- **WinJS.Application.loaded**—Triggered by the standard browser DOMContentLoaded event, right after the HTML document has finished loading.

- **WinJS.Application.activated**—Triggered when your application is activated.

- **WinJS.Application.ready**—Triggered after the loaded and activated events.

- **WinJS.Application.unload**—Triggered by the standard browser beforeunload event, right before a page is unloaded.

You also can handle these other application events which are triggered by particular events:

- `WinJS.Application.error`—Triggered by an unhandled error in your application.
- `WinJS.Application.checkpoint`—Triggered when your application is being suspended.
- `WinJS.Application.settings`—Triggered when application settings are changed.

None of these events are raised unless you call `WinJS.Application.start()`. The events are queued and the events are not raised until the `WinJS.Application.start()` method is called.

The following JavaScript code illustrates how you can create a handler for each of these events and log when the event happens to the Visual Studio JavaScript console window:

```javascript
WinJS.Application.addEventListener("loaded", function (evt) {
    console.log("loaded");
});
WinJS.Application.addEventListener("activated", function (evt) {
    console.log("activated");
});
WinJS.Application.addEventListener("ready", function (evt) {
    console.log("ready");
});
```

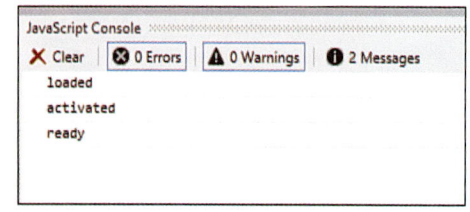

FIGURE 9.1 Logging WinJS Application events

Handling the Activated Event

The activated event is raised when a Windows Store app is activated (started). A Windows Store app can be activated in several different ways and you can use the `ActivationKind` property to determine exactly how the app was activated:

```javascript
WinJS.Application.addEventListener("activated", function (evt) {
    var activationKind = Windows.ApplicationModel.Activation.ActivationKind;
    switch (evt.detail.kind) {
        case activationKind.launch:
            console.log("Launched from a tile");
            break;
        case activationKind.search:
```

```
            console.log("Activated from a search");
            break;
        default:
            console.log("Activated for some other reason");
    }
});
```

The most common way in which a Windows Store app is activated is when a user clicks the tile for the app in the Start screen. In that case, the `ActivationKind` enumeration has the value Launch.

However, there are other ways that a Windows Store app can be activated. For example, an app can be activated in response to a user performing a search from the Search charm, or in response to a user sharing something from the Share charm, or in response to a user clicking on a file from another app like an email app. In these cases, you can use the `ActivationKind` property to determine the exact reason that the app was activated.

Handling the Error Event

By default, when there is an unhandled error in a Windows Store app—an error which is not handled within a try…catch block—the following three things happen:

1. The error is logged by calling the `WinJS.log()` method
2. The debugger statement is called to break into the debugger when the app is running in Visual Studio in Debug mode.
3. The app is terminated by calling the `MSApp.terminateApp()` method.

After the `terminateApp()` method is called, the user is thrown back to the Windows Start Screen (violently, unexpectedly, and without explanation).

You can handle the application error event to provide a better user experience. For example, here's how you can display a message to the user when an unhandled error happens:

```
WinJS.Application.addEventListener("error", function (evt) {
    var message = new Windows.UI.Popups.MessageDialog(
        "There was an error."
    );
    message.showAsync();
    return true;
});

WinJS.Application.addEventListener("ready", function () {
    throw new WinJS.ErrorFromName("MyError", "Yikes! An Error!");
});

WinJS.Application.start();
```

The previous code displays a model dialog when there is an error with the message "There was an error." (see Figure 9.2).

FIGURE 9.2 Displaying an error message

Notice that the error handler returns the value true. When the error handler returns true, the error is considered handled and the app is not terminated. If you want to terminate the app after executing your custom error handler code, then don't return true.

> **WARNING**
> If the error happens before the `WinJS.application.start()` method is called, then your custom error handler won't be invoked.

Deferring Events with Promises

`WinJS.Application` events are different than normal DOM events because they support promises. You can execute an asynchronous task during a `WinJS.Application` event and delay the next event until a promise completes.

For example, the `default.js` file created when you create a new Windows Store app project delays the completion of the `WinJS.Application.activated` event until the asynchronous call to `WinJS.UI.processAll()` completes. This ensures that all of the controls in the page are processed before the splash screen is torn down.

Here's what the `WinJS.Application.activated` event handler looks like in the default.js file with some code removed:

```
app.onactivated = function (args) {
    if (args.detail.kind === activation.ActivationKind.launch) {
        args.setPromise(WinJS.UI.processAll());
    }
};
```

In the code above, the `args.setPromise()` method is used to execute a method which returns a promise: the `processAll()` method. The `processAll()` method executes asynchronously and the ready event is not raised until the `processAll()` method completes.

Creating Custom Events

You can create and listen to custom application events. You can make up any type of event that you please.

For example, if you are creating a game, you might want to create a heartbeat event which is raised every second so that you can refresh the game board. The following code demonstrates how you can raise and listen to a custom heartbeat event:

```
window.setInterval(function () {
    WinJS.Application.queueEvent({ type: "heartbeat" });
}, 1000);

WinJS.Application.addEventListener("heartbeat", function (evt) {
    console.log("heartbeat");
});

WinJS.Application.start();
```

The code above uses the `setInterval()` method to execute code once every second. The `queueEvent()` method is called to queue up a custom heartbeat event.

The `addEventListener()` method is used to listen to the event. Every second, the message "heartbeat" is written to the Visual Studio JavaScript Console window.

You can supply additional event details by supplying a detail property when queuing an event like this:

```
WinJS.Application.queueEvent({
    type: "heartbeat",
    detail: { numberOfPlayers: 12 }
});
```

Suspending, Terminating, and Resuming an App

When you are building a Windows Store app, you need to maintain the illusion that the app is always running even when the user might be switching compulsively among multiple open apps. Normally, you do not explicitly close a Windows Store app—instead, you just switch to a new one.

If you switch from one app to another, Windows will suspend the app but keep the app in memory. If memory resources become low because of other running apps, Windows will quietly terminate the app in the background.

From the perspective of a user, an app should behave in the same way regardless of whether the app was suspended or terminated. You expect the app to be in the same state when you switch back to it—even if you don't switch back to the app for many hours. For example, if the user was reading a particular news story, the same story should be selected when the user switches back to the app.

Detecting When an App Is Suspended and Terminated

You can detect when an app is suspended by handling the `WinJS.Application.checkpoint` event. You should use this event to save the state of your app, in case your app is terminated after suspension, so you can reload the state when the app starts again.

There is no method within a Windows Store app to detect when an app is terminated. In particular, there is no app terminated event. For this reason, if you need to save the state of your app so the state can be reloaded after termination, then you should save your app state during the checkpoint event.

Here's some sample code for handling this event:

```javascript
WinJS.Application.addEventListener("checkpoint", function () {
    // Save app state
});
```

Detecting the Previous Execution State

When a Windows Store app is activated, you can use the `previousExecutionState` property to determine whether the app is being newly launched, whether it was previously closed by the user, or whether it is coming back after being suspended and terminated.

Depending on the value of `previousExecutionState`, you might want to load default values or load the previous app state. For example, if you are creating a news app, then you probably want to load the previous article that the user was reading. If, on the other hand, the user has never run the app, then you might want to load a default page such as the home page.

Here's what the code looks like for checking the previous state:

```javascript
WinJS.Application.addEventListener("activated", function (evt) {
    var appState = Windows.ApplicationModel.Activation.ApplicationExecutionState;
    if (evt.detail.previousExecutionState == appState.notRunning) {
        // The app has not been run in the current user session
        // or it crashed.
        // Should load defaults.
    }
    if (evt.detail.previousExecutionState == appState.closedByUser) {
        // The app was closed by the user.
        // Should load defaults.
    }
    if (evt.detail.previousExecutionState == appState.terminated) {
        // The app was suspended and terminated.
        // Should restore previous state.
    }
});
```

Suspending, Terminating, and Resuming an App   259

The code above contains a handler for the `WinJS.Application.activated` event. The `event.previousExecutionState` property represents the previous state of the application. All of the previous states are represented by the `ApplicationExecutionState` enumeration.

Here are all of the possible values of the `ApplicationExecutionState` enumeration:

- `notRunning`—The user activates the app after installing the app from the Windows Store, rebooting the computer, logging in and out, ending the task, the app crashing, or closing the app and restarting it within 10 seconds of closing it.

- `running`—The app is already running and the user activates it through a secondary tile or through one of the activation contracts or extensions.

- `suspended`—The app is suspended and the app is activated through a secondary tile or through one of the activation contracts or extensions.

- `terminated`—The app was terminated by Windows.

- `closedByUser`—The app was closed by the user and not restarted for more than 10 seconds.

> **NOTE**
>
> You cannot detect whether an app is being activated after suspension. You can detect only when an application is activated after suspension *and termination*. The activated event is not raised for apps which get suspended without termination.

Testing Application State with Visual Studio

You can use Visual Studio to test how your Windows Store app behaves when it is suspended, terminated, or resumes. When you run an app from Visual Studio, the dropdown in Figure 9.3 appears (it is part of the Debug Location toolbar).

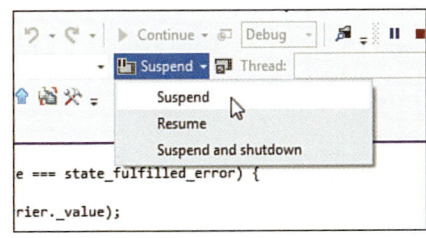

FIGURE 9.3   Change app state options

If you want to simulate app suspension and resumption, then you can click the Suspend option to suspend your application and then click the Resume option to resume your application again. When you click the Suspend option, the checkpoint event is raised. When you click the Resume option, the activated event is *not* raised (your app does not know when it was resumed after suspension).

CHAPTER 9 App Events and States

If you want to simulate app suspension and termination, then you can click the Suspend and shutdown button. When you click the Suspend and shutdown button, the checkpoint event is raised and your app stops. When you run the app again, by actually running your app again in Visual Studio, the previous execution state property will have the value terminated.

Storing State with Session State

If an app is suspended, then the app does not lose state. However, if an app is suspended and terminated, then the state of the app is lost. Any variables will lose their values and the app will start from scratch.

There is a special object, the `WinJS.Application.sessionState` object, which you can use to store state across app suspension. Anything you add to session state survives until the app is activated again.

The following code illustrates how you can use session state to store the user's current game score:

```
(function () {
    "use strict";

    var _gameScore;

    WinJS.Application.addEventListener("activated", function (evt) {
        var appState = Windows.ApplicationModel.Activation.ApplicationExecutionState;
        if (evt.detail.previousExecutionState == appState.notRunning ||
            evt.detail.previousExecutionState == appState.closedByUser) {
            // Set default game score
            _gameScore = 0;
        }
        if (evt.detail.previousExecutionState == appState.terminated) {
            // Load game score from session state
            _gameScore = WinJS.Application.sessionState.gameScore;
        }
    });

    WinJS.Application.addEventListener("checkpoint", function () {
        // Save game score to session state
        WinJS.Application.sessionState.gameScore = _gameScore;
    });

    WinJS.Application.addEventListener("ready", function (evt) {
        // Killed alien, +1 to game score
        document.getElementById("btnKillAlien").addEventListener("click", function () {
            _gameScore++;
```

```
        });
    });

    WinJS.Application.start();
})();
```

The previous code includes three event handlers:

- `click`—When you click the btnKillAlien button, the current game score goes up by 1.

- `checkpoint`—Called when the app is suspended. This event handler stores the current game score in session state.

- `activated`—Called when the app is activated. If the app is activated after termination, then the current game score is loaded from session state. Otherwise, a default value for the game score is assigned.

Session state is only loaded when an app is activated after termination. Session state is not preserved, for example, when a user explicitly closes an app or reboots their machine.

> **NOTE**
> Behind the scenes, session state is stored in local storage in a file named _sessionState.json. After the checkpoint event, session state is written to this file automatically. When an app is activated after termination, session state is loaded from this file automatically.

Application View States

A Windows Store app can be displayed in several different view states. The different view states determine the horizontal and vertical screen real estate available to your application.

A well-designed Windows Store app will intelligently adapt to the available real estate. For example, if a fat app is forced to get skinny, it will hide extra content automatically.

In this section, you learn about the different Windows Store app view states and how you can take advantage of media queries to adapt to different view states automatically.

Snapped, Filled, Portrait, and Landscape

A Windows Store app can be in snapped view state, filled view state, or full screen. Each of these states corresponds to a different horizontal screen resolution. For example, one Windows Store app can be snapped to the left or right edge of the screen while a second Windows Store app fills the remainder of the screen. The first app is in a *snapped view state* and the second app is in a *filled view state*.

Figure 9.4 illustrates the difference between snapped and filled view state. In Figure 9.4, Internet Explorer is in a filled view state and the Weather app is in a snapped view state.

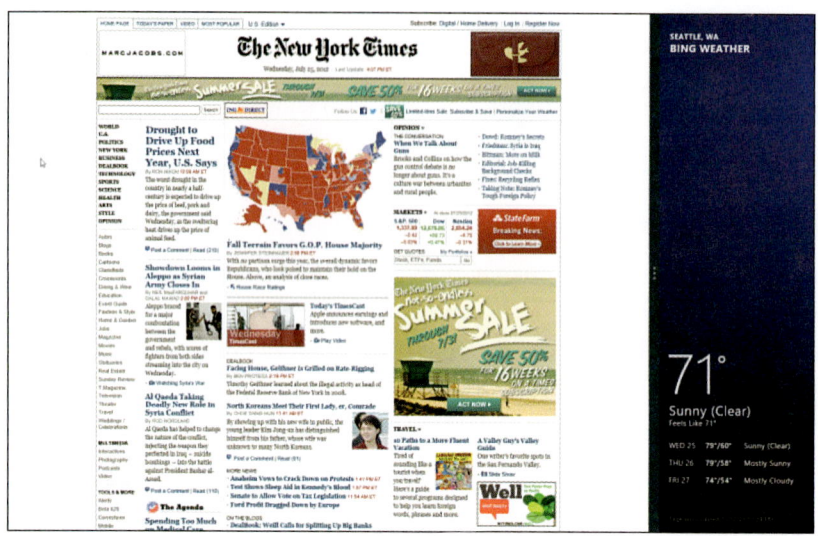

FIGURE 9.4   Snapped versus fill view state

> **WARNING**
>
> You can switch an app to snapped state only on a Windows device with a horizontal resolution of 1,366 pixels or higher. Otherwise, there is not enough screen real estate to see more than one app at a time.

When using the keyboard, you can switch the current app from being in a left-snapped, right-snapped, or full-screen view state by pressing the Win + . (period) key. Using touch, you can drag an app slowly from the left of the screen.

A snapped app always has a horizontal resolution of 320 pixels. The splitter eats up another 22 pixels. Finally, the filled app has a resolution of 1,024 pixels or higher (limited only by your screen resolution). See Figure 9.5.

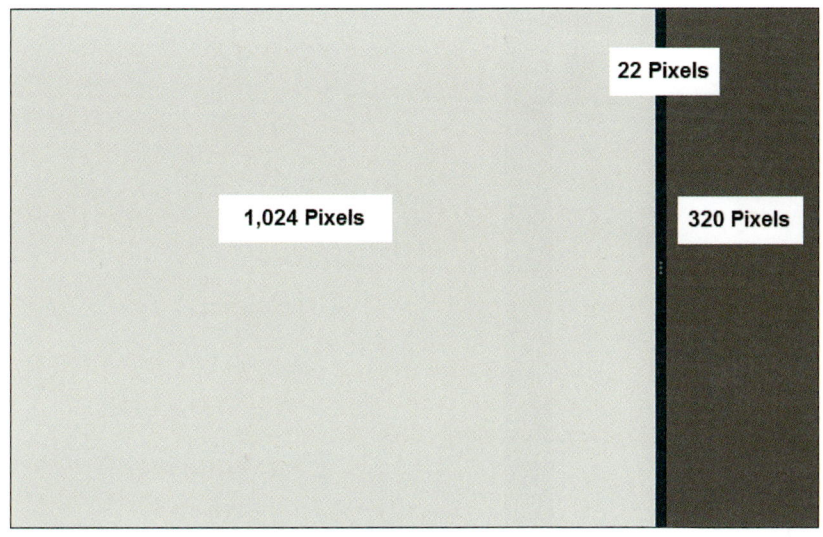

FIGURE 9.5   Dimensions of a snapped app

When you create a Windows Store app, your app might be displayed in either landscape or portrait mode. For example, when I rotate my tablet, I expect any open Windows Store app to switch from landscape to portrait automatically (see Figures 9.6 and 9.7).

FIGURE 9.6   Landscape

FIGURE 9.7 Portrait

A well-designed Windows Store app style will look good in full-screen, snapped, or filled view state. It also will look good in both landscape and portrait mode.

Using Media Queries

You can take advantage of *media queries* in conjunction with Cascading Style Sheets to adapt to different view states automatically. You can use media queries to detect the characteristics of a device and modify the presentation of content.

> **NOTE**
>
> Media queries is a W3C recommendation. You can use media queries not only with Windows Store apps, but also with normal websites. Media queries are supported by Google Chrome 4+, Mozilla Firefox 3.5+, Apple Safari 4+, and Microsoft Internet Explorer 9+.

Imagine, for example, that you want to display different content depending on the horizontal resolution of a device. In that case, you can group styles by using the @media rule.

For example, the following HTML page contains three sets of style rules. One set applies to all devices, one set applies to medium resolution devices, and one set applies to high resolution devices:

```html
<!DOCTYPE html>
<html>
    <head>
        <title></title>
        <style type="text/css">
            /* Default Styles */
            .displayInMedium, .displayInHigh {
                display:none;
            }
            /* Greater than or equal to 1,366px */
            @media screen and (min-width:1366px) {
              .displayInMedium {
                display: block;
              }
            }
            /* Greater than or equal to 1,920px */
            @media screen and (min-width:1920px) {
              .displayInMedium, .displayInHigh {
                display: block;
              }
            }

        </style>
    </head>
    <body>
        <div>
            <h1>You can see me at all resolutions.</h1>
        </div>

        <div class="displayInMedium">
            <h1>You can see me at medium resolutions.</h1>
        </div>

        <div class="displayInHigh">
            <h1>You can see me at high resolutions.</h1>
        </div>
    </body>
</html>
```

You can simulate different devices sizes by running your Windows Store app using the Visual Studio simulator and selecting different resolutions (see Figure 9.8). When you switch to different resolutions, the content in different DIV elements is displayed.

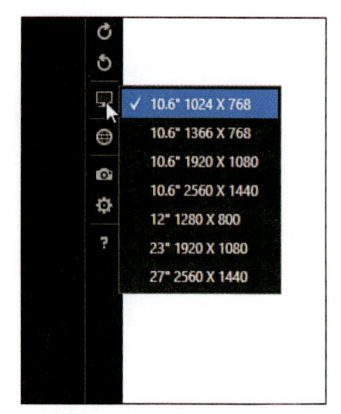

FIGURE 9.8 Changing screen resolution in the simulator

> **WARNING**
>
> Not all computers support all resolutions listed by the device simulator. For example, on my laptop, I am unable to switch to 10.6" 2560x1440 but I can switch to 27" 2560x1440.

Microsoft has its own extensions to media queries. The default CSS file which you get when you create a new Windows Store app—located at \css\default.css—includes the following style rules:

```css
@media screen and (-ms-view-state: fullscreen-landscape) {
}
@media screen and (-ms-view-state: filled) {
}
@media screen and (-ms-view-state: snapped) {
}
@media screen and (-ms-view-state: fullscreen-portrait) {
}
```

The –ms-view-state media feature enables you to detect when a page is full screen (landscape or portrait), filled, or snapped. You can display or hide different content (using `display:none`) automatically when your app switches been these different view states.

Using the JavaScript `mediaMatch` Method

In the previous section, you learned how to perform media queries with Cascading Style Sheets. You also can perform media queries using JavaScript by taking advantage of the `window.matchMedia()` method. This method returns a `MediaQueryList` which has a matches method that represents success or failure.

For example, the following code checks whether the current device is in portrait mode:

```
if (window.matchMedia("(orientation:portrait)").matches) {
    console.log("portrait");
} else {
    console.log("landscape");
}
```

If the matches property returns true, then the device is in portrait mode and the message "portrait" is written to the Visual Studio JavaScript Console window. Otherwise, the message "landscape" is written to the JavaScript Console window.

You can create an event listener which triggers code whenever the results of a media query change. For example, the following code writes a message to the JavaScript Console whenever the current device is switched into Portrait mode:

```
window.matchMedia("(orientation:portrait)").addListener(function (mql) {
    if (mql.matches) {
        console.log("Switched to portrait");
    }
});
```

Be aware that the event listener is triggered whenever the result of the media query changes. So the event listener is triggered both when you switch from landscape to portrait to landscape and when you switch from landscape to portrait. For this reason, you need to verify that the matches property has the value true before writing the message.

Defining a Viewport

You can take advantage of the `@-ms-viewport` rule to scale content to fit different device resolutions—devices with different widths and heights—automatically. Using the `@-ms-viewport` rule is also valuable when you want to scale content to fit different view states such as snapped or filled.

The `@-ms-viewport` rule enables you to define a *viewport*. A viewport determines the width and height of the available screen real estate used to display content independent of the actual screen size.

For example, the following page displays some text and a picture of a Tesla:

```
<!DOCTYPE html>
<html>
    <head>
        <title>viewport</title>
    </head>
    <body>
        <h1>A fast, red Tesla</h1>
        <img src="../images/tesla.jpg" />
    </body>
</html>
```

When the page is displayed in a full-screen state (see Figure 9.9) then everything looks fine. When you switch to a snapped state, however, then the picture is cut off (see Figure 9.10).

FIGURE 9.9 Full-screen page

FIGURE 9.10 Snapped page

Here's how you can use the `@-ms-viewport` rule to scale the page automatically:

```html
<!DOCTYPE html>
<html>
    <head>
        <title>viewport</title>
        <style type="text/css">
            @-ms-viewport {
                width: 1024px;
            }
        </style>
    </head>
    <body>
        <h1>A fast, red Tesla</h1>
        <img src="../images/tesla.jpg" />
    </body>
</html>
```

In the page above, the viewport is set to 1,024px by 768px. If the page is displayed at a lower resolution than 1,204px by 768px, then the content of the page is shrunk (see Figure 9.11).

FIGURE 9.11 Snapped and shrunk

If the page is displayed at a resolution higher than 1,024px by 768px, then the content of the page (including the picture) is expanded (see Figure 9.12).

FIGURE 9.12 Full-screen and expanded

If you want to specify a viewport (scale page content) only when an app is snapped, then you can use the `@-ms-viewport` rule in combination with the `-ms-view-state` media feature described previously. For example, the following CSS rules change the width of the viewport only when an app is snapped:

```css
@media screen and (-ms-view-state: snapped) {
    @-ms-viewport {
        width: 1024px;
    }
}
```

> **NOTE**
>
> The `@-ms-viewport` rule is a Microsoft extension to Cascading Style Sheets which is based on the forthcoming `@viewport` rule from the W3C. The draft specification for the `@viewport` rule is part of the CSS Device Adaptation specification which can be found here: http://dev.w3.org/csswg/css-device-adapt/.

Summary

This chapter was all about Windows Store app events and view state. In the first part, I explained the standard types of events which are raised whenever you run a Windows Store app. You learned how to handle the application loaded, activated, and ready events.

Next, I discussed how Windows Store apps get suspended and terminated automatically in Windows 8. You learned how to take advantage of session state to store and retrieve app data.

Finally, you learned about the different application view states for a Windows Store app such as the snapped and filled view states. I demonstrated how you can take advantage of media queries—from both CSS and JavaScript—to detect different application view states and display different content.

CHAPTER 10
Page Fragments and Navigation

IN THIS CHAPTER

▶ Using the `HtmlControl` Control

▶ Creating a Page Control

▶ Creating Multipage Apps

The goal of this chapter is to explain three controls: the `HtmlControl`, the Page Control, and the `PageControlNavigator` control. All three controls enable you to display the contents of one HTML page in another HTML page using Ajax.

The `HtmlControl` enables you to add a chunk of HTML to a page. You can use this control to reuse the same HTML markup in multiple places in your app.

Creating custom Page Controls enables you to easily create new WinJS controls out of an HTML page, JavaScript file, and style sheet. Create a Page Control when you want to encapsulate both markup and behavior in a new control.

Finally, the `PageControlNavigator` control enables you to build single page apps which contain multiple pages. The `PageControlNavigator` enables you to load Page Controls to simulate the experience of navigating between pages.

Using the `HtmlControl` Control

If you want to include the same chunk of HTML in multiple pages in a Windows Store app, or you want to break up an existing page into more manageable parts, then you can use the WinJS `HtmlControl` control. This control requires you to set one option: a URI. You set the URI to indicate the content that you want to load.

> **NOTE**
>
> The code discussed in this section can be found in the Chapter10\Fragments folder in the GitHub source.

274   CHAPTER 10   Page Fragments and Navigation

Imagine, for example, that you want to display a page that includes a form for entering both a billing and shipping address. In other words, you want to display the same address form twice (see Figure 10.1).

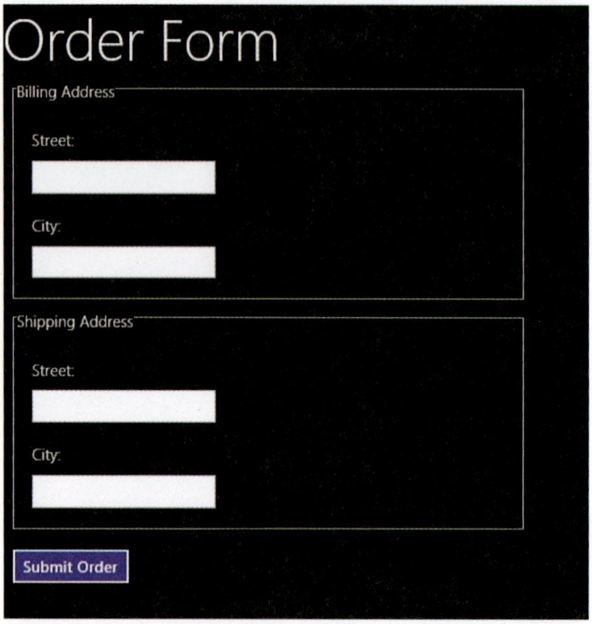

![Order Form with Billing Address and Shipping Address sections, each containing Street and City fields, and a Submit Order button]

FIGURE 10.1   Using the `HtmlControl` to display address forms

In this case, you can create the Address form in a separate HTML file named addressForm.html:

```html
<div>
    <div class="label">
        <label for="inpStreet">Street:</label>
    </div>
    <div class="field">
        <input class="inpStreet" required />
    </div>
</div>
<div>
    <div class="label">
        <label for="inpCity">City:</label>
    </div>
    <div class="field">
        <input class="inpCity" required />
    </div>
</div>
```

Using the `HtmlControl` Control 275

> **NOTE**
> Notice that I am using class names for the form fields instead of IDs because I want to avoid creating conflicting IDs when the form is displayed twice.

Next, you can load this form into the same page twice using the `HtmlControl` control like this:

```html
<h1>Order Form</h1>
<form id="frmOrder">
<fieldset>
    <legend>Billing Address</legend>
    <div id="divBillingAddress"
        data-win-control="WinJS.UI.HtmlControl"
        data-win-options="{
            uri: 'address.html'
        }"></div>
</fieldset>

<fieldset>
    <legend>Shipping Address</legend>
    <div id="divShippingAddress"
        data-win-control="WinJS.UI.HtmlControl"
        data-win-options="{
            uri: 'address.html'
        }"></div>
</fieldset>

<input type="submit" value="Submit Order" />
</form>
```

Finally, here is how you can handle the form submit event to grab the values of both the billing and shipping address forms:

```js
WinJS.UI.processAll().done(function () {
    var frmOrder = document.getElementById("frmOrder");

    // Get the order
    frmOrder.addEventListener("submit", function (e) {
        e.preventDefault();
        var order = {
            billing_street: document.querySelector("#divBillingAddress .inpStreet").
➥value,
            billing_city: document.querySelector("#divBillingAddress .inpCity").
➥value,
```

```
            shipping_street: document.querySelector("#divShippingAddress.
➥inpStreet").value,
            shipping_city: document.querySelector("#divShippingAddress .inpCity").
➥value
        };
    });

    // Save to Database
});
```

In the code above, the `querySelector()` method is used to retrieve the values of both the billing and shipping address form fields. The values of all of the fields are assigned to an object named orders.

> **WARNING**
>
> Don't forget to call `WinJS.UI.processAll()` or the `HtmlControl` will never become a control.

> **NOTE**
>
> In a Windows Store app, you can't use a server-side `#INCLUDE` directive to include content from other files. If you want to include content, then you need to use an `HtmlControl` control.

Creating a Page Control

A Page Control, as its name suggests, enables you to create a control from a page. A Page Control provides you with an easy method of creating custom WinJS controls. When you create a Page Control, you create a new WinJS control out of an HTML page, JavaScript file, and CSS file.

Creating a new Page Control makes sense when you need to do more than simply add a chunk of HTML to a page. A Page Control enables you to encapsulate both appearance and behavior in a control.

Furthermore, a Page Control has its own event lifecycle. For example, a Page Control has its own ready event which you can handle to initialize the control.

Imagine, for example, that you want to create an Alert control. When someone clicks the button rendered by the Alert control, a WinRT modal dialog appears which displays a message (see Figure 10.2). I'll walk through each of the steps required to create the Alert control as a Page Control.

Creating a Page Control 277

FIGURE 10.2 Displaying an alert with a custom Page Control

First, we need to create the following three files:

- alert.html
- alert.js
- alert.css

You can create these three files by adding an HTML Page, a JavaScript File, and a Style Sheet to your project.

The alert.html page contains all of the markup for our new control:

```html
<!DOCTYPE html>
<html>
<head>
    <meta charset="utf-8" />
    <title>confirmButton</title>
    <link href="alert.css" rel="stylesheet" />
    <script src="alert.js"></script>
</head>
<body>
    <button class="alert"></button>
</body>
</html>
```

Notice that the alert.html page looks like a normal HTML page with both a HEAD and BODY section. The HEAD section contains all of the style sheets and JavaScript files required by the page. The BODY section contains all of the markup required by the Alert control.

> **NOTE**
> All of the scripts and style sheets referred to in the head of a Page Control HTML file are removed from the HTML file and added to the parent page. In other words, all of the scripts and styles are promoted up from the control to the containing page.

The alert.css file looks like this (not super exciting):

```css
.alert {
    background-color: red
}
```

The CSS file changes the background color of the Alert button to the color red.

Finally, the alert.js file looks like this:

```javascript
/// <reference path="//Microsoft.WinJS.1.0/js/base.js" />
/// <reference path="//Microsoft.WinJS.1.0/js/ui.js" />
(function () {
    "use strict";

    var Alert = WinJS.UI.Pages.define("myControls/alert.html", {

        ready: function (element, options) {
            var btn = WinJS.Utilities.query("button", element);

            // Set option defaults
            options.buttonLabel = options.buttonLabel || "Show Alert";
            options.message = options.message || "Alert!!!";

            // Update button label text
            btn[0].innerText = options.buttonLabel;

            // Setup click handler
            btn.listen("click", function () {
                var md = new Windows.UI.Popups.MessageDialog(
                    options.message
                );
                md.showAsync();
            });
        }
    });

    WinJS.Namespace.define("MyControls", {
        Alert: Alert
    });
})();
```

The alert.js JavaScript file creates the Alert control. The Alert control is created by calling the `WinJS.Pages.define()` method with the path to the alert.html file.

When you create a Page Control, you can create an event handler for the Page Control ready event. This event is raised after the control has been rendered so you can access any elements in the alert.html file.

In the code above, the ready handler configures a click handler for the button. When you click the button, a `Windows.UI.Popups.MessageDialog` is displayed.

There is one other important section in the alert.js file. The following code exposes the Alert control in the global namespace so that the control can be used declaratively in other HTML pages:

```
WinJS.Namespace.define("MyControls", {
    Alert: Alert
});
```

Now that I have created the Alert control, I can use it in a page. The following page displays a button with the label Click Here! When you click the button, the alert You Clicked the Button! is displayed:

```
<!DOCTYPE html>
<html>
<head>
    <meta charset="utf-8" />
    <title>Fragments</title>

    <!-- WinJS references -->
    <link href="//Microsoft.WinJS.1.0/css/ui-dark.css" rel="stylesheet" />
    <script src="//Microsoft.WinJS.1.0/js/base.js"></script>
    <script src="//Microsoft.WinJS.1.0/js/ui.js"></script>

    <script type="text/javascript" src="pageControl.js"></script>
    <script type="text/javascript" src="/pageControl/alert.js"></script>
</head>
<body>

    <div id="btnDelete"
        data-win-control="MyControls.Alert"
        data-win-options="{
            buttonLabel: 'Click Here!',
            message: 'You clicked the button!'
        }"></div>

</body>
</html>
```

Notice that the page above refers to the alert.js JavaScript file. You must include a reference to your custom Page Control in any page which uses the control declaratively.

The Alert Page Control is created declaratively in the body of the page just like any other standard WinJS control such as the `ListView` or `DatePicker` control.

> **WARNING**
> Remember to call `WinJS.UI.processAll()` or your Page Controls, just like any other WinJS control, won't get processed and turned into a control.

Creating Multipage Apps

You can create a Windows Store app which contains multiple HTML pages and create links between the pages. However, Microsoft strongly discourages you from doing this. Instead, they encourage you to create a single page app and dynamically load different Page Controls which represent individual pages.

Why does Microsoft make this recommendation? When you are building a Windows Store app, you are not building a website (even though you are using many of the same technologies). Instead, you are building a Windows application.

Users have different expectations when using a Windows application than a web application. In a web application, it is normal to click a link and wait (and wait, and wait) for another page to load. While you are waiting, the application freezes. When the new page loads, you start over in a completely new context—the context of the new page.

In a Windows application, this experience would be unacceptable. Microsoft Word, for example, never freezes when you click a button (well, hardly ever). You don't navigate between pages in a Windows application. Instead, you navigate content by opening dialogs and switching between tabs.

To create this same type of Windows application experience in a Windows Store app, you are encouraged to create a single page app.

Creating a Navigation App

The easiest way to create a single page app which contains multiple pages is to take advantage of the Visual Studio Navigation App project template (see Figure 10.3). There are several differences between this template and the Blank App template.

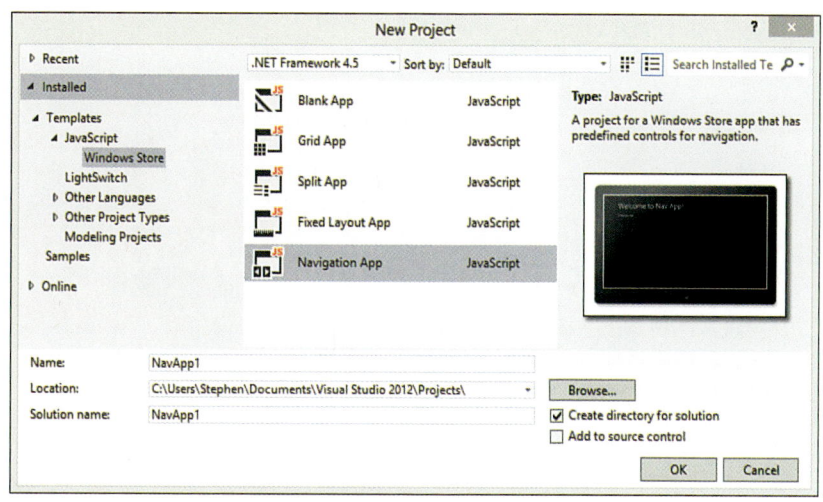

FIGURE 10.3   Creating a Navigation App

First, the Navigation App template contains a *pages* folder. The *pages* folder contains all of the Page Controls which represent the pages in your application. Each Page Control is contained in a separate subfolder of the pages folder.

The Navigation App includes a pages/home folder which contains a Page Control which represents the home page. This Page Control is loaded by default when you start a Navigation App.

The Navigation App template, like the Blank App template, does include a default.html file. However, this file mainly acts as a shell for loading up different Page Controls from the pages folder. When you navigate from page to page, the content in the body of the default.html file is loaded with new content.

Finally, the Navigation App template includes a WinJS control which is not included in the Blank App template named the `PageControlNavigator` control. This control is located in a file named js/navigator.js. The `PageControlNavigator` control handles all of the details of loading the Page Controls into the default.html page.

Let me dig a little deeper into how all of this works.

Understanding the Navigation App default.html Page

As I mentioned previously, the default.html page in a Navigation App is mainly a shell for the content contained in the Page Controls. The entire contents of the default.html page are contained in Listing 10.1.

LISTING 10.1   The default.html Page

```html
<!DOCTYPE html>
<html>
<head>
    <meta charset="utf-8" />
    <title>MultiPage</title>

    <!-- WinJS references -->
    <link href="//Microsoft.WinJS.1.0/css/ui-dark.css" rel="stylesheet" />
    <script src="//Microsoft.WinJS.1.0/js/base.js"></script>
    <script src="//Microsoft.WinJS.1.0/js/ui.js"></script>

    <!-- MultiPage references -->
    <link href="/css/default.css" rel="stylesheet" />
    <script src="/js/default.js"></script>
    <script src="/js/navigator.js"></script>
</head>
<body>
    <div id="contenthost" data-win-control="Application.PageControlNavigator"
➥data-win-options="{home: '/pages/home/home.html'}"></div>
    <!-- <div id="appbar" data-win-control="WinJS.UI.AppBar">
        <button data-win-control="WinJS.UI.AppBarCommand"
➥data-win-options="{id:'cmd', label:'Command', icon:'placeholder'}"></button>
    </div> -->
</body>
</html>
```

The body of the page in Listing 10.1 contains two controls. The first control is the `PageControlNavigator` control. This control has the ID contenthost and it acts as the host for the content loaded up from the Page Controls. I'll discuss the `PageControlNavigator` control in more depth shortly.

The second control (which is commented out) is an `AppBar` control. Any content which you place in the default.html page will be displayed for every page in the application. Because an AppBar should be the same across all of the pages in a Windows Store app, the default.html page is a good place to declare it.

> **NOTE**
> I discussed the `AppBar` control in Chapter 6, "Menus and Flyouts."

Any other content that you add to the default.html page will also be displayed for all pages in a Navigation App. For example, if you want to create a standard header, footer, or sidebar, then it makes sense to add this standard content to the default.html page.

Adding New Page Controls to a Navigation App

A single page app which contained only a single Page Control, the home page, would not be worth the effort. So let me show you how to add a second page.

The easiest way to add a new Page Control to your project is to take advantage of the Visual Studio Page Control item template. Create a new subfolder named anotherPage located at pages/anotherPage. Select the menu item Project, Add New Item, and select the Page Control template (see Figure 10.4). Name your new Page Control with the name anotherPage.html.

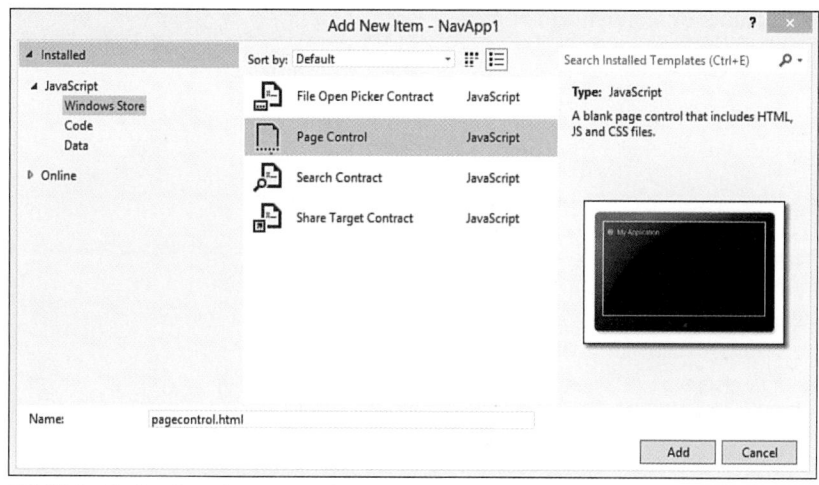

FIGURE 10.4 Creating a new Page Control with Visual Studio

When you add a Page Control named anotherPage.html to a project, you get the following three files:

- anotherPage.html
- anotherPage.js
- anotherPage.css

Of course, you could create these exact same three files by hand, but using the Visual Studio item template saves you a little time.

The entire contents of anotherPage.html is contained in Listing 10.2. Notice that the body of the page contains an HTML5 HEADER tag (not to be confused with the HEAD tag). The HEADER tag contains a back button and the page title (see Figure 10.5).

FIGURE 10.5 The header of a Page Control

LISTING 10.2 The Contents of anotherPage.html

```html
<!DOCTYPE html>
<html>
<head>
    <meta charset="utf-8" />
    <title>anotherPage</title>

    <!-- WinJS references -->
    <link href="//Microsoft.WinJS.1.0/css/ui-dark.css" rel="stylesheet" />
    <script src="//Microsoft.WinJS.1.0/js/base.js"></script>
    <script src="//Microsoft.WinJS.1.0/js/ui.js"></script>
    <link href="anotherPage.css" rel="stylesheet" />
    <script src="anotherPage.js"></script>
</head>
<body>
    <div class="anotherPage fragment">
        <header aria-label="Header content" role="banner">
            <button class="win-backbutton" aria-label="Back" disabled></button>
            <h1 class="titlearea win-type-ellipsis">
                <span class="pagetitle">Welcome to anotherPage</span>
            </h1>
        </header>
        <section aria-label="Main content" role="main">
            <p>Content goes here.</p>
        </section>
    </div>
</body>
</html>
```

So that we can tell when we have navigated to anotherPage.html, I am going to modify the body of the page by replacing the text "Content goes here" with the text "Hello from Another Page!".

The contents of the anotherPage.js JavaScript file are contained in Listing 10.3.

Creating Multipage Apps 285

LISTING 10.3 The Contents of anotherPage.js

```
(function () {
    "use strict";

    WinJS.UI.Pages.define("/pages/anotherPage/anotherPage.html", {
        // This function is called whenever a user navigates to this page. It
        // populates the page elements with the app's data.
        ready: function (element, options) {
            // TODO: Initialize the page here.
        },

        updateLayout: function (element, viewState, lastViewState) {
            /// <param name="element" domElement="true" />
            /// <param name="viewState" value="Windows.UI.ViewManagement.
➥ApplicationViewState" />
            /// <param name="lastViewState" value="Windows.UI.ViewManagement.
➥ApplicationViewState" />

            // TODO: Respond to changes in viewState.
        },

        unload: function () {
            // TODO: Respond to navigations away from this page.
        }
    });
})();
```

Notice that the JavaScript file in Listing 10.3 contains the code to define a new Page Control. The Page Control has three event handlers: `ready`, `updateLayout`, and `unload`. I modify the ready event handler to support page navigation in the next section.

Navigating to Another Page

I now have a page named home and a page named anotherPage in my app; how do I navigate between these two pages? You navigate between pages by using the `WinJS.Navigate.navigate()` method.

Let me modify the home page so we can navigate from the home page to anotherPage. Add a hyperlink to the main section of the home page which looks like this:

```
<section aria-label="Main content" role="main">
    <p>Content goes here.</p>
    <a id="lnkAnotherPage">Visit Another Page</a>
</section>
```

This hyperlink has an ID attribute but no HREF attribute.

> **NOTE**
>
> The code discussed in this section can be found in the Chapter10\Multipage folder in the GitHub source.

Next, I'll modify the code in the home.js file so it sets up a click handler for the hyperlink in its ready handler:

```
WinJS.UI.Pages.define("/pages/home/home.html", {
    ready: function (element, options) {
        var lnkAnotherPage = document.getElementById("lnkAnotherPage");
        lnkAnotherPage.addEventListener("click", function (evt) {
            evt.preventDefault();
            WinJS.Navigation.navigate("/pages/anotherPage/anotherPage.html");
        });
    }
});
```

The click event handler first calls `preventDefault()` to prevent normal link navigation from happening. Remember that we are fake navigating here.

Next, the `WinJS.Navigation.navigate()` method is called to navigate to the anotherPage.html page.

When you click the link in the home page, then you navigate to the anotherPage page (see Figure 10.6). What's even cooler, on the anotherPage page, the back button works. If you click the back button, you return to the home page.

FIGURE 10.6 Navigating between pages

Understanding the Navigation API

The `WinJS.Navigatation.navigate()` method is just one method of the WinJS Navigation API. You can use all of the following methods to control user navigation:

- `back()`—Enables you to navigate back in history. If you supply an integer parameter, then you can go back in history a certain number of entries.

- `forward()`—Enables you to navigate forward in history. If you supply an integer parameter, then you can go forward in history a certain number of entries.

▶ `navigate()`—Enables you to navigate to a particular page (Page Control). You can also supply a custom object which represents the initial state of the page.

And, you can use the following properties with navigation:

▶ `canGoBack`—Returns true when you can navigate back.

▶ `canGoForward`—Returns true when you can navigate forward.

▶ `history`—Returns an object which represents all of the history entries. The history object has a current, `backStack`, and `forwardState` property.

▶ `location`—Return the URL associated with the current page.

▶ `state`—Returns the state associated with the current page.

Finally, the Navigation API supports the following three navigation events:

▶ `beforenavigate`

▶ `navigating`

▶ `navigated`

For each of these three events, you can use the event detail property to read the location and state properties.

Understanding the `PageControlNavigator` Control

The `PageControlNavigator` control is included with the Navigation App, Grid App, and Split App Visual Studio project templates—but it is not included with the Blank App or Fixed Layout App templates. This control does two main things.

First, the `PageControlNavigator` control handles the navigated event and takes care of loading the right Page Control in response to this event. For example, if you call `WinJS.Navigation.navigate("/pages/somePage/somePage.html")` then the `PageControlNavigator` control loads the somePage.html Page Control into the default. html page.

Second, this control enables or disables the back button. If `WinJS.Navigation.canGoBack` has the value true, then the back button is enabled. Otherwise, the back button is disabled.

Understanding Navigation State

When building a multipage app with the Navigation API, you can take advantage of Navigation state to preserve state as you navigate back and forth between pages. Each entry in history has a state property associated with it. You can assign whatever value that you want to this state property.

Imagine, for example, that you are building a simple product catalog. The app consists of only two pages: a home page which displays a list of categories and a details page which

288 CHAPTER 10 Page Fragments and Navigation

displays a list of matching products (see Figures 10.7 and 10.8). When you click a category on the home page, then you see a list of matching products on the details page.

Master

Beverages

Fruit

Meat

FIGURE 10.7 The store app home page

Details

Apples

Oranges

Grapes

FIGURE 10.8 The store app details page

After you select a category on the home page, and you navigate to the details page and back again, then you want the same category to be selected. That way, the customer knows which category was just selected. The customer does not lose his place in the list of categories (see Figure 10.9).

FIGURE 10.9 Preserving state in the store app

> **NOTE**
>
> The code discussed in this section can be found in the Chapter10\NavigationState folder in the GitHub source.

Let me build this app, starting with the home page. The home page contains a `ListView` which displays a list of product categories:

```
<div id="tmplCategory"
    data-win-control="WinJS.Binding.Template">
    <div class="categoryItem">
        <span data-win-bind="textContent:categoryName"></span>
    </div>
</div>

<div id="lvCategories"
    data-win-control="WinJS.UI.ListView"
    data-win-options="{
        itemTemplate: select('#tmplCategory'),
        selectionMode: 'single',
        tapBehavior: 'directSelect',
        swipBehavior: 'select'
    }"></div>
```

The `ListView` is initialized in the home Page Control's ready event handler:

```
WinJS.UI.Pages.define("/pages/home/home.html", {
    ready: function (element, options) {
        var lvCategories = document.getElementById("lvCategories").winControl;

        // Bind the categories to the ListView
```

```javascript
        var dsCategories = new WinJS.Binding.List(MyApp.categoriesAndProducts);
        lvCategories.itemDataSource = dsCategories.dataSource;

        // Retrieve selected category index from state
        WinJS.Navigation.state = WinJS.Navigation.state || {};
        var selectedCategoryIndex = WinJS.Navigation.state.selectedCategoryIndex;
        if (selectedCategoryIndex > -1) {
            lvCategories.selection.set(selectedCategoryIndex);
        }

        // Navigate when item selected
        lvCategories.addEventListener("selectionchanged", function () {
            if (lvCategories.selection.count() > 0) {
                lvCategories.selection.getItems().done(function (items) {
                    // Store index of selected category in history
                    var selectedCategoryIndex = items[0].index;
                    WinJS.Navigation.state = { selectedCategoryIndex:
➥selectedCategoryIndex };

                    // Navigate with selected category name
                    var selectedCategoryName = items[0].data.categoryName;
                    WinJS.Navigation.navigate(
                        "/pages/details/details.html",
                        { selectedCategoryName: selectedCategoryName }
                    );
                });
            }
        });

    }
});
```

Actually, there are several things happening in the previous code. The first couple of lines in the ready event handler are used to bind the `ListView` control to the `categoriesAnd-Products` data.

> **NOTE**
>
> Notice that you do not need to call `WinJS.UI.processAll()` to initialize the `ListView` control when working with Page Controls. The Page Control handles calling this method for you.

Next, if a selected category index has been stored in Navigation state, then the selected category index is retrieved and assigned to the `ListView` control.

The next section of code contains a listener for the `ListView selectionchanged` event. When a new category is selected in the `ListView`, the index of the selected category is stored in navigation state.

The `selectionchanged` handler also handles navigating to the details page. When the `WinJS.Navigation.navigate()` method is called, the selected category name is passed to the details page.

The details page also contains a `ListView` which is used to display the list of products which match the selected category. The details ready event handler takes care of binding the products to the `ListView`:

```
WinJS.UI.Pages.define("/pages/details/details.html", {
    ready: function (element, options) {
        var lvProducts = document.getElementById("lvProducts").winControl;

        // Get selected category
        var selectedCategoryName = options.selectedCategoryName;

        // Filter products by category
        var selectedCategory = MyApp.categoriesAndProducts.filter(function
➥(category) {
            return category.categoryName == selectedCategoryName;
        });

        // Bind products to ListView
        var dsProducts = new WinJS.Binding.List(selectedCategory[0].products);
        lvProducts.itemDataSource = dsProducts.dataSource;
    }

});
```

The selected category name is retrieved from the options passed to the ready event handler. The matching category and products are retrieved and assigned to the `ListView` control's `itemDataSource` property.

Summary

This chapter focused on two topics: how to reuse the same fragment of HTML across multiple pages and how to build apps with multiple pages. In the first part of this chapter, I discussed the `HtmlControl` which enables you to include one HTML page in another HTML page.

Next, I discussed how you can create Page Controls. Page Controls provide you with an easy way of creating new WinJS controls out of an HTML page, JavaScript file, and style sheet.

Finally, I explained how you can create a single page app which contains multiple pages. You learned how to use the `PageControlNavigator` control—in conjunction with the Navigation API—to load Page Controls dynamically and simulate the experience of navigating to separate pages.

CHAPTER 11

Using the Live Connect API

IN THIS CHAPTER

▶ Installing the Live SDK
▶ Authenticating a User
▶ Passing an Authentication Token to a Web Service
▶ Retrieving Basic User Information
▶ Uploading and Downloading Files from SkyDrive

The Live Connect API enables you to connect to Live Services from your Windows Store apps. Live Services provides you with services for authenticating users, retrieving user information (including a user's calendars and contacts), and interacting with a user's SkyDrive.

In the first part of this chapter, I explain the steps required to install and set up the Live SDK. For example, you learn how to register your Windows Store app at the Live Connect website.

Next, I discuss how you can take advantage of a feature called *zero-click single sign-on*. This feature enables you to authenticate the users of your Windows Store app without requiring the users to enter their user names and passwords.

I also explain how you take advantage of authentication when your Windows Store app communicates with a remote web service. I demonstrate how you can pass an authentication token from your Windows Store app to a web service.

You also learn how you can retrieve user information from Live Services. For example, I show you how you can retrieve the current user's first and last name, birthday, and profile picture.

Finally, I discuss SkyDrive. You learn how you can upload and download files from your Windows Store app to the hard drive in the sky which is SkyDrive.

Installing the Live SDK

Before you can use the Live Connect API, you need to download the latest version of the Live SDK for Windows and Windows Phone from the Microsoft website. You can download the SDK from the Dev Center for Windows Store apps at http://msdn.microsoft.com/en-us/windows/apps/.

Adding a Reference to the Live SDK

After you download the Live SDK, you need to add a reference to the Live SDK JavaScript library to your Visual Studio Windows Store app project. Select the menu option Project, Add Reference. After picking Windows, Extensions, check the checkbox next to Live SDK (see Figure 11.1).

> **WARNING**
>
> After downloading the Live SDK, you need to stop and start Visual Studio for the Live SDK to appear in the Reference Manager.

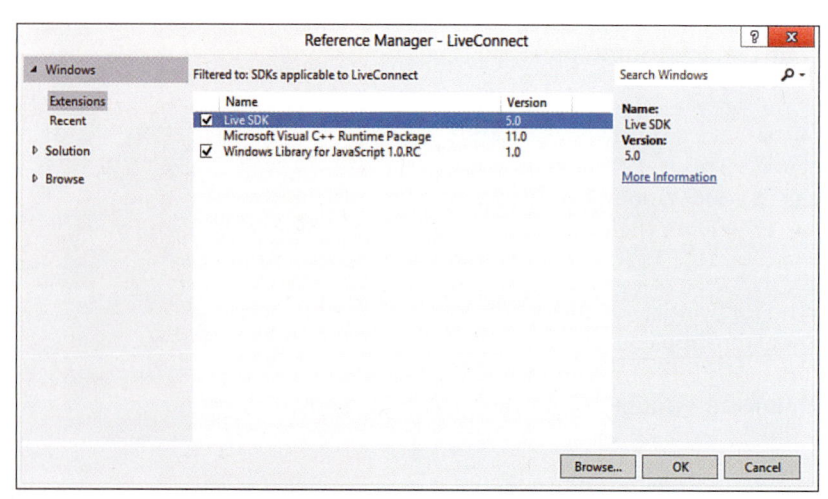

FIGURE 11.1 Adding a reference to the Live SDK JavaScript library

Next, expand your References, Live SDK, JS folder and drag the wl.js file onto your default.html page. This will add the following JavaScript reference:

```
<script type="text/javascript" src="/LiveSDKHTML/js/wl.js"></script>
```

Registering Your App

Before you can start using the Live Connect API, you must first register your app with Live Connect. Visit the following website: https://manage.dev.live.com/build.

Don't let the title of the website—Windows Push Notifications & Live Connect—confuse you; this is the right place. Follow the instructions at the website to register your Windows Store app. Don't forget to follow the instructions in Step 3 for updating the information in your Windows Store app's manifest.

After you register, your client secret is displayed (see Figure 11.2). Record this client secret because you will need it later (we use it with the web service).

Congratulations
Your application has been configured and you can use the information below to access Windows Push Notification S

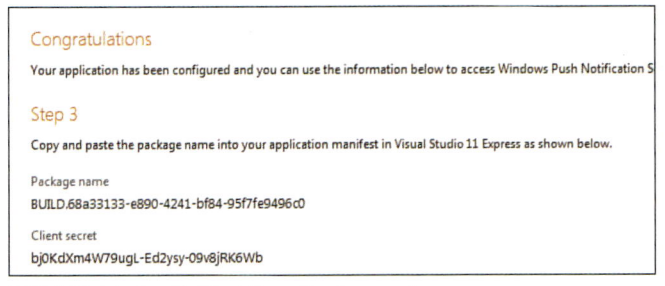

Step 3
Copy and paste the package name into your application manifest in Visual Studio 11 Express as shown below.

Package name
BUILD.68a33133-e890-4241-bf84-95f7fe9496c0

Client secret
bj0KdXm4W79ugL-Ed2ysy-09v8jRK6Wb

FIGURE 11.2 Getting the client secret

> **NOTE**
>
> I hope this goes without saying, but keep your client secret secret. I regenerated the one that you see in the screenshot.

You need to configure one more thing. You must enter your Redirect Domain by visiting the following website: https://manage.dev.live.com/Applications/Index.

Click on your application name, click Edit Settings, click the API Settings tab, and enter a value for the Redirect Domain field. You can enter any domain that you please just as long as the domain has not already been taken (see Figure 11.3).

LiveConnect
My applications ▶ LiveConnect ▶ API Settings

Settings
Basic Information
API Settings
Localization

Your changes were saved.

Client ID:
00000000440CF112

Client secret:
bj0KdXm4W79ugL-Ed2ysy-09v8jRK6Wb

Create a new client secret

Redirect domain:
http://livesdkdemo.superexpert.com/

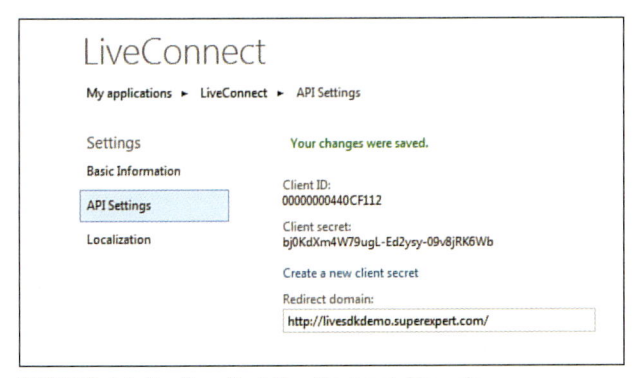

FIGURE 11.3 Creating the Redirect Domain

For the purposes of the code in this chapter, I entered the Redirect Domain http://livesdkdemo.superexpert.com/.

> **WARNING**
>
> The Redirect Domain must be a domain and not a URL. If you run out of domain ideas, remember that you can vary the host name and remember that the domain does not need to point to anything real.

> **NOTE**
>
> If you have already submitted your app to the Windows Store, then the process of registering your app with Live Connect is different. From the Dashboard, edit your app and click Advanced Features. Follow the instructions for configuring Live Connect services.

Initializing the Live Connect SDK

Before you can call any of the services available from the Live Connect API, you must first initialize your connection. You initialize your connection by calling the `WL.init()` method as illustrated in Listing 11.1:

LISTING 11.1   Initializing Your Connection

```
var REDIRECT_DOMAIN = "http://liveSDKDemo.Superexpert.com";
var scopes = ["wl.signin"];
WL.init({
    scope: scopes,
    redirect_uri: REDIRECT_DOMAIN
});

WL.login().then(
    function (loginResults) {
        // Success! Now do something...
    },
    function (loginResponse) {
        throw WinJS.ErrorFromName("Failed to login!");
    }
);
```

The `WL.init()` method in Listing 11.1 is called with two arguments: a `redirect_uri` and an array of scopes. The `redirect_uri` must match (exactly) the Redirect Domain that you configured in the previous section. I discuss the array of scopes in the next section.

Specifying Different Scopes

The array of scopes that you pass to the `WL.init()` method determines the information that you have permission to access. There is all sorts of fun and scary information that you can extract from a Windows Live user account including the user birthday, email addresses, mailing address, photos, and contacts.

Here's a partial list of scopes:

- `wl.signon`—Single sign-in behavior
- `wl.basic`—Read access to basic profile information and contacts.
- `wl.offline_access`—Ability to read and update user information even when a user is not signed in and using your app.
- `wl.birthday`—Read access to user birthday.
- `wl.calendars`—Read access to user calendars and events.
- `wl.calendars_update`—Read and write access to user calendars and events.
- `wl.contacts_birthday`—Read access to user birthday and user contacts birthdays.
- `wl.contacts_create`—Write access to user contacts.
- `wl.contacts_calendars`—Read access to user calendars and events and contacts calendars and events.
- `wl.contacts_photos`—Read access to user media and media shared by other users.
- `wl.contacts_skydrive`—Read access to user SkyDrive and files shared by other users.
- `wl.emails`—Read access to user email addresses.
- `wl.events_create`—Write access for creating events.
- `wl.messenger`—Enables you to sign in to the user messenger service.
- `wl.phone_numbers`—Read access to user phone numbers.
- `wl.photos`—Read access to user media.
- `wl.postal_addresses`—Read access to user mailing addresses.
- `wl.share`—Enables you to update a user's status message.
- `wl.skydrive`—Read access to user files in SkyDrive.
- `wl.skydrive_update`—Read and write access to user files in SkyDrive.
- `wl.work_profile`—Read access to a user's work and employment information.

> **NOTE**
>
> For a complete listing of scopes, see http://msdn.microsoft.com/en-us/library/live/hh243646.aspx

Obviously, not all users of a Windows Store app will want to share all information about themselves. Your Windows Store app, therefore, must get consent to access the information.

When you first run a Windows Store app which requires a particular scope, a modal dialog appears asking the user to provide permission. For example, the form in Figure 11.4 is displayed when you call `WL.init()` with the `wl.signon` scope.

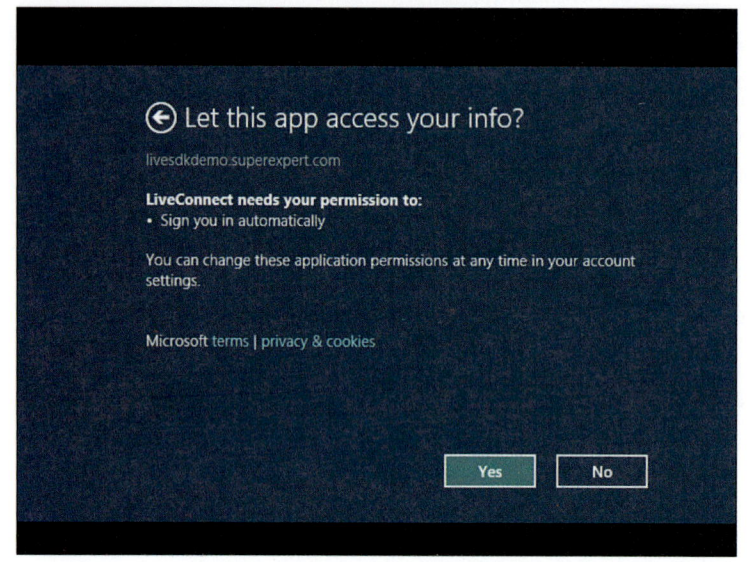

FIGURE 11.4 Windows Store app asking permission to sign you in

Even if you give a Windows Store app permission to access your Windows Live user information, you can revoke this information at a later date. To revoke a permission, log into your account at the Live.com website, pick the app, and remove the permissions (see Figure 11.5).

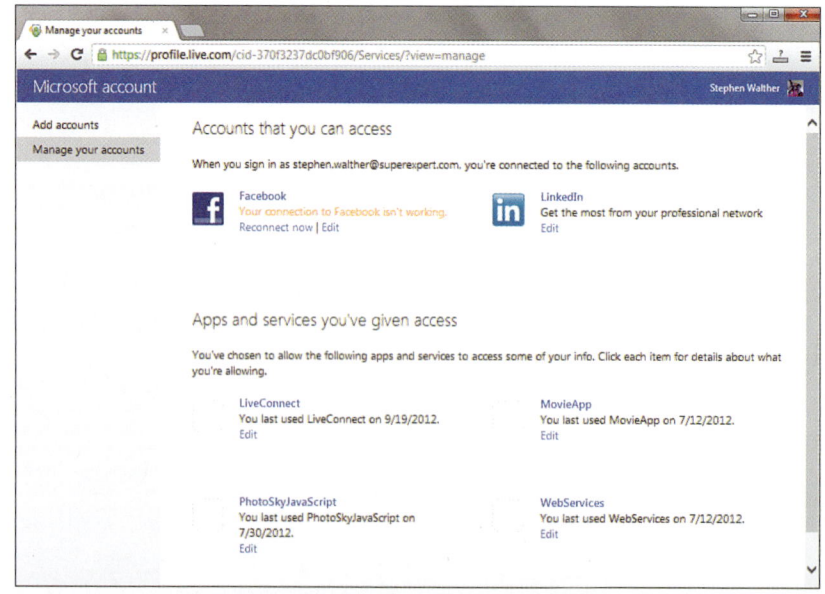

FIGURE 11.5 Revoking Windows Store app permissions

Authenticating a User

The most valuable service that Live Connect provides you is authentication. Live Connect supports something called *zero-click single sign-on*.

If you log into your Windows 8 computer using your Windows Live account, or your Windows Live Account is associated with your Windows account, then you don't need to sign in to Windows Live when using a Windows Store app. You never need to enter your user name or password when running a Windows Store app.

> **NOTE**
> The very first time that the user accesses your Windows Store app, the user *does* need to give permission to the Windows Store app to sign in automatically (refer back to Figure 11.4). However, the user does not need to enter their credentials.

Using `WL.login()`

There are two ways to log into Live Connect: programmatically or declaratively. You can use the `WL.login()` method or you can use the `WL.UI.SignOn` control. If you want to authenticate the user immediately after the user starts your app, then you should use the `WL.login()` method.

For example, the code in Listing 11.2 illustrates how you can log in the current user. If everything works, then the message "Connected" is displayed in the page.

LISTING 11.2 Using the `WL.login()` Method

```
(function () {
    "use strict";

    var REDIRECT_DOMAIN = "http://liveSDKDemo.Superexpert.com";

    function init() {
        var REDIRECT_DOMAIN = "http://liveSDKDemo.Superexpert.com";
        var spanResults = document.getElementById("spanResults");

        var scopes = ["wl.signin"];
        WL.init({
            scope: scopes,
            redirect_uri: REDIRECT_DOMAIN
        });

        WL.login().then(
            function (loginResults) {
                spanResults.innerText = "Connected";
            },
            function (loginResponse) {
```

CHAPTER 11 Using the Live Connect API

```
            spanResults.innerText = "Error when calling WL.login";
        }
    );

}

document.addEventListener("DOMContentLoaded", init);
})();
```

Using the `SignIn` Control

For some Windows store apps, it does not make sense to force everyone to be authenticated before the app can be used. You might want to make authentication optional. If someone authenticates, then the person might get a better experience (you can show their name).

In this scenario, it makes sense to use the Windows Live `SignIn` control. You can place the `SignIn` control in a settings `Flyout` so a user can sign in from the standard Settings charm (see Figure 11.6).

FIGURE 11.6 Sign in from the Settings charm

> **NOTE**
>
> I talked about the `SettingsFlyout` control in Chapter 6, "Menus and Flyouts."

Listing 11.3 contains the HTML for the `signInSettingsFlyout`. Notice that the HMTL contains an element named `divSignInControl`.

LISTING 11.3 The signInSettingsFlyout HTML File

```
<!DOCTYPE html>
<html>
    <head>
        <title>Security</title>
        <script type="text/javascript" src="signInSettings.js"></script>
```

```
    </head>
    <body>
        <div id="divSignIn"
            data-win-control="WinJS.UI.SettingsFlyout"
            data-win-options="{
                width:'narrow'
            }">
            <div class="win-header"
                style="background-color:#464646">
                <button
                    onclick="WinJS.UI.SettingsFlyout.show()"
                    class="win-backbutton"></button>
                <div class="win-label">Sign-in</div>
            </div>
            <div class="win-content">

                <div id="divSignInControl"></div>

            </div>
        </div>
    </body>
</html>
```

The Windows Live `SignIn` control is created within the signInSettings.js JavaScript file in Listing 11.4.

LISTING 11.4 The signInSettingsFlyout JavaScript File

```
(function () {
    'use strict';

    WinJS.UI.Pages.define("signInSettings.html",
    {
        ready: function (element, options) {

            WL.ui({
                name: "signin",
                element: "divSignInControl",
                theme: "dark"
            });
        }
    });
}());
```

The Windows Live `SignIn` control is created by calling the `WL.ui` with the following options:

- `name`—The type of control to create (signin is currently the only option).
- `element`—The DOM element to associate with the control.
- `theme`—Use either the "light" or "dark" theme.

> **WARNING**
>
> If you have already given an app single sign-on permissions, then the `SignIn` control won't do anything useful—it will show a Sign out button which doesn't actually sign you out.

Authentication Events

The Live Connect API supports the following events:

- `auth.login`—Raised when a user signs in.
- `auth.logout`—Raised when a user signs out.
- `auth.sessionChange`—Raised when a user's access token is changed.
- `auth.statusChange`—Raised when a user's status has changed.
- `wl.log`—Raised when an error occurs when calling a Live service.

The following code demonstrates how you can subscribe to the `auth.login` and `auth.logout` events and display different messages:

```
var spanResults = document.getElementById("spanResults");

WL.Event.subscribe("auth.login", function () {
    spanResults.innerText = "Signed In";
});

WL.Event.subscribe("auth.logout", function () {
    spanResults.innerText = "Signed Out";
});
```

Notice that you don't use `addEventListener()` to listen to an event. Instead, you subscribe to the event using the Windows Live `WL.Event.subscribe()` method.

Passing an Authentication Token to a Web Service

Imagine that you want to call a remote web service from your Windows Store app. For example, if you are building a task list app, then you might want to call the remote web service to get a list of tasks associated with a user from a database.

How do you authenticate the user in the web service? You need to make sure that users cannot read each other's tasks. Within the remote web service, you need a way to identify the Windows Store app user who is requesting the tasks.

When you log in using the Live Connect API, you get an authentication token. The authentication token includes a hash of your client secret (refer back to the section "Registering Your App").

> **NOTE**
>
> The authentication token uses an open standard called the JSON Web Token (JWT) standard. This standard is detailed at: http://tools.ietf.org/search/draft-jones-json-web-token-00.

You can pass this authentication token to the remote service. Within the remote web service, you can reproduce the hash using the client secret and verify the authentication token.

Following this process, you can securely identify the user associated with a web service call. Let me walk through this process step-by-step.

Sending the Authentication Token from a Windows Store App

Let me start with the Windows Store app. In Chapter 8, "Creating Data Sources," I showed you how you can use a Web Service Data Source to communicate with a remote web service. Let me use that Web Service Data Source again here.

The HTML page in Listing 11.5 contains a `ListView` control which displays a list of tasks (see Figure 11.7).

LISTING 11.5 HTML Page for Displaying a List of Tasks

```
<div id="tmplTask" data-win-control="WinJS.Binding.Template">
    <div class="taskItem">
        Id: <span data-win-bind="innerText:id"></span>
        <br /><br />
        Name: <span data-win-bind="innerText:name"></span>
        <br /><br />
        Date Created: <span data-win-bind="innerText:dateCreated"></span>
    </div>
</div>
```

```
<div id="lvTasks"
    data-win-control="WinJS.UI.ListView"
    data-win-options="{
        itemTemplate: select('#tmplTask'),
        selectionMode: 'none'
    }"></div>
```

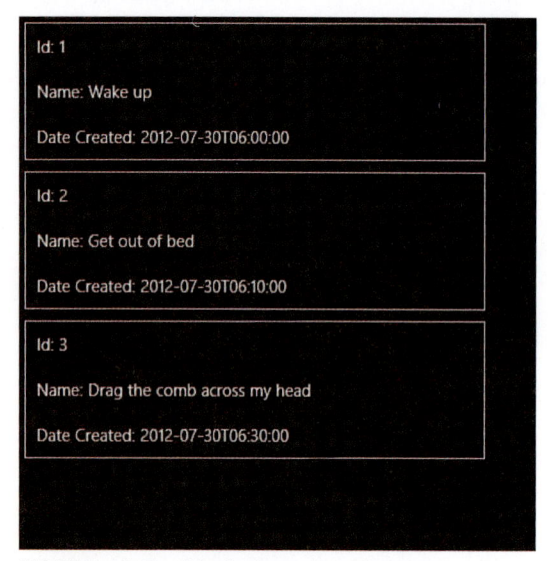

```
Id: 1
Name: Wake up
Date Created: 2012-07-30T06:00:00

Id: 2
Name: Get out of bed
Date Created: 2012-07-30T06:10:00

Id: 3
Name: Drag the comb across my head
Date Created: 2012-07-30T06:30:00
```

FIGURE 11.7　Displaying a list of tasks

The list of tasks is retrieved from a remote web service with the code in Listing 11.6. This code takes advantage of the Web Service Data Source which we created in Chapter 8.

LISTING 11.6　Retrieving the List of Tasks

```
(function () {
    "use strict";

    var serviceURL = "http://localhost:51308/api/tasks";
    var REDIRECT_DOMAIN = "http://liveSDKDemo.Superexpert.com";

    function init() {
        WinJS.UI.processAll().done(function () {
            var lvTasks = document.getElementById("lvTasks").winControl;

            // Init Live Connect
            var scopes = ["wl.signin"];
            WL.init({
                scope: scopes,
                redirect_uri: REDIRECT_DOMAIN
```

```
            });

            // Login to Live Connect
            WL.login().then(
                function (loginResults) {
                    // Bind ListView to web data source
                    var tasksDataSource = new DataSources.WebServiceDataSource(
                        serviceURL,
                        "id",
                        loginResults.session.authentication_token
                    );
                    lvTasks.itemDataSource = tasksDataSource;
                },
                function (loginResponse) {
                    spanResults.innerText = "Error when calling WL.login";
                }
            );
        });
    }

    document.addEventListener("DOMContentLoaded", init);
})();
```

Notice that the `WL.login()` method is used to sign in the current user to Windows Live. After the user signs in, the Windows Live authentication token associated with the user is retrieved from the `session.authentication_token` property.

The authentication token is used when an instance of the Web Service Data Source is created. Each of the methods in the Web Service Data Source uses the authentication token when making a call to the remote service.

For example, Listing 11.7 contains the code for the Web Service Data Source `getCount()` method. Notice how the authentication token is added to the headers collection in the options for the `WinJS.xhr()` call.

LISTING 11.7 Web Service Data Source `getCount()` Method

```
getCount: function () {
    var that = this;

    return new WinJS.Promise(function (complete, error) {
        var options = {
            url: that._url + "/getCount",
            headers: { authenticationToken: that._authenticationToken }
        };
        return WinJS.xhr(options).then(function (xhr) {
            var count = JSON.parse(xhr.response);
```

```
            complete(count);
        },
        function (xhr) {
            console.log("Could not call getCount()");
            debugger;
        });
    });
},
```

The important thing is that each time you call the remote web service, you need to include the authentication token. This token identifies the user making the remote call.

Verifying the Authentication Token in a Web Service

The second half to getting this security process to work is to verify the authentication token in the web service. The Windows Store app calls a Tasks web service which returns the set of tasks.

The web service is implemented using the ASP.NET Web API. In particular, the web service is implemented as an API controller class named `TasksController`. This class is written using C#.

Within the `TasksController`, you need to validate the authentication token. Fortunately, the Windows Live team includes a sample class for validating an authentication token as part of the Live SDK. The name of the class is `JsonWebToken`.

> **NOTE**
>
> You can download the `JsonWebToken` class from the Windows Live GitHub account located at https://github.com/liveservices/LiveSDK. Look under the ASP.NET samples.

Listing 11.8 contains an action filter named `AuthenticationTokenAttribute` which takes advantage of the `JsonWebToken` class. This action filter retrieves the authentication token from the header of a request and uses the `JsonWebToken` class to verify the token.

LISTING 11.8 The `AuthenticationTokenAttribute` Action Filter

```
using System;
using System.Collections.Generic;
using System.Linq;
using System.Web.Configuration;
using JWTSample;

namespace WebServices.Infrastructure {
    public class AuthenticationTokenAttribute : System.Web.Http.Filters.
➥ActionFilterAttribute {
        public override void OnActionExecuting(System.Web.Http.Controllers.
➥HttpActionContext actionContext) {
```

Passing an Authentication Token to a Web Service

```csharp
            // Get the Windows Live authentication token from header
            string authenticationToken = null;
            try {
                authenticationToken = actionContext.Request.Headers.GetValues(
➥"authenticationToken").FirstOrDefault();
            }
            catch {
                actionContext.Response = new System.Net.Http.
➥HttpResponseMessage(System.Net.HttpStatusCode.Unauthorized);
            }

            // Load client secret from Web.config
            var clientSecret = WebConfigurationManager.AppSettings["CLIENT_SECRET"];
            if (String.IsNullOrWhiteSpace(clientSecret)) {
                throw new Exception("Missing Client Secret for Authentication");
            }

            // Validate token
            var d = new Dictionary<int, string>();
            d.Add(0, clientSecret);
            try {
                var myJWT = new JsonWebToken(authenticationToken, d);
            }
            catch {
                actionContext.Response = new System.Net.Http.
➥HttpResponseMessage(System.Net.HttpStatusCode.Unauthorized);
            }
        }
    }
}
```

Notice that the `AuthenticationTokenAttribute` loads up the client secret (which you got when you registered your Windows Store app) from the Web.config file. You need to add your client secret to the app settings section of the Web.config like this:

```xml
<appSettings>
  <add key="aspnet:UseTaskFriendlySynchronizationContext" value="true" />
  <add key="webpages:Version" value="2.0.0.0" />
  <add key="webpages:Enabled" value="false" />
  <add key="PreserveLoginUrl" value="true" />
  <add key="ClientValidationEnabled" value="true" />
  <add key="UnobtrusiveJavaScriptEnabled" value="true" />
  <add key="CLIENT_SECRET" value="bj0KdXm4W79ugL-Ed2ysy-09v8jRK6Wb" />
</appSettings>
```

After you create the `AuthenticationTokenAttribute` action filter, you can use the action filter with any ASP.NET Web API controller method. For example, the `GetCount()` method is decorated with the `AuthenticationTokenAttribute` filter like this:

```
[HttpGet]
[AuthenticationToken]
public int GetCount() {
    return _db.Tasks.Count();
}
```

If you attempt to access any of the `TasksController` action methods without supplying the right authentication token, then the action method will return a 401 Unauthorized result. If you are running your Windows Store app using the Visual Studio debugger, and you don't supply a valid authentication token, then you get the error illustrated in Figure 11.8.

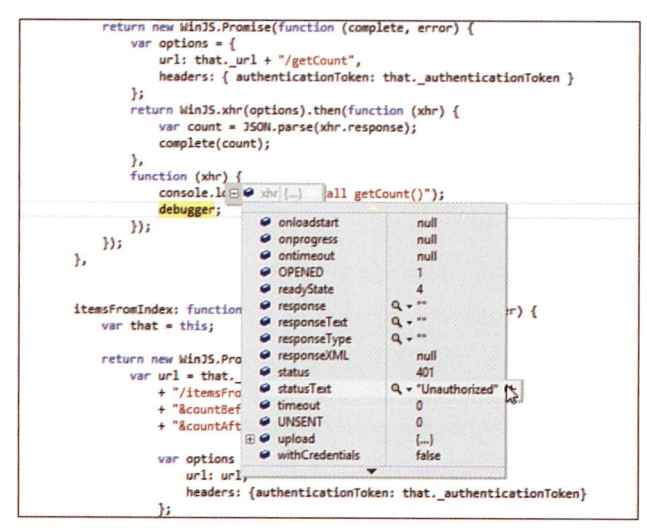

FIGURE 11.8 Web service request with an invalid authentication token

Retrieving the User ID

The authentication token passed to the web service includes several bits of useful information:

- **AppID**—For example, "00000000440CF112"

- **Audience**—For example, "livesdkdemo.superexpert.com"

- **ClientIdentifier**—For example, "ms-app:
  //S-1-15-2-3755963394-994919851-1648241179-1781318319-2690871552-1993569707-2142578964"

- **Expiration**—For example, 7/31/2012 12:51:31 AM
- **expUnixTime**—For example, 1343695891
- **Issuer**—For example, "urn:windows:liveid"
- **UserId**—For example, "ed63ad02ac2a852d56e2fa9886998532"
- **Version**—For example, 1

The `UserId` property is particularly valuable because you can use the `UserId` to uniquely identify a user and associate data in a web service with that user. The `UserId` is a unique value like "ed63ad02ac2a852d56e2fa9886998532"—unfortunately, it is not the user name or email address.

The code in Listing 11.9 demonstrates how you can extract the value of the `UserID` property from an authentication token.

LISTING 11.9 Retrieving the User ID

```
// Get the user id
var authenticationToken = Request.Headers.GetValues("authenticationToken").
➥FirstOrDefault();
var clientSecret = WebConfigurationManager.AppSettings["CLIENT_SECRET"];
var d = new Dictionary<int, string>();
d.Add(0, clientSecret);
var myJWT = new JsonWebToken(authenticationToken, d);
var user = myJWT.Claims.UserId;
```

Retrieving Basic User Information

There is a wealth of user information that you can retrieve from Live Connect including the user's name, birthday, email addresses, and list of friends. In this section, I demonstrate how you can retrieve this information by taking advantage of the `WL.api()` method.

The `WL.api()` method enables you to interact with the Live Connect REST API. When you call the `WL.api()` method, you can supply the following four options:

- **path**—A path to a REST object.
- **method**—An HTTP method such as GET, POST, MOVE, COPY.
- **body**—The body of the request (serialized to JSON).
- **type**—Used only when creating folders or albums.

The `path` object is the most important option because it determines the object you are interacting with. For example, if you want to get the user's photo, then you need to supply the path "me/picture". If you want to set a user's status message, then you would use the path "me/share" (me refers to the current user).

CHAPTER 11 Using the Live Connect API

> **NOTE**
>
> The documentation for all of the REST objects supported by Live Connect is located at http://msdn.microsoft.com/en-us/library/live/hh243648.aspx.

Let me show you how this works by creating a page which displays several bits of user information (see Figure 11.9). The JavaScript source is contained in Listing 11.10.

FIGURE 11.9 Displaying user info from Live Connect

LISTING 11.10 Retrieving Basic User Information from Live Connect

```javascript
(function () {
    "use strict";
    var REDIRECT_DOMAIN = "http://liveSDKDemo.Superexpert.com";
    function init() {
        var spanFirstName = document.getElementById("spanFirstName");
        var spanLastName = document.getElementById("spanLastName");
        var spanBirthday = document.getElementById("spanBirthday");
        var spanStatus = document.getElementById("spanStatus");
        var imgPhoto = document.getElementById("imgPhoto");

        // Initialize Windows Live
        var scopes = ["wl.signin", "wl.basic", "wl.birthday"];
        WL.init({
            scope: scopes,
            redirect_uri: REDIRECT_DOMAIN
        });

        // Log in to Windows Live
        WL.login().then(function (loginResults) {
            // Show basic info
            callLiveConnect("me", "GET").then(function (results) {
                spanFirstName.innerText = results.first_name;
                spanLastName.innerText = results.last_name;
                spanBirthday.innerText = results.birth_month
                    + "/" + results.birth_day;
```

```
            });

            // Show profile picture
            callLiveConnect("me/picture", "GET").then(function (results) {
                imgPhoto.src = results.location;
            });

        });

        // Call Live
        function callLiveConnect(path, method) {
            return new WinJS.Promise(function (complete, error) {
                WL.api({
                    path: path,
                    method: method
                }).then(
                    function(results) {
                        complete(results);
                    },
                    function(results) {
                        // Error calling WL.api()
                        debugger;
                    }
                );
            });
        }

    }

    document.addEventListener("DOMContentLoaded", init);
})();
```

In Listing 11.10, all of the heavy lifting is being performed by the `callLiveConnect()` method. This method uses the `WL.api()` method to call a REST service.

The `callLiveConnect()` method is called twice: the first time to get basic user information and the second time to get the user photo.

Uploading and Downloading Files from SkyDrive

Microsoft SkyDrive enables you to store files in the cloud so the files can be easily shared across devices. Everybody on earth gets 7 gigabytes of free SkyDrive storage to play with. You can add photos, documents, or any other type of file that you please to SkyDrive.

You can take advantage of the Live Connect API to interact with a user's SkyDrive. For example, you can use the API to upload, download, copy, move, and delete files on SkyDrive.

Imagine, for example, that you want to create a Windows Store app for displaying photos. You want a user to be able to view their photo gallery anywhere from any computer. In that case, it makes sense to store the photos on SkyDrive.

In this section, I explain how you can list files and folders from a user's SkyDrive, how you can download files, and how you can upload new files.

> **NOTE**
>
> You can access your SkyDrive by navigating to http://SkyDrive.Live.com.

Listing SkyDrive Folders and Files

Let me start with the basics; let me explain how you can get a list of the files and the folders on a user's SkyDrive (see Figure 11.10).

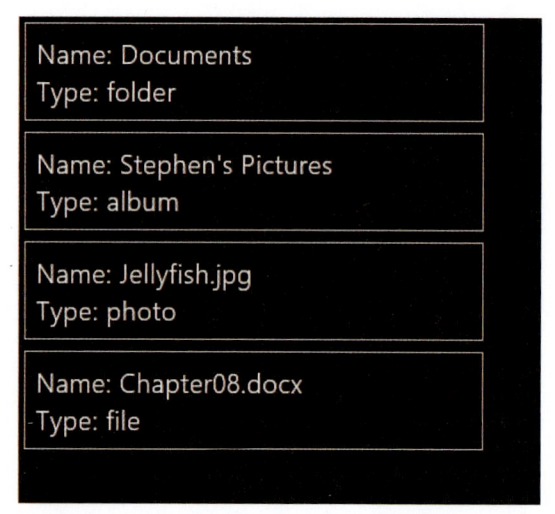

Name: Documents
Type: folder

Name: Stephen's Pictures
Type: album

Name: Jellyfish.jpg
Type: photo

Name: Chapter08.docx
Type: file

FIGURE 11.10 Displaying a list of SkyDrive files and folders

I'll display the list of SkyDrive folders and files with a `ListView` control. The HTML page in Listing 11.11 contains a Template and a `ListView` control. The template displays the name and type of each item retrieved from SkyDrive.

LISTING 11.11 HTML for Displaying Files from SkyDrive

```html
<div id="tmplFile" data-win-control="WinJS.Binding.Template">
    <div class="fileItem">
        Name: <span data-win-bind="innerText:name"></span>
        <br />
        Type: <span data-win-bind="innerText:type"></span>
    </div>
</div>
```

Uploading and Downloading Files from SkyDrive 313

```
<div id="lvFiles"
    data-win-control="WinJS.UI.ListView"
    data-win-options="{
        itemTemplate: select('#tmplFile'),
        selectionMode: 'none'
    }"></div>
```

The JavaScript file in Listing 11.12 retrieves the list of files and folders from the current user's root SkyDrive folder.

LISTING 11.12 JavaScript for Retrieving a List of Files from SkyDrive

```javascript
(function () {
    "use strict";
    var REDIRECT_DOMAIN = "http://liveSDKDemo.Superexpert.com";

    function init() {
        WinJS.UI.processAll().done(function () {
            var lvFiles = document.getElementById("lvFiles").winControl;

            // Initialize Live Connect
            var scopes = ["wl.signin", "wl.skydrive"];
            WL.init({
                scope: scopes,
                redirect_uri: REDIRECT_DOMAIN
            });

            // Log in to Live Connect
            WL.login().then(function (loginResults) {
                // Get List of top-level SkyDrive files
                callLiveConnect("me/skydrive/files", "GET").then(function (results) {
                    var items = [];
                    for (var key in results.data) {
                        items.push(results.data[key]);
                    }
                    var dsItems = new WinJS.Binding.List(items);
                    lvFiles.itemDataSource = dsItems.dataSource;
                });
            });

        });

        // Call Live Connect
        function callLiveConnect(path, method) {
            return new WinJS.Promise(function (complete, error) {
```

```
                    WL.api({
                        path: path,
                        method: method
                    }).then(
                        function (results) {
                            complete(results);
                        },
                        function (results) {
                            // Error calling WL.api()
                            debugger;
                        }
                    );
                });
            }

        }

        document.addEventListener("DOMContentLoaded", init);
    })();
```

The first section in the code above initializes the connection to Live Connect by calling the `wl.init()` method with the `wl.skydrive` scope. To read files and folders from SkyDrive, the user must consent to the `wl.skydrive` permission. To update files and folders in SkyDrive, the user must consent to the `wl.skydrive_update` permission.

Next, the user is logged in by calling `wl.login()`. After the user is logged in, the list of files and folders from the user's SkyDrive is retrieved by invoking the `callLiveConnect()` method with the path "me/skydrive/files". This call retrieves the items (both files and folders) from the user's root SkyDrive folder.

The list of files and folders is returned in the data property. Oddly, the list of files and folders is not returned as a JavaScript array. Instead, the list is returned as a JavaScript object. For this reason, the list is converted to an array with the following code:

```
for (var key in results.data) {
    items.push(results.data[key]);
}
```

Finally the items array is converted into a List data source and bound to the `ListView`. The list of files and folders is displayed.

Downloading Files from SkyDrive

You can use the `WL.backgroundDownload()` method to download files from a user's SkyDrive. When you call this method, you supply the path to the file on the user's SkyDrive and the StorageFile where the file is saved.

Let me modify the `ListView` which we discussed in the previous section so it supports downloading files. I'll modify the `ListView` so that when you click a file in the `ListView`, a save file screen will appear which enables you to save the file from the SkyDrive to your local hard drive (see Figure 11.11).

FIGURE 11.11   Saving a file from SkyDrive

First, I need to modify the options for the `ListView` so it supports raising the `iteminvoked` event when you click/tap a `ListView` item:

```
<div id="lvFiles"
    data-win-control="WinJS.UI.ListView"
    data-win-options="{
        itemTemplate: select('#tmplFile'),
        tapBehavior: 'invokeOnly'
    }"></div>
```

Next, I need to implement a handler for the `iteminvoked` event which saves the clicked/tapped item to the hard drive (see Listing 11.13).

LISTING 11.13   The `iteminvoked` Event Handler

```
// Set up invoke handler
lvFiles.addEventListener("iteminvoked", function (evt) {
    evt.detail.itemPromise.done(function (invokedItem) {
        var itemData = invokedItem.data;

        // Don't download folders and albums
        if (itemData.type == "folder" || itemData.type == "album") {
            return;
        }

        // Create save picker
        var savePicker = new Windows.Storage.Pickers.FileSavePicker();
```

```
        savePicker.suggestedStartLocation = Windows.Storage.Pickers.
➥PickerLocationId.documentsLibrary;
        savePicker.suggestedFileName = itemData.name;
        savePicker.fileTypeChoices.insert("PNG file", [".png"]);
        savePicker.fileTypeChoices.insert("JPEG file", [".jpg", ".jpeg"]);
        savePicker.fileTypeChoices.insert("Microsoft Word Document", [".docx",
➥".doc"]);

        // Display picker
        savePicker.pickSaveFileAsync().then(function (file) {
            if (file) {
                WL.backgroundDownload({
                    path: itemData.id + "/content",
                    file_output: file
                });
            }
        });
    })
});
```

When the `iteminvoked` event is raised, the code in Listing 11.13 retrieves the `ListView` item which was clicked/tapped with the help of the `itemPromise()` method.

Next, a `FileSavePicker` is created for saving the selected file. The `FileSavePicker` is configured to handle PNG, JPEG, and Microsoft Word Documents. If you want to handle downloading other types of files, then you need to add the new file types to the `FileSavePicker`'s `fileTypeChoices` collection.

The file save screen is displayed by calling the `pickSaveFileAsync()` method. When the user clicks the Save button, the Live Connect `WL.backgroundDownload()` method is called. This method downloads the file contents from SkyDrive and saves the file to the location that the user selected with the save file picker.

Notice the path used to save the file: itemData.id + "/content". You retrieve the contents of a file (instead of a description of the file) by using the id of the file followed by "/content".

Uploading Files to SkyDrive

So how do you upload files to SkyDrive?

Before you can upload files to SkyDrive, you must get the user's consent to a stronger permission request. You need to initialize your connection to the Live API with `wl.skydrive_update` scope like this:

```
// Initialize Live Connect
var scopes = ["wl.signin", "wl.skydrive_update"];
WL.init({
```

Uploading and Downloading Files from SkyDrive

```
    scope: scopes,
    redirect_uri: REDIRECT_DOMAIN
});
```

To enable users to upload files, I'll modify the app from the previous section so that it includes an app bar with an upload command (see Figure 11.12). The app bar is declared like this:

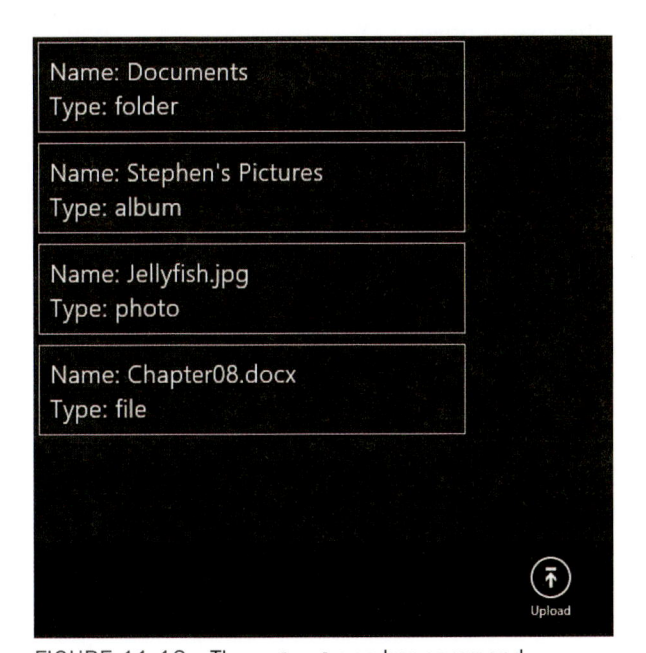

```
<div data-win-control="WinJS.UI.AppBar">
    <button data-win-control="WinJS.UI.AppBarCommand"
        data-win-options="{
            id:'cmdUpload',
            label:'Upload',
            icon:'upload',
            tooltip:'Upload File'
        }">
    </button>
</div>
```

FIGURE 11.12   The `upload` app bar command

Finally, I need to write the code that handles invoking the upload command. The code for handling the `upload` command, and uploading a file to SkyDrive, is contained in Listing 11.14.

LISTING 11.14 Handling the `upload` Command

```javascript
// Set up upload handler
var cmdUpload = document.getElementById("cmdUpload");
cmdUpload.addEventListener("click", function () {
    var openPicker = new Windows.Storage.Pickers.FileOpenPicker();
    openPicker.fileTypeFilter.replaceAll(["*"]);
    openPicker.pickSingleFileAsync().then(function (file) {
        WL.backgroundUpload({
            path: "me/skydrive",
            file_name: file.name,
            file_input: file
        }).then(function () {
            getFileList();
        });
    });
});
```

The code in Listing 11.14 displays a file open picker which enables you to pick a file from your hard drive. When you pick a file, the Live Connect `WL.backgroundUpload()` method is called with three parameters:

- `path`—The path on SkyDrive where you want to upload the file.
- `file_name`—The name of the new file to create on SkyDrive.
- `file_input`—The storage file picked from the open file picker.

After the file is uploaded, the `getFileList()` method is called to refresh the list of files displayed by the `ListView` control so the `ListView` control will display the newly uploaded file.

Summary

This chapter focused on the subject of the Live Connect API. You learned how to use the Live Connect API to support zero-click single sign-on to authenticate users without requiring users to enter their user names and passwords. You also learned how to pass an authentication token from a Windows Store app to a remote web service.

Next, you learned how you can extract a treasure trove of information about the current user from Live Services. For example, I demonstrated how you can retrieve the current user's first and last name, birthday, and profile picture from Live Services.

Finally, I explained how you can interact with SkyDrive from a Windows Store app. You learned how to list, download, and upload files to a user's SkyDrive account.

CHAPTER 12
Graphics and Games

In this chapter, you learn how to create a simple game using a Windows Store app. You learn how to create a game named *Brain Eaters*.

The goal of the *Brain Eaters* game is to avoid getting eaten by zombies while eating food pellets. If you eat all 5 food pellets, then you win the game. If your character gets eaten by a zombie, then you lose (see Figure 12.1).

IN THIS CHAPTER

- ▶ Overview of the Game
- ▶ Creating the Game Tiles
- ▶ Playing the Game Sounds
- ▶ Creating the Game Canvas
- ▶ Capturing User Interaction
- ▶ Creating the Update Loop
- ▶ Creating the Render Loop

320 CHAPTER 12 Graphics and Games

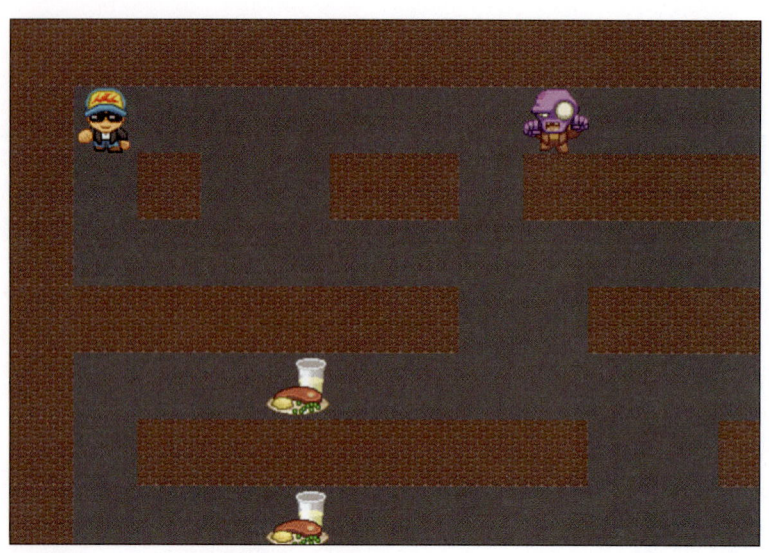

FIGURE 12.1 *Brain Eaters* game

The game works with keyboard, mouse, touch, and stylus. You can move your character using the arrow keys on your keyboard. Alternatively, if you are using a slate, then you can touch the screen to indicate the direction which your character should move.

The game also works at different display resolutions. The game board resizes automatically to fit the available screen size so you can play the game on both low resolution and high resolution screens.

> **NOTE**
>
> All of the code for the *Brain Eaters* game is included in the source code for this book in the Chapter12\Game folder.

Overview of the Game

I created the *Brain Eaters* game with the Visual Studio Navigation App template. The game includes the following four pages:

- **Home**—The home page contains an introduction screen which explains the rules for the game. You click the Start Game button to navigate to the play page.
- **Play**—The play page contains the actual game. Here is where you need to run away from the zombies.
- **Lose**—If the zombies catch you, then you lose the game and end up on the lose page. You can click the Play Again? button to return to the play page.
- **Win**—If you eat all of the food pellets, then you win the game and you are navigated to the win page.

The home, lose, and win pages are boring—they are simple HTML pages which link to the play page (see Figure 12.2). The play page is where the game is actually played.

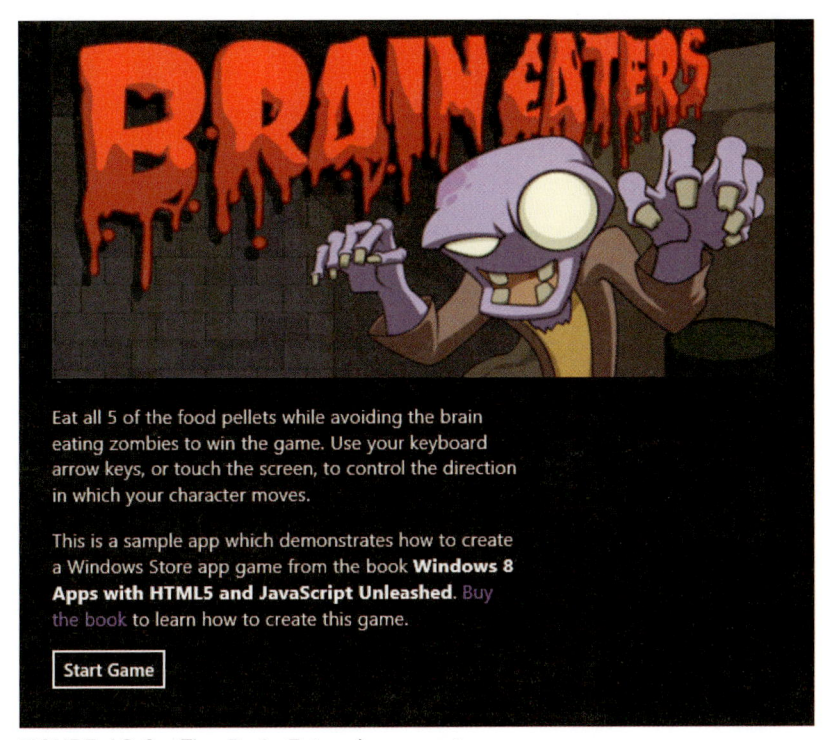

FIGURE 12.2 The *Brain Eaters* home page

Almost all of the code for the game is included in a JavaScript file named game.js which contains the JavaScript Game class. This class contains the code for starting the game, stopping the game, updating the positions of the zombies, and rendering the game.

Creating the Game Tiles

The *Brain Eaters* game is rendered out of a set of image tiles. An image tile is simply a 50 pixel by 50 pixel image. The game board is rendered from background and wall tiles. The game also includes tiles for the zombies, player, and food.

All of the game tiles are created in a JavaScript file named tiles.js (see Listing 12.1).

LISTING 12.1 The tiles.js File

```
(function () {
    "use strict";

    function Tile(url) {
        this.image = new Image();
        this.image.src = url;
```

```
    }

    var tiles = {};
    tiles.background = new Tile("/images/background.jpg");
    tiles.wall = new Tile("/images/brick.jpg");
    tiles.player = new Tile("/images/hero.png");
    tiles.zombie = new Tile("/images/zombie.jpg");
    tiles.hamburger = new Tile("/images/hamburger.gif");

    WinJS.Namespace.define("Unleashed", {
        Tiles: tiles
    });

})();
```

Each tile represents an image loaded from the images folder. For example, the wall tile represents an image named brick.jpg.

Notice that the game includes PNG, GIF, and JPG images. You can create tiles using any type of image supported by a modern browser.

The set of tiles is exposed as properties from the `Unleashed.Tiles` object. For example, you can refer to the wall tile with the `Unleashed.Tiles.wall` property.

Playing the Game Sounds

When you get eaten by a zombie, you get to die a noisy death. And, when you eat a food pellet, your character says "Yum!"

The game sounds are contained in a file named sounds.js (see Listing 12.2).

LISTING 12.2 The sounds.js File

```
(function () {
    "use strict";

    WinJS.Namespace.define("Unleashed", {
        Sounds: {
            yum: new Audio("/sounds/yum.wav"),
            eaten: new Audio("/sounds/eaten.wav"),
            cheer: new Audio("/sounds/cheer.wav")
        }
    });

})();
```

Notice that the game sounds are WAV sound files. I recorded the sound files using a program named Audacity which is a free, open-source sound recorder and editor.

The sounds are exposed as properties of the `Unleashed.Sounds` object. For example, the Yum sound is played with the following code:

```
Unleashed.Sounds.yum.play();
```

NOTE

I created the sound files by recording my children Jon, Ada, and Athena making zombie noises.

Creating the Game Canvas

The game graphics are rendered using an HTML5 Canvas element. The Canvas element is created in the play.html page like this:

```
<div
    data-win-control="WinJS.UI.ViewBox">
    <canvas id="canvas" width="1000" height="750"></canvas>
</div>
```

Notice that the Canvas element is contained in a `WinJS ViewBox` control. The ViewBox control scales the Canvas to fit the resolution of the screen automatically. You can play the game on a 1,024px by 768px screen in portrait mode (see Figure 12.3) and a 2,560px by 1,440 screen in landscape mode (see Figure 12.4). The ViewBox scales the Canvas to fit the available screen automatically.

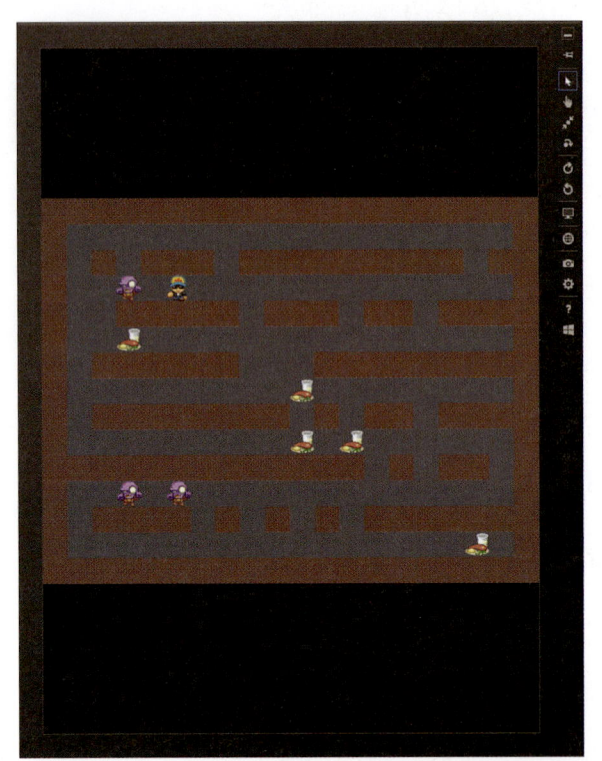

FIGURE 12.3 Game scaled to 1,024px by 768px screen in portrait mode

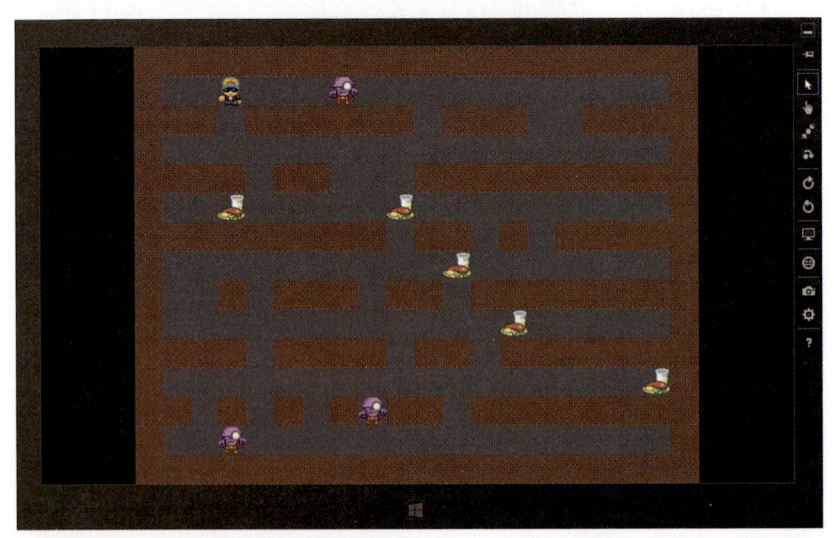

FIGURE 12.4 Game scaled to 2,560px by 1,440px screen in landscape mode

The Canvas element is declared with a width of 1,000 pixels and a height of 750 pixels. All of the game tiles—such as the zombie and wall tiles—are painted on this Canvas element.

When the Game class is initialized in the game.js file, a 2-D context is retrieved from the Canvas element with the following code:

```
// Setup Canvas
this._canvas = document.getElementById("canvas");
this._ctx = this._canvas.getContext("2d");
```

The 2-D context contains the graphics API for drawing on the Canvas. For example, the graphics API includes methods such as `lineTo()`, `rect()`, and `arc()` for drawing lines, rectangles, and arcs.

The *Brain Eaters* game only takes advantage of a single method of the Canvas API: the `drawImage()` method. The `drawImage()` method paints an image on the canvas at a particular location.

For example, the player tile is rendered with the following code:

```
renderPlayer: function () {
    this.drawImage(this._player.tile.image, this._player.x, this._player.y);
},

drawImage: function (image, x, y) {
    this._ctx.drawImage(image, x * TILE_WIDTH, y * TILE_HEIGHT);
}
```

The `renderPlayer()` method calls the `drawImage()` method passing an image and x and y coordinates. The `drawImage()` method draws the image on the Canvas by calling the 2-D context `drawImage()` method.

> **NOTE**
>
> Unfortunately, you cannot use animated GIFs with the Canvas `drawImage()` method. According to the HTML5 spec "When the `drawImage()` method is passed an animated image as its image argument, the user agent must use the poster frame of the animation, or, if there is no poster frame, the first frame of the animation." Bummer.

Capturing User Interaction

The *Brain Eaters* game supports keyboard, mouse, touch, and stylus interaction. If you are using the keyboard, then you can move your character by using the arrow keys.

The following code is used to capture keyboard interaction:

```
document.addEventListener("keydown", this.movePlayerKeyboard.bind(this));
```

When you press a key down, the `movePlayerKeyboard()` method is called. This method detects the arrow key that was pressed and changes the direction of the player:

```
movePlayerKeyboard: function (e) {
    switch (e.keyCode) {
        case WinJS.Utilities.Key.upArrow:
            this._player.direction = Unleashed.Direction.up;
            break;
        case WinJS.Utilities.Key.downArrow:
            this._player.direction = Unleashed.Direction.down;
            break;
        case WinJS.Utilities.Key.leftArrow:
            this._player.direction = Unleashed.Direction.left;
            break;
        case WinJS.Utilities.Key.rightArrow:
            this._player.direction = Unleashed.Direction.right;
            break;
        case WinJS.Utilities.Key.space:
            this._player.direction = Unleashed.Direction.none;
            break;
    }
},
```

The `movePlayerKeyboard()` method takes advantage of the `WinJS.Utilities.Key` enumeration to detect which keyboard key was pressed. This enumeration contains a list of human friendly names for the key codes so you can use `WinJS.Utilities.Key.upArrow` instead of 38.

If you are using a tablet device, then you want to use touch instead of a keyboard. In that case you can touch the screen to indicate the direction in which you want your character to move.

The following code is used to capture the `MSPointerDown` event. This event is raised when you press down on your mouse button, touch the screen with your finger, or touch the screen with a stylus:

```
this._canvas.addEventListener("MSPointerDown", this.movePlayerTouch.bind(this));
```

When the `MSPointerDown` event is raised, the `movePlayerTouch()` method is called. This method takes care of changing the direction in which your character moves:

```
movePlayerTouch: function(e) {
    var playerX = this._player.x * TILE_WIDTH;
    var playerY = this._player.y * TILE_HEIGHT;
    var absX = Math.abs(e.offsetX - playerX);
    var absY = Math.abs(e.offsetY - playerY);
```

```
        if (absX > absY) {
            if (e.offsetX > playerX) {
                this._player.direction = Unleashed.Direction.right;
            } else {
                this._player.direction = Unleashed.Direction.left;
            }
        } else {
            if (e.offsetY > playerY) {
                this._player.direction = Unleashed.Direction.down;
            } else {
                this._player.direction = Unleashed.Direction.up;
            }
        }
    },
```

Depending on where you touch the screen, your character moves in different directions. For example, if you touch the screen below your character, then your character changes direction to move down. If you touch to the right of your character, then your character moves to the right (see Figure 12.5).

FIGURE 12.5 Touching the screen to change direction

Creating the Update Loop

The *Brain Eaters* game uses two loops during game play. The game executes an *update loop* to update the positions of the player and the zombies. The game also executes a *render loop* to render the game.

The update loop executes every 250 milliseconds. The `executeUpdateLoop()` method is triggered with the following call to the `window.setInterval()` method when you start a game:

```
this._updateLoopId = window.setInterval(this.executeUpdateLoop.bind(this),
➥UPDATE_LOOP_RATE);
```

> **NOTE**
>
> The `bind()` method called on the `executeUpdateLoop()` method is used to bind the current instance of the Game object to the `executeUpdateLoop()` method when the `executeUpdateLoop()` method is called. In other words, it ensures that the *this* variable will refer to the current instance of the Game object within the `executeUpdateLoop()` method.

The `UPDATE_LOOP_RATE` constant has the value 250 milliseconds. If you want the zombies to chase you faster, then you can reduce this value (the game definitely gets harder the lower that you make this number).

The `executeUpdateLoop()` method looks like this:

```
executeUpdateLoop: function () {
    this.updateMonsterPositions();
    this.updatePlayerPosition();
},
```

This method updates the positions of the zombies and the player. For example, the `updateMonsterPositions()` method moves all of the zombies in the direction of the player.

While updating the positions of the zombies and the player, the update loop also checks for collisions. The update loop must check whether there is a collision between the player and a zombie or between the player and a food pellet.

For example, the `updatePlayerPosition()` method calls the following `collideWithFood()` method to detect whether the player has walked into a food pellet:

```
collideWithFood: function () {
    for (var i = 0; i < this._food.length; i++) {
        var food = this._food[i];
        if (this._player.x === food.x && this._player.y === food.y) {
            Unleashed.Sounds.yum.play();
            this._food.splice(i, 1);
        }
    }

    // If no more food then player wins!
    if (this._food.length === 0) {
        this.win();
    }
},
```

The `collideWithFood()` method loops through the JavaScript _food array and checks whether the x and y position of any food pellet corresponds to the x and y position of the player. If there is a match then a "Yum!" sound is played and the food pellet is removed from the food array using `_food.splice()`. If all of the food is eaten, then the player wins.

The update loop does not render anything to the screen. The update loop is responsible only for the state of the game. Rendering the game is the responsibility of the render loop.

Creating the Render Loop

The render loop is responsible for rendering the game board. Unlike the update loop, which is triggered by the `window.setInterval()` method, the render loop is executed by calling the `requestAnimationFrame()` method.

The `requestAnimationFrame()` method is defined as part of the W3C Timing Control for Script-Based Animation standard. This method was introduced specifically for the purpose of creating animated games.

When you use the `requestAnimationFrame()` method, you don't specify how often the screen should be rendered. Instead, you let the browser determine the best frame rate.

The idea is that the browser can do a better job than you in determining the best frame rate. The browser can take into account all of the animations being rendered and, therefore, render all of the animations more smoothly. If the page is not currently visible, then the browser can throttle the animations and conserve CPU power.

In the *Brain Eaters* game, the render loop is started with the following code:

```
this._animationLoopId = window.requestAnimationFrame(this.executeRenderLoop.
➥bind(this));
```

The `executeRenderLoop()` method is passed to the `requestAnimationFrame()` method. The `executeRenderLoop()` method looks like this:

```
executeRenderLoop: function () {
    this.render();
    this._animationLoopId = window.requestAnimationFrame(this.executeRenderLoop.
➥bind(this));
},
```

The `executeRenderLoop()` method calls the `render()` method and then immediately calls the `window.requestAnimationFrame()` method again. It is up to the `window.requestAnimationFrame()` method to decide how quickly the `executeRenderLoop()` method gets called again.

> **NOTE**
>
> The `window.requestAnimationFrame()` method is similar to the `window.setTimeout()` method with the crucial difference that you don't specify a timeout value. The `window.requestAnimationFrame()` method figures out its own timeout value.

The `render()` method is responsible for drawing the screen and it looks like this:

```
render: function () {
    this.renderBoard();
    this.renderFood();
    this.renderMonsters();
    this.renderPlayer();
},
```

The `render()` method draws the game board, the food pellets, the monsters, and the player.

The `renderBoard()` method draws the 20 by 15 tile game board by calling the `drawImage()` method for each tile in the game board. Here's what the `renderBoard()` method looks like:

```
renderBoard: function () {
    for (var y = 0; y < VERTICAL_TILES; y++) {
        for (var x = 0; x < HORIZONTAL_TILES; x++) {
            var tile = this.getTile(x, y);
            if (tile) {
                this.drawImage(tile.image, x, y);
            } else {
                this.drawImage(Unleashed.Tiles.background.image, x, y);
            }
        }
    }
},
```

The `renderFood()` and `renderMonsters()` methods are very similar; both methods loop through an array and render each element in the array to the screen. Here's what the `renderMonsters()` method looks like:

```
renderMonsters: function () {
    for (var i = 0; i < this._monsters.length; i++) {
        var monster = this._monsters[i];
        this.drawImage(monster.tile.image, monster.x, monster.y);
    }
},
```

In the previous code, the `_monsters` array contains an array of monster objects. The `drawImage()` method is used to draw each monster to the Canvas element.

Finally, the `renderPlayer()` method renders the player (the hero of the game) to the screen like this:

```
renderPlayer: function () {
    this.drawImage(this._player.tile.image, this._player.x, this._player.y);
},
```

> **NOTE**
>
> The `requestAnimationFrame()` method is defined in the Timing Control for Script-Based Animation standard located at http://dvcs.w3.org/hg/webperf/raw-file/tip/specs/RequestAnimationFrame/Overview.html

Summary

The goal of this chapter was to create a simple game by creating a Windows Store app. I showed you how to create image and sound files for the game and I showed you how to render the images using the HTML5 Canvas element.

You also learned how to create both an update loop and a render loop. The update loop is used to update the positions of the monsters and player on the game board. The render loop is used to render the game board by calling the `requestAnimationFrame()` method to draw the image tiles.

Good luck winning the game! If you win the game, you get to hear my children cheer.

Index

A

About Page settings, creating, 176-178
accessing SkyDrive, 312
adapting view states automatically with media queries, 264-266
adding
    objects to object store, 242-243
    Page Controls to Navigation App, 283-285
    reference to Live SDK, 294
Ajax requests, performing with xhr() function, 69-74
any() method, 63
app bar, 8-9
    commands, 170-173
    contextual commands, displaying, 173-175
    creating, 168-169
app events, 253-257
    activated event, handling, 254-255
    custom events, creating, 257
    deferring with promises, 256
    error event, handling, 255-256
AppBar control, 167-175
    app bar
        commands, 170-173
        creating, 168-169
    contextual commands, displaying, 173-175
applying templates with query selectors, 104-106
apps
    multipage apps, creating, 280-291
        Navigation App, 280-282
    permissions, revoking, 298
    previous execution state, detecting, 258-259

publishing, certification process, 41-42

registering, 294-296

skeuomorphism, 7

state, storing with session state, 260-261

submitting to Windows Store for publishing, 39-40

suspended apps, detecting, 258

view states, 261-270

asynchronous programming, 56-63

   callbacks, 57

   promises, 57-63

      canceling, 62

      composing, 63

      creating, 60-61

      then() versus done() method, 58-60

      timeout promises, creating, 61-62

attributes, HTML form validation

   pattern attribute, 142-143

   required attribute, 142

audio, playing *Brain Eaters* game sounds, 322-323

authenticating users

   authentication events, 302

   authentication tokens

      passing to web service, 303-309

      verifying in a web service, 306-308

   logging into Live Connect

      SignIn control, 300-302

      WL.login() method, 299-300

authentication tokens, passing to web service, 303-309

   verification process, 306-308

authentication tokens, retrieving UserID, 308-309

B

binding converters, 96-100

   date and price binding converters, creating, 99-100

Brain Eaters game

   Canvas element, creating, 323-325

   game tiles, creating, 321-322

   pages, 320-321

   render loop, creating, 329-331

   sounds, playing, 322-323

   update loop, creating, 327-329

   user interaction, capturing, 325-327

breakpoints, setting for Windows Store app debugging, 37

building

   promises from other promises, 63

   Windows Store apps with Visual Studio, selecting project template, 26-33

buttons, creating for FlipView control, 137-139

bypassing observables, 82-83

C

callbacks, 57

canceling promises, 62

Canvas, 21

Canvas element (*Brain Eaters* game), creating, 323-325

capabilities of Windows Store apps, declaring, 15-16

capturing

   contents of HTML forms, 91-94

   date (DatePicker control), 127-128

   user interaction (*Brain Eaters* game), 325-327

certification process for Windows Store apps, 41-42

chaining together promises, 60
change() method, implementing, 228
charms, 9-11
classes, 51-56
    defining, WinJS.Classdefine() method, 51-52
    deriving from other classes, 53-54
    VirtualizedDataSource class, 224
closing Windows Store apps, 12
coalescing notifications, 81-82
collections, observable collections, 83-86
combining methods into single JavaScript object, 54-56
commands for app bar, 170-173
comparing done() versus then() methods, 58-60
complete callbacks, 58
composing promises, 63
connecting to IndexedDB database, 242
contextual commands, displaying, 173-175
controls
    creating imperatively, 113-114
    DatePicker control, 123-128
    declaring, 109, 111-113
    FlipView control, 132-139
    HtmlControl control, 273-276
    ListView control, 185-196
        grid layout, 190-193
        items, filtering, 206-208
        items, grouping, 208-211
        items, loading incrementally, 219-221
        items, selecting, 197-204
        items, sorting, 204-205
        list layout, 190-193
        master/detail view, creating, 198-202
        multiple items, selecting, 202-204
        overlapping items, preventing, 193-196
        templates, switching dynamically, 216-219
    options, 114-115
    PageControlNavigator, 287
    Rating control, 120-123
    references, 110-111
    SignIn control, logging into Live Connect, 300-302
    TimePicker control, 128-131
    ToggleSwitch control, 118-120
    Tooltip control, 116-118
CORS (W3C Cross-Origin Resource Sharing), 71
craftsmanship, Microsoft design style principles, 6
creating
    app bar, 168-169
    Canvas element (*Brain Eaters* game), 323-325
    custom app events, 257
    custom data sources
        change() method, implementing, 228
        error handling, 228-229
        IListDataAdapter interface, 224-225
        insertAtEnd() method, implementing, 227
        itemsFromIndex() method, implementing, 225-226
        remove() method, implementing, 227-228
        setNotificationHandler() method, implementing, 229-230
    data adapter, 224-225
    date and price binding converters, 99-100
    external templates, 106-107
    file data sources, 230-236
    game tiles (*Brain Eaters* game), 321-322
    IndexedDB data source, 241-252
    mixins, 54-56
    multipage apps, 280-291
    observables, 78-79
        listeners, 79-81
    Page Controls, 276-280

creating

promises, 60-61
   timeout promises, 61-62
render loop (*Brain Eaters* game), 329-331
rich text editor, 155-156
update loop (*Brain Eaters* game), 327-329
web service data sources, 236-241
Windows Store apps
   app capabilities, declaring, 15-16
   HTML page, 16-17
   JavaScript file, 18-20
   style sheet, 17-18
   Visual Studio project, 13-14
WinJS controls, imperative creation, 113-114

CSS3 (Cascading Style Sheets 3)
   as element of Windows Store app, 22
   view states, adapting automatically with media queries, 264-266

custom app events, creating, 257
custom data sources, creating
   data adapter, creating, 224-225
   error handling, 228-229
   getCount() method, implementing, 225
   insertAtEnd() method, implementing, 227
   itemsFromIndex() method, implementing, 225-226
   setNotificationHandler() method, implementing, 229-230
custom form validation (HTML), 143-144
customizing
   date display (DatePicker control), 126-127
   form validation error styles, 144-146
   ratings (Ratings control), 121
   XmlHttpRequest object properties, 73-74

D

data adapter, creating, 224-225
data binding
   binding converters, 96-100
   declarative data binding, 86-100
      binding converters, 96-100
      HTML documents, capturing contents of, 91-94
      and WinJS controls, 94-95
data sources
   custom data sources, creating
      change() method, implementing, 228
      data adapter, creating, 224-225
      error handling, 228-229
      getCount() method, implementing, 225
      insertAtEnd() method, implementing, 227
      itemsFromIndex() method, implementing, 225-226
      remove() method, implementing, 227-228
      setNotificationHandler() method, implementing, 229-230
   file data sources, creating, 230-236
   IndexedDB data source, creating, 241-252, 245-252
   web service data sources, creating, 236-241
data-*, 21
databases
   IndexedDB, 241-245
databases, IndexedDB
   connecting to, 242
   indexes, 244-245
   key ranges, 244-245
   objects, adding to object store, 242-243
   objects, retrieving from object store, 243-244

error style   337

data-win-bind attribute (SPAN elements), 87-88
date and price binding converters, creating, 99-100
DatePicker control, 123-128
   date
      capturing, 127-128
      display, customizing, 126-127
      formatting, 124-126
debugging Windows Store apps, 35-38
   breakpoints, setting, 37
   DOM Explorer, 37-38
   Visual Studio JavaScript console, 35-36
declarative data binding, 86-100
   binding converters, 96-100
   HTML forms, capturing contents of, 91-94
   and observables, 89-91
   and WinJS controls, 94-95
declarative templates, 103-104
declaring
   Menu control, 164-165
   Windows Store app capabilities, 15-16
   WinJS controls, 109, 111-113
deferring app events with promises, 256
defining
   JavaScript classes, WinJS.Classdefine() method, 51-52
   namespaces
      WinJS.Namespace.define() method, 46-48
      WinJS.Namespace.defineWithParent() method, 48
   viewports, 267-270
deriving classes from other classes, 53-54
detecting
   previous app execution state, 258-259
   suspended apps, 258
determinate progress indicators, 157

Devices charm, 10
dialogs, displaying, 182-183
displaying
   app bar contextual commands, 173-175
   form progress, 156-158
   modal dialogs, 182-183
   page numbers (FlipView control), 135-137
   popups, Flyout control, 161-163
doing more with less, Microsoft design style principles, 6
DOM Explorer, debugging Windows Store apps, 37-38
done() versus then() method, 58-60
downloading files from SkyDrive, 314-316

E

elements of Windows Store apps
   CSS3, 22
   HTML5, 21-22
   JavaScript, 21
   jQuery, 23-25
   Windows Runtime, 22-23
   WinJS, 23
email addresses, entering in HTML forms, 151-153
encapsulating functions, 48-51
entering numbers in HTML forms, 149-150
error callbacks, 58
error events, handling, 255-256
error handling
   custom data sources, 228-229
   done() versus then() method, comparing, 58-60
error style, customizing for HTML form validation, 144-146

How can we make this index more useful? Email us at indexes@samspublishing.com

events, app events, 253-257
    activated event, handling, 254-255
    custom events, creating, 257
    deferring with promises, 256
    error event, handling, 255-256
external templates, creating, 106-107

F

features
    of CSS3, 22
    of HTML5, 21-22
    of Windows Store apps, 8-12
Fiddler2 tool, 236
fields (HTML forms), labeling, 148-149
File API (HMTL5), 21
file data sources, creating, 230-236
files
    Microsoft SkyDrive
        downloading, 314-316
        listing, 312-314
        uploading, 316-318
    selecting from forms, 154-155
filled view state, 11-12, 261-264
filtering ListView control items, 206-208
Fixed Layout template (Visual Studio), 31-33
FlexBox, 22
FlipView control, 132-139
    custom buttons, creating, 137-139
    page numbers, displaying, 135-137
fluidity, Microsoft design style principles, 6
Flyout control, 161-163
folders, listing for Microsoft SkyDrive, 312-314
form validation (HTML5)
    custom validation, 143-144
    error style, customizing, 144-146

forms, resetting, 146-147
    pattern attribute, 142-143
    required attribute, 142
formatting
    date (DatePicker control), 124-126
    time (TimePicker control), 131
forms
    input elements, 147-155
        email addresses, 151-153
        fields, labeling, 148-149
        files, selecting, 154-155
        numbers, entering, 149-150
        search terms, 151-153
        telephone numbers, 151-153
        URLs, 151-153
        value from list of values, entering, 153-154
    progress indicators, 156-158
    rich text editor, creating, 155-156
full-screen view state, 11-12
functions
    encapsulating, 48-51
    xhr(), specifying response types, 72-73

G

game tiles, creating (*Brain Eaters*), 321-322
getCount() method, implementing, 225
getters, 56
Grid App project template (Visual Studio), 27-28
grid layout (ListView control), 190-193
grouping ListView control items, 208-211

H

handling
- activated app events, 254-255
- error events, 255-256

hiding internal methods, 48-51

HTML documents
- controls, retrieving, 115-116
- query selectors, 63-69
  - QueryCollection class, 68-69
  - WinJS.Utilities.children() method, 67-68
  - WinJS.Utilities.id() method, 66-67
  - WinJS.Utilities.query() method, 64-66

HTML forms, capturing contents of, 91-94

HTML page, creating for Windows Store apps, 16-17

HTML5
- *Brain Eaters* Canvas element, creating, 323-325
- as element of Windows Store app, 21-22
- form validation
  - custom validation, 143-144
  - error style, customizing, 144-146
  - forms, resetting, 146-147
  - pattern attribute, 142-143
  - required attribute, 142
- forms
  - input elements, 147-155
  - progress indicators, 156-158
  - rich text editor, creating, 155-156
- SPAN elements, data-win-bind attribute, 87-88
- templates, 100-107
  - declarative templates, 103-104
  - imperative templates, 100-103

HtmlControl control, 273-276

I

IListDataAdapter interface, methods, 224-225

imperative templates, 100-103

imperative WinJS control creation, 113-114

indeterminate progress indicators, 157

Indexed Database API, 21

IndexedDB data source, creating, 241-252

indexes, 244-245

initializing Live Connect SDK, 296

input elements, HTML forms, 147-155
- email addresses, 151-153
- files, selecting, 154-155
- form fields, labeling, 148-149
- numbers, entering, 149-150
- search terms, 151-153
- telephone numbers, 151-153
- URLs, 151-153
- value from list of values, entering, 153-154

insertAtEnd() method, implementing, 227

installing Live SDK, 294-298

intellisense files, 24

internal methods, hiding, 48-51

J

JavaScript
- classes
  - defining, 51-56
  - deriving from other classes, 53-54
- as element of Windows Store app, 21
- mixins, creating, 54-56

JavaScript file, creating for Windows Store apps, 18-20

join() method, 63

jQuery, as element of Windows Store app, 23-25

How can we make this index more useful? Email us at indexes@samspublishing.com

K-L

key ranges, 244-245
keyboard, support for, 8
labeling form fields, 148-149
landscape view state, 261-264
light dismiss, 161
list layout (ListView control), 190-193
listeners, creating, 79-81
listing Microsoft SkyDrive files and folders, 312-314
ListView control, 185-196
    grid layout, 190-193
    items
        filtering, 206-208
        grouping, 208-211
        loading incrementally, 219-221
        selecting, 197-204
        sorting, 204-205
    list layout, 190-193
    master/detail view, creating, 198-202
    multiple items, selecting, 202-204
    overlapping items, preventing, 193-196
    templates, switching dynamically, 216-219
    views, switching with Semantic Zoom, 211-216
Live Connect API
    authentication events, 302
    Live SDK, installing, 294-298
    logging into
        SignIn control, 300-302
        WL.login() method, 299-300
    user information, retrieving, 309-311
    users, authenticating, 299-302
Live SDK
    initializing, 296
    installing, 294-298
    reference, adding, 294

Live Services, 293
loading ListView control items incrementally, 219-221
logging in to Live Connect
    SignIn control, 300-302
    WL.login() method, 299-300

M

master/detail view (ListView control), creating, 198-202
media queries, 22
    performing with mediaMatch() method, 266-267
    view states, adapting, 264-266
mediaMatch() method, 266-267
menu commands support (Menu control), 164
Menu control
    declaring, 164-165
    flyouts, displaying, 165-166
    supported menu commands, 164
methods
    change() method, implementing, 228
    done() versus then(), comparing, 58-60
    encapsulating, 48-51
    getCount() method, 225
    getCount() method, implementing, 225
    IListDataAdapter interface, 224-225
    insertAtEnd() method, implementing, 227
    mediaMatch(), 266-267
    for QueryCollection class, 68-69
    remove() method, implementing, 227-228
    setNotificationHandler() method, implementing, 229-230
    timeout() method, 61-62
    window.setInterval(), 61
    WinJS.Class.define(), 51-52

WinJS.Class.derive(), 53-54
WinJS.Class.mix(), 54-56
WinJS.Namespace.define(), 46-48
WinJS.Namespace.defineWithParent() method, 48
WinJS.Utilities.children(), 67-68
WinJS.Utilities.id(), 66-67
WinJS.Utilities.query(), 64-66
WL.api(), 309
WL.login(), 299-300

Microsoft design style principles, 6-7

Microsoft SkyDrive
- accessing, 312
- files
  - downloading, 314-316
  - listing, 312-314
  - uploading, 316-318

mixins, creating, 54-56

modal dialogs, displaying, 182-183

mouse, support for, 8

multipage apps, creating, 280-291
- Navigation App, 280-282

multiple inheritance, supporting with mixins, 55

multiple items (ListView controls), selecting, 202-204

N

namespaces, 46
- defining
  - WinJS.Namespace.define() method, 46-48
  - WinJS.Namespace.defineWithParent() method, 48

nav bar, 8-9

navigating between pages, 285-286

Navigation API, 286-287
- Navigation state, 287-291

Navigation App
- creating, 280-282
- navigating between pages, 285-286
- Page Controls, adding, 283-285
- PageControlNavigator control, 287

Navigation state, 287-291

notifications
- bypassing, 82-83
- coalescing, 81-82

numbers, entering in HTML forms, 149-150

O

objects
- adding to object store, 242-243
- observables
  - creating, 78-79
  - and declarative data binding, 89-91
- WinJS.Binding.List, 83-85

observables
- collections, working with, 83-86
- creating, 78-79
- and declarative data binding, 89-91
- listeners, creating, 79-81
- notifications
  - bypassing, 82-83
  - coalescing, 81-82

options
- WinJS controls, 114-115
- xhr() function, 71-72

overlapping items (ListView control), preventing, 193-196

P

Page Controls
    adding to Navigation App, 283-285
    creating, 276-280
page numbers, displaying (FlipView control), 135-137
PageControlNavigator control, 287
pages
    Brain Eaters game, 320-321
    navigating between, 285-286
passing authentication token to web service, 303-306
    verification process, 306-308
pattern attribute, HTML form validation, 142-143
permissions, revoking for Windows Store apps, 298
personal settings, creating for Windows Store apps, 178-181
popups, Flyout control, 161-163
portrait view state, 261-264
preventing overlapping items (ListView control), 193-196
pride in craftsmanship, Microsoft design style principles, 6
private methods, 48
progress callbacks, 58
progress indicators, 156-158
project template, selecting in Visual Studio, 26-33
    Fixed Layout template, 31-33
    Grid App project template, 27-28
    Split App project template, 30-31
promises
    app events, deferring, 256
    canceling, 62
    chaining together, 60
    composing, 63

    creating, 60-61
    timeout promises, creating, 61-62
prototype inheritance, deriving classes from other classes, 53-54
public methods, 48
publishing Windows Store apps to Windows Store, 38-42
    certification process, 41-42
    submitting your app, 39-40

Q

query selectors, 63-69
    QueryCollection class, 68-69
    syntax, 64
    templates, applying, 104-106
    WinJS.Utilities.children() method, 67-68
    WinJS.Utilities.id() method, 66-67
    WinJS.Utilities.query() method, 64-66
QueryCollection class, 68-69

R

Rating control, 120-123
    ratings
        customizing, 121
        submitting, 121-123
references, adding to Live SDK, 294
registering
    Windows Store apps, 294-296
    as Windows Store developer, 38-39
remove() method, implementing, 227-228
render loop (*Brain Eaters* game), creating, 329-331
requests (Ajax), performing with xhr() function, 69-74

required attribute, HTML form validation, 142
resetting HTML5 forms, 146-147
resolution
 changing in Visual Studio simulator, 265
 viewports, defining, 267-270
retrieving
 objects from object store, 243-244
 user information from Live Connect, 309-311
 UserID from authentication token, 308-309
 WinJS controls from HTML documents, 115-116
revoking permissions for Windows Store apps, 298
rich text editor, creating, 155-156
running
 Windows Store apps
 in Visual Studio, 34-35
running Windows Store apps, 20-21

S

scopes, specifying for Windows Store apps, 296-298
screen resolution, changing in Visual Studio simulator, 265
Search charm, 10
search terms, entering in HTML forms, 151-153
selecting items in ListView control, 197-204
Semantic Zoom, switching ListView control views, 211-216
session state, 260-261
setNotificationHandler() method, implementing, 229-230
setters, 56
setting breakpoints, debugging Windows Store apps, 37
setting time (TimePicker control), 130-131

settings (Windows Store apps)
 About Page settings, creating, 176-178
 personal settings, creating, 178-181
Settings charm, 10
Share charm, 10
SignIn control, logging into Live Connect, 300-302
skeuomorphism, 7
SkyDrive
 accessing, 312
 files
 downloading, 314-316
 listing, 312-314
 uploading, 316-318
snapped view state, 11-12, 261-264
sorting ListView control items, 204-205
sounds (*Brain Eaters* game), playing, 322-323
SPAN elements (HTML), data-win-bind attribute, 87-88
specifying
 scopes for Windows Store app, 296-298
 xhr() function response types, 72-73
speed and fluidity, Microsoft design style principles, 6
Split App project template (Visual Studio), 30-31
Start charm, 10
state of ToggleSwitch control, determining, 118-120
storing app state with session state, 260-261
style sheet, creating for Windows Store apps, 17-18
styling Tooltip control, 117
stylus, support for, 8
submitting
 apps to Windows Store, 39-40
 ratings (Ratings control), 121-123
supporting multiple inheritance with mixins, 55
suspended apps, detecting, 258

How can we make this index more useful? Email us at indexes@samspublishing.com

switching
    ListView control templates dynamically, 216-219
    ListView control views with Semantic Zoom, 211-216
syntax, query selectors, 64

T

telephone numbers, entering in HTML forms, 151-153
templates
    applying with query selectors, 104-106
    declarative templates, 103-104
    external templates, creating, 106-107
    imperative templates, 100-103
    ListView control, switching dynamically, 216-219
templates (HTML), 100-107
testing Windows Store apps with Visual Studio, 259-260
then() method versus done(), 58-60
timeout promises, creating, 61-62
TimePicker control, 128-131
    time
        formatting, 131
        setting, 130-131
ToggleSwitch control, 118-120
Tooltip control, 116-118

U

update loop (*Brain Eaters* game), creating, 327-329
uploading, files to SkyDrive, 316-318
URLs, entering in HTML forms, 151-153

user experience, Microsoft design style principles, 6-7
user information, retrieving from Live Connect, 309-311
user interaction (*Brain Eaters* game), capturing, 325-327
UserID, retrieving from authentication token, 308-309

V

validation attributes (HTML5), 21
value from list of values, entering in HTML forms, 153-154
variable scope, 49
verifying authentication token in a web service, 306-308
view states, 11-12, 261-270
    adapting automatically with media queries, 264-266
    filled view state, 261-264
    landscape view state, 261-264
    portrait view state, 261-264
    snapped view state, 261-264
    viewports, defining, 267-270
viewing charms, 9
viewports, defining, 267-270
views (ListView control), switching with Semantic Zoom, 211-216
VirtualizedDataSource class, 224
Visual Studio
    building Windows Store apps, selecting project template, 26-33
    DOM Explorer, debugging Windows Store apps, 37-38
    JavaScript console, debugging Windows Store apps, 35-36
    project for Windows Store apps, creating, 13-14

W

Windows Store apps
    running, 34-35
    testing, 259-260

warnings, displaying with Flyout control, 162
web service data sources, creating, 236-241
web services, authentication tokens
    passing to, 303-306
    verifying, 306-308
web workers, 22
Windows Azure Mobile Services, 241
Windows Runtime, 22-23
Windows Store apps, 5-12
    About Page settings, creating, 176-178
    app bar, 8-9
    app events, 253-257
        activated event, handling, 254-255
        custom events, creating, 257
        deferring with promises, 256
        error event, handling, 255-256
    authentication tokens, passing to web service, 303-306
        verification process, 306-308
    capabilities, declaring, 15-16
    charms, 9-11
    closing, 12
    debugging, 35-38
        breakpoints, setting, 37
        DOM Explorer, 37-38
        Visual Studio JavaScript console, 35-36
    elements of
        CSS3, 22
        HTML5, 21-22
        JavaScript, 21

        jQuery, 23-25
        Windows Runtime, 22-23
        WinJS, 23
    features of, 8-12
    HTML page, creating, 16-17
    JavaScript file, creating, 18-20
    nav bar, 8-9
    personal settings, creating, 178-181
    previous execution state, detecting, 258-259
    publishing, submitting your app, 39-40
    publishing to Windows Store, 38-42
    registering, 294-296
    running, 20-21
    scopes, specifying, 296-298
    state, storing with session state, 260-261
    style sheet, creating, 17-18
    suspended apps, detecting, 258
    testing with Visual Studio, 259-260
    view states, 11-12, 261-270
        adapting view states automatically with media queries, 264-266
        filled view state, 261-264
        landscape view state, 261-264
        portrait view state, 261-264
        snapped view state, 261-264
    Visual Studio project, creating, 13-14
Windows Store developer, registration, 38-39
window.setInterval() method, 61
WinJS (Windows Library for JavaScript), 23
    classes, 51-56
    controls
        creating imperatively, 113-114
        DatePicker control, 123-128
        and declarative data binding, 94-95
        declaring, 109, 111-113
        FlipView control, 132-139
        ListView control. *See* ListView control

How can we make this index more useful? Email us at indexes@samspublishing.com

        options, 114-115
        Rating control, 120-123
        retrieving from HTML documents, 115-116
        TimePicker control, 128-131
        ToggleSwitch control, 118-120
        Tooltip control, 116-118
    modules, encapsulating functions, 48-51
    namespaces, defining, 46-48
    Navigation API, 286-287
WinJS.Binding.List object, 83-85
WinJS.Classdefine() method, 51-52
WinJS.Class.derive() method, 53-54
WinJS.Class.mix() method, 54-56
WinJS.Namespace.define() method, 46-48
WinJS.Namespace.defineWithParent() method, 48
WinJS.Utilities.children() method, 67-68
WinJS.Utilities.id() method, 66-67
WinJS.Utilities.query() method, 64-66
winning as one, Microsoft design style principles, 7
WL.api() method, 309
WL.login() method, logging into Live Connect, 299-300
writing custom data sources, 183

X

xhr() function
    Ajax requests, performing, 69-74
    options, 71-72
    response types, specifying, 72-73
    XmlHttpRequest object properties, customizing, 73-75

Y-Z

yes/no dialogs, creating, 183
zero-click single sign-on, 299

UNLEASHED

Unleashed takes you beyond the basics, providing an exhaustive, technically sophisticated reference for professionals who need to exploit a technology to its fullest potential. It's the best resource for practical advice from the experts, and the most in-depth coverage of the latest technologies.

informit.com/unleashed

Microsoft Visual Studio LightSwitch Unleashed
ISBN-13: 9780672335532

OTHER UNLEASHED TITLES

Windows Phone 7.5 Unleashed
ISBN-13: 9780672333484

ASP.NET Dynamic Data Unleashed
ISBN-13: 9780672335655

Microsoft System Center 2012 Unleashed
ISBN-13: 9780672336126

System Center 2012 Configuration Manager (SCCM) Unleashed
ISBN-13: 9780672334375

Windows Server 2012 Unleashed
ISBN-13: 9780672336225

Microsoft Exchange Server 2013 Unleashed
ISBN-13: 9780672336119

MVVM Unleashed
ISBN-13: 9780672334382

System Center 2012 Operations Manager Unleashed
ISBN-13: 9780672335914

Microsoft Dynamics CRM 2011 Unleashed
ISBN-13: 9780672335389

SharePoint Designer 2010 Unleashed
ISBN-13: 9780672331053

ASP.NET 4.0 Unleashed
ISBN-13: 9780672331121

Silverlight 4 Unleashed
ISBN-13: 9780672333361

Windows 8 Apps with XAML and C# Unleashed
ISBN-13: 9780672336010

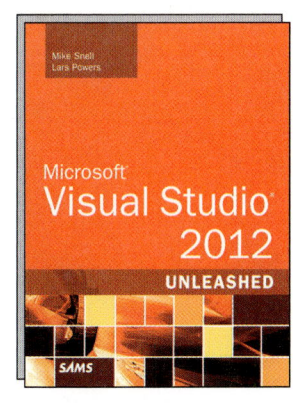

Microsoft Visual Studio 2012 Unleashed
ISBN-13: 9780672336256

SAMS
informit.com/sams

Get Help Building Windows Store Apps

from Stephen Walther, the Author of **Windows 8 Apps with HTML5 and JavaScript Unleashed**

If you need training on building Windows Store Apps, we can fly to your company to provide hand-on training. Learn more at SuperexpertTraining.com

Our team of developers can help you build a Windows Store App. Learn more at Superexpert.com.

SAMS

REGISTER THIS PRODUCT

informit.com/register

Register the Addison-Wesley, Exam Cram, Prentice Hall, Que, and Sams products you own to unlock great benefits.

To begin the registration process, simply go to **informit.com/register** to sign in or create an account. You will then be prompted to enter the 10- or 13-digit ISBN that appears on the back cover of your product.

Registering your products can unlock the following benefits:
- Access to supplemental content, including bonus chapters, source code, or project files.
- A coupon to be used on your next purchase.

Registration benefits vary by product. Benefits will be listed on your Account page under Registered Products.

About InformIT — THE TRUSTED TECHNOLOGY LEARNING SOURCE

INFORMIT IS HOME TO THE LEADING TECHNOLOGY PUBLISHING IMPRINTS Addison-Wesley Professional, Cisco Press, Exam Cram, IBM Press, Prentice Hall Professional, Que, and Sams. Here you will gain access to quality and trusted content and resources from the authors, creators, innovators, and leaders of technology. Whether you're looking for a book on a new technology, a helpful article, timely newsletters, or access to the Safari Books Online digital library, InformIT has a solution for you.

informIT.com
THE TRUSTED TECHNOLOGY LEARNING SOURCE

Addison-Wesley | Cisco Press | Exam Cram
IBM Press | Que | Prentice Hall | Sams
SAFARI BOOKS ONLINE

informIT.com
THE TRUSTED TECHNOLOGY LEARNING SOURCE

InformIT is a brand of Pearson and the online presence for the world's leading technology publishers. It's your source for reliable and qualified content and knowledge, providing access to the top brands, authors, and contributors from the tech community.

Addison-Wesley | Cisco Press | EXAM/CRAM | IBM Press | QUE | PRENTICE HALL | SAMS | Safari Books Online

LearnIT at InformIT

Looking for a book, eBook, or training video on a new technology? Seeking timely and relevant information and tutorials? Looking for expert opinions, advice, and tips? **InformIT has the solution.**

- Learn about new releases and special promotions by subscribing to a wide variety of newsletters. Visit **informit.com/newsletters**.

- Access FREE podcasts from experts at **informit.com/podcasts**.

- Read the latest author articles and sample chapters at **informit.com/articles**.

- Access thousands of books and videos in the Safari Books Online digital library at **safari.informit.com**.

- Get tips from expert blogs at **informit.com/blogs**.

Visit **informit.com/learn** to discover all the ways you can access the hottest technology content.

Are You Part of the IT Crowd?

Connect with Pearson authors and editors via RSS feeds, Facebook, Twitter, YouTube, and more! Visit **informit.com/socialconnect**.

informIT.com
THE TRUSTED TECHNOLOGY LEARNING SOURCE

PEARSON

Addison-Wesley | Cisco Press | EXAM/CRAM | IBM Press | QUE | PRENTICE HALL | SAMS | Safari

Try Safari Books Online FREE for 15 days

Get online access to Thousands of Books and Videos

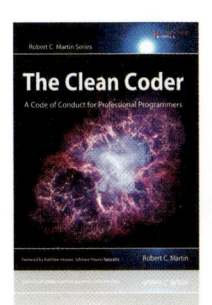

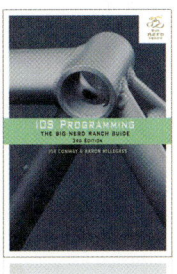

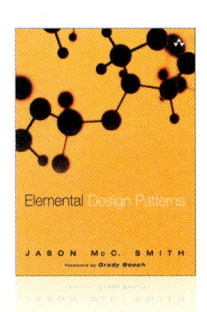

Safari Books Online

FREE 15-DAY TRIAL + 15% OFF*
informit.com/safaritrial

▸ Feed your brain

Gain unlimited access to thousands of books and videos about technology, digital media and professional development from O'Reilly Media, Addison-Wesley, Microsoft Press, Cisco Press, McGraw Hill, Wiley, WROX, Prentice Hall, Que, Sams, Apress, Adobe Press and other top publishers.

▸ See it, believe it

Watch hundreds of expert-led instructional videos on today's hottest topics.

WAIT, THERE'S MORE!

▸ Gain a competitive edge

Be first to learn about the newest technologies and subjects with Rough Cuts pre-published manuscripts and new technology overviews in Short Cuts.

▸ Accelerate your project

Copy and paste code, create smart searches that let you know when new books about your favorite topics are available, and customize your library with favorites, highlights, tags, notes, mash-ups and more.

*Available to new subscribers only. Discount applies to the Safari Library and is valid for first 12 consecutive monthly billing cycles. Safari Library is not available in all countries.

FREE Online Edition

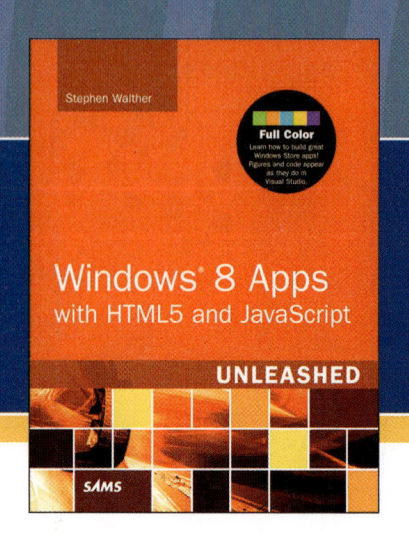

Your purchase of **Windows® 8 Apps with HTML5 and JavaScript Unleashed** includes access to a free online edition for 45 days through the **Safari Books Online** subscription service. Nearly every Sams book is available online through **Safari Books Online**, along with thousands of books and videos from publishers such as Addison-Wesley Professional, Cisco Press, Exam Cram, IBM Press, O'Reilly Media, Prentice Hall, Que, and VMware Press.

Safari Books Online is a digital library providing searchable, on-demand access to thousands of technology, digital media, and professional development books and videos from leading publishers. With one monthly or yearly subscription price, you get unlimited access to learning tools and information on topics including mobile app and software development, tips and tricks on using your favorite gadgets, networking, project management, graphic design, and much more.

Activate your FREE Online Edition at informit.com/safarifree

STEP 1: Enter the coupon code: QSRFXBI.

STEP 2: New Safari users, complete the brief registration form. Safari subscribers, just log in.

If you have difficulty registering on Safari or accessing the online edition, please e-mail customer-service@safaribooksonline.com